Civil Society, Education and Human Formation

Education has been widely criticised as being too narrowly focused on skills, capacities and the transference of knowledge that can be used in the workplace. As a result of the dominance of economic rationalism and neo-liberalism, it has become commodified and marketed to potential customers. As a consequence, students have become consumers of an educational product and education has become an industry. There is deep dissatisfaction with these neo-liberal developments. What is missing is any conception of education as a key factor in the 'human formation' that will lead students to develop the virtues and values that they will need to not only lead successful lives, but also be responsible members of their communities – working for the common good and acting to transform them into just societies.

This volume draws together a number of different perspectives on what is meant by 'human formation', argues for a much richer conception of education and addresses the lack of attention to human fulfilment. It also highlights the importance of philosophy in the articulation of novel ways of conceptualising education – providing alternatives to the dominant neo-liberal and economic rationalist models. The central question with which the book is concerned is a renewed understanding of education as the formation of persons, of civil society and the role of philosophy in fostering that renewal.

In this volume there are a variety of voices from diverse traditions and cultures. Both East and West are represented, and it might be expected that this would result in a divergence of opinion about the purpose of education. However, in spite of the diversity, there is some significant convergence in thinking about the ways in which education ought to serve the needs of both individuals and their communities. What is also particularly useful, and what is fresh about the essays presented here, is that there is also diversity in the philosophical approaches to the problem. This means that the convergence on the importance of 'human formation' as the cornerstone of education does not rely on a privileged philosophical method.

Jānis (John) Tālivaldis Ozoliņš, M.Sc., Ph.D., Dip. Ed. (Melbourne), G. Dip. Ed. Admin. (Deakin), FHERDSA, FPESA, FACE, Foreign Member of the Latvian Academy of Sciences, is Professor of Philosophy at Australian Catholic University and permanent Honorary Fellow of the Institute of Philosophy and Sociology, University of Latvia. His teaching and research interests include eastern philosophy, metaphysics of Aquinas, applied ethics and bioethics, social and political philosophy and the philosophy of education.

Routledge International Studies in the Philosophy of Education

For a full list of titles in this series, please visit www.routledge.com

35 **Posthumanism and Educational Research**
    Edited by Nathan Snaza and John A. Weaver

36 **Parallels and Responses to Curricular Innovation**
    The Possibilities of Posthumanistic Education
    Brad Petitfils

37 **The Educational Prophecies of Aldous Huxley**
    The Visionary Legacy of Brave New World,
    Ape and Essence, and Island
    Ronald Lee Zigler

38 **Popper's Approach to Education**
    A Cornerstone of Teaching and Learning
    Stephanie Chitpin

39 **Neuroscience and Education**
    A Philosophical Appraisal
    Edited by Clarence W. Joldersma

40 **Teachability and Learnability**
    Can Thinking Be Taught?
    Paul Fairfield

41 **Reinventing Intercultural Education**
    A Metaphysical Manifest for Rethinking Cultural Diversity
    Neal Dreamson

42 **Creating the Practical Man of Modernity**
    The Reception of John Dewey's Pedagogy in Mexico
    Victor J. Rodriguez

43 **Civil Society, Education and Human Formation**
    Philosophy's Role in a Renewed Understanding of Education
    Edited by Jānis (John) Tālivaldis Ozoliņš

Civil Society, Education and Human Formation

Philosophy's Role in a Renewed Understanding of Education

Edited by Jānis (John) Tālivaldis Ozoliņš

LONDON AND NEW YORK

First published 2017
by Routledge
2 Park Square, Milton Park, Abingdon, Oxon OX14 4RN

and by Routledge
711 Third Avenue, New York, NY 10017

Routledge is an imprint of the Taylor & Francis Group, an informa business

© 2017 selection and editorial matter, Jānis (John) Tālivaldis Ozoliņš; individual chapters, the contributors

The right of the editor to be identified as the author of the editorial material, and of the authors for their individual chapters, has been asserted in accordance with sections 77 and 78 of the Copyright, Designs and Patents Act 1988.

All rights reserved. No part of this book may be reprinted or reproduced or utilised in any form or by any electronic, mechanical, or other means, now known or hereafter invented, including photocopying and recording, or in any information storage or retrieval system, without permission in writing from the publishers.

Trademark notice: Product or corporate names may be trademarks or registered trademarks, and are used only for identification and explanation without intent to infringe.

British Library Cataloguing-in-Publication Data
A catalogue record for this book is available from the British Library

Library of Congress Cataloging-in-Publication Data
A catalog record for this book has been requested

ISBN: 978-1-138-71310-9 (hbk)
ISBN: 978-1-315-19940-5 (ebk)

Typeset in Bembo
by Apex CoVantage, LLC

In memory of Jacob Jānis Ozoliņš (1981–2013), for my family, Barbara my wife, and especially my grandchildren in Australia and Latvia, Ryley, Braeden, Talia and Patrīcija, whose balanced education is particularly important.

Contents

Acknowledgements ix
Preface x
Notes on contributors xii

Introduction 1
JĀNIS (JOHN) TĀLIVALDIS OZOLIŅŠ

1 **Democracy, civil society and education** 11
JĀNIS (JOHN) TĀLIVALDIS OZOLIŅŠ

2 **The relevance of a Catholic philosophy of education** 31
WILLIAM SWEET

3 **Confucian secular formation and Catholic education: (or the spiritual education of the *Jun Zi*)** 49
ALFREDO P. CO

4 **Education and human formation: a Freirean perspective** 66
PETER ROBERTS

5 **Holistic formation in Asia** 84
NOEL SHETH, S. J.

6 **MacIntyre, rationality and universities** 104
STEVEN STOLZ

7 **Values as a basis for human education: personalistic approach** 122
WLADYSLAW ZUZIAK

8 The promise and risk of the university: secular education in Paul Ricoeur 137
JECKO BELLO

9 Teleological pragmatism: A MacIntyre-shaped university education 151
PHILIP MATTHEWS

10 Values education and Christological personhood: philosophical and practical implications 163
RENEE KOHLER-RYAN AND SANDY LYNCH

11 Adorno's critique of *Halbbildung*: Mapping an emancipatory educational program for critical consciousness 178
RANIER CARLO V. ABENGAÑA

12 Contestation of the ends of higher education and the disciplinary voice 196
JOHN G. QUILTER

13 "The confessing animal": Michel Foucault and the making of a responsible individual 209
WENDYL LUNA

Index 221

Acknowledgements

We would like to gratefully acknowledge the support of the Australian Catholic University Vice Chancellor's Fund, the Philosophy of Education Society of Australasia and most importantly, Conférence Mondiale des Institutions Universitaires Catholiques de Philosophie (COMIUCAP), without whom the regional conference would not have been held and the opportunity to present these essays would not have occurred. We also thank the anonymous reviewers for reviewing these essays and the publishing team for their work in bringing this volume to fruition.

Preface

The modern education system without doubt has been corrupted through being subordinated to the dictates of economic positivism, a pernicious doctrine which holds that unless something is measureable it is meaningless. As a result, we see education systems around the world busying themselves with rankings, benchmarks and outcomes to justify to the government and a sceptical public that the teaching and learning taking place within their institutions are of high quality. The achievement of a high ranking in external university rankings, in government measures of research and of teaching become ends in themselves as institutions seek to attract students and funds as well as position themselves in the marketplace.

Much of the rhetoric surrounding the preoccupation with measurements of various kinds is couched in terms of quality and the need to be vigilant about its maintenance. Institutions need to be confident that students graduating from their ranks have successfully gained the skills and capacities which will enable them to obtain employment in the workforce. Quality assurance practices, therefore, need to measurably show that learning outcomes have been met and that the teaching is of the highest standard. There are two problems here: firstly, that education is primarily concerned with preparing the next generation of workers and hence serves the needs of business, and secondly, that readiness to enter the workforce can be solely measured through the quantification of the skills and capacities they have developed. Education is reduced to what is measureable.

The corrupting influence of the market can also be seen in the way in which research has been subordinated to commercial interests. Governments urge institutions to develop partnerships with business and industry for the sake of the economic well-being of the nation. Research must be commercialisable so that the funding allocated to it is efficiently utilised and there is a return on the investment that has been made. Research which does not make a return on investment is an indulgence which, given the competing demands on government budgets, cannot be justified. The difficulty with this metaphysical ontological reality is that it presumes that what does not have an obvious economic benefit is of no value and in fact becomes invisible since what is not valued can have no being and so no longer has the possibility of entering conscious perception. Academic researchers are therefore urged to undertake, as far as possible, research which has commercial impact. The problem is that this might well mean that important research is never undertaken.

The commercialisation of research and the reduction of education to training for the workplace have significant implications for the kind of society that we are creating. It is one thing to be critical of the directions in which modern education has been led by neo-liberalism but another to provide some alternatives. This volume, which contains a selection of revised essays presented at a regional conference of Conférence Mondiale des Institutions Universitaires Catholiques de Philosophie (COMIUCAP) in Melbourne seeks to provide some alternative ways of thinking about education. Crucially, in their different ways, they argue that education needs to be concerned as much with human formation as with providing young people with employable skills and capacities. Additionally, and equally importantly, they also show how philosophy is central to a critical evaluation of not only the present neoliberal paradigm but also to framing a new vision of education. In particular, the Catholic Intellectual Tradition is drawn upon to argue for the importance of justice, for commitment to the common good and to truth. Through providing an alternative, more ontologically diverse metaphysical framework, the essays bring into being what hitherto has disappeared from view, namely that education must concern itself with forming human persons committed to building just, democratic societies.

Jānis (John) Tālivaldis Ozoliņš
Melbourne, 2016

Notes on contributors

Ranier Carlo V. Abengaña is affiliated with the Department of Philosophy of the University of Santo Tomas (Manila, Philippines) as a graduate student in philosophy and as a part-time/ substitute member of staff for the department. His research interest covers the philosophy of G.W.F. Hegel, with special focus on recognition theory, theory of *Bildung*, philosophy of history and aesthetics. He also finds interest in the philosophy of Adorno, critical theory, general social and political philosophy, social ontology, moral philosophy and philosophy of education. He is a member of the Philosophical Association of the Philippines (PAP, Inc.) and the Philosophical Association of the Visayas and Mindanao (PHAVISMINDA). He is also the current layout editor for *Kritike: An Online Journal of Philosophy* (ISSN 1908–7330), which is the official open access journal of the Department of Philosophy of the University of Santo Tomas, a Commission on Higher Education (CHEd, Philippines) Center of Excellence for Philosophy. As a member of the department, he has participated in several local (as presenter and organiser) and international conferences.

Jecko Bello is a member of the Department of Philosophy at the Pontifical University of Santo Tomas, Manila, Philippines, where he teaches philosophy. As well as his interest in the work of Paul Ricoeur and its influence in Asian cultures, his research interests include continental philosophy, ethical theory and political philosophy.

Alfredo P. Co is an eminent professor of Chinese philosophy and comparative philosophy at the Pontifical University of Santo Tomas, Manila, Philippines. He is president of the prestigious Philippine Academy of Philosophical Research and chair of the Technical Committee for Philosophy of the Philippine Commission on Higher Education. Alfredo P. Co graduated with a Ph.D. in philosophy from the University of Santo Tomas in 1976. He was a special scholar of the Soka University of Japan at the Chinese University of Hong Kong from 1977 to 1978 and has a postdoctorate degree in classical Chinese philosophy from the latter institution. From 1979 to 1981 he took a second postdoctorate degree in comparative philosophy in Sorbonne (*Université de Paris* III and *Université de Paris* IV) as a French government scholar, where he wrote a thesis in French titled *La Notion de Yi chez Kong Zi et la Conception de la Liberte chez Jean-Jacques Rousseau: La Politique du Devoir et la Politique du Droi*. He was a special fellow of the Pacific Cultural Foundation of Taiwan and a special fellow of the International Society for Intercultural Studies and Research (India). A well-published scholar, his works have been widely published in prestigious journals locally and internationally. Professor Co is also the editor of *Karunungan – A Journal of Philosophy*.

Renee Kohler-Ryan (Ph.D.) is a senior lecturer in philosophy and assistant dean of the School of Philosophy and Theology at University of Notre Dame Australia, Sydney campus. She also holds a licentiate from the Catholic University of Leuven. Her publications reflect her academic interests in the ideas, art and architecture of the Middle Ages, the philosophy of the human person and of culture, political philosophy and the dynamic relationship between faith and reason in the Catholic intellectual tradition. In particular, she is the author of commentary on the work of contemporary philosopher William Desmond, including "An Archaeological Ethics: Augustine, Desmond, and Digging Back to the Agapeic Origin" in *Between System and Poetics: Themes in the Work of William Desmond* (Ashgate, 2007.)

Wendyl Luna is undertaking his Ph.D. at the School of Humanities and Languages, Faculty of Arts and Social Sciences, University of New South Wales in Sydney, Australia. In 2015, he graduated with a master's by research degree from the same university with a thesis titled, "Foucault's Reconceptualisation of Kantian Critique." He also holds a master of arts in philosophy, summa cum laude, from the University of Santo Tomas-Graduate School in Manila, Philippines. He has published various articles, including "Foucault and Ethical Subjectivity" and "On the Differences between *A Priori* and *A Posteriori* Thomism." His research interests include contemporary French philosophy, particularly the philosophy of Michel Foucault. For his Ph.D., he is undertaking an in-depth examination of the nature and significance of Foucault's 'pragmatic anthropology,' with the aim of demonstrating that it may be fairly construed as his 'translation' of Kantian anthropology. Examining the implications of this translation for the philosophy of both Foucault and Kant, he proposes to give a fresh interpretation of Kantian anthropology while at the same time uncovering Foucault's 'pragmatic anthropology' and demonstrating its importance and novel contribution to Kantian scholarship.

Sandy Lynch (Ph.D.) is Director of the Institute for Ethics and Society and Professor of Philosophy at the University of Notre Dame Australia, Sydney campus. Her research interests lie in applied and professional ethics, moral philosophy, values education and friendship. She is author of *Philosophy and Friendship* (Edinburgh UP, 2005); *Strategies for a Thinking Classroom* (Primary English Teachers Association, Australia, 2008); "Friendship and Happiness from a Philosophical Perspective" in *Friendship and Happiness* (Springer, 2015) and "Philosophy, Play and Ethics in Education" in *Philosophical Perspectives on Play* (Routledge, 2015).

Philip Matthews is currently Acting Dean of the School of Philosophy and Theology of the Fremantle campus for the University of Notre Dame, Australia. Previously head of the Bioethics Teaching and Research Unit at Curtin University and clinical ethicist on the Reproductive Technology Council of Western Australia, Dr Matthews's primary research involves the integration of philosophical analysis to complex issues in health care. He is involved in 'second generation bioethics,' a concept articulated by the Hastings Centre after the first generation of bioethics was shown to be inappropriately confident about the role that reason plays in debates over bioethical issues. Recent publications include "Justice: Thin Pragmatism Between Thick Practices" in D. Neville (ed.). *The Bible, Justice and Public Theology*, Sheffield Phoenix Press (2014).

Jānis (John) Tālivaldis Ozoliņš, FHERDSA, FPESA, FACE, Foreign Member of the Latvian Academy of Sciences, is Professor of Philosophy in the School of Philosophy (National) at Australian Catholic University, Honorary Fellow, Institute of Philosophy and Sociology, University of Latvia, and was Inaugural Crawford Miller Visiting Research Fellow at St. Cross College, Oxford. He has been a visiting professor at Wuhan University, Wuhan China and University of St. Thomas, Houston, Texas. He is Reviews Editor of *Educational Philosophy and Theory*, Editor of *Res Disputandae*, formerly *Ethics Education*, and an editorial consultant on a number of international refereed journals. He has interests in the metaphysics of Aquinas, Eastern philosophy, philosophy of education and applied ethics and has numerous publications in these areas. His work has been translated into French, Spanish, Turkish, Polish and Chinese. He has also published in his native language, Latvian. His most recent publications include *Foundations of Health Care Ethics* (CUP, 2015) and *Religion and Culture in Dialogue* (Springer, 2016).

John G. Quilter has taught philosophy at Sydney University, Pittsburgh University and, since 1991, Australian Catholic University, Sydney. Quilter is a former Fulbright scholar and has held a number of travelling research scholarships. Quilter was a visiting lecturer in philosophy at Auckland University, a visiting fellow in the Philosophy Department in the Research School of Social Sciences at Australian National University and a visiting lecturer at the University of Örebro, Sweden. Quilter has published in philosophy of religion, philosophy of education, health-care ethics, ancient philosophy, ancient Greek tragedy, moral philosophy and international ethics. He has been has been a judge in the Eureka Prize for Ethics, chief examiner of the New South Wales Higher School Certificate (NSW HSC) Studies of Religion and is chairperson of the Australia Hearing Human Research Ethics Committee. Current interests include luck in morality and epistemology and philosophical issues in dialogue between traditions.

Peter Roberts is Professor of Education and Director of the Educational Theory, Policy and Practice Research Hub at the University of Canterbury in New Zealand. His primary areas of scholarship are philosophy of education and educational policy studies. His most recent books include *Happiness, Hope, and Despair: Rethinking the Role of Education* (2016); *Education, Ethics and Existence: Camus and the Human Condition* (with Andrew Gibbons and Richard Heraud, 2015); *Better Worlds: Education, Art, and Utopia* (with John Freeman-Moir, 2013); *The Virtues of Openness: Education, Science, and Scholarship in the Digital Age* (with Michael Peters, 2011); *Paulo Freire in the 21st Century: Education, Dialogue, and Transformation* (2010); and *Neoliberalism, Higher Education and Research* (with Michael Peters, 2008). In 2012 Peter was a Rutherford visiting scholar at Trinity College, Cambridge, and in 2016 he was a Canterbury fellow at the University of Oxford. He is the immediate past president of the Philosophy of Education Society of Australasia.

Noel Sheth, S. J., who completed his Ph.D. in Sanskrit at Harvard University, is a Jesuit priest and president/principal emeritus of Jnana-Deepa Vidyapeeth, Pune, India, where he is a professor of Indian Religions and Philosophies. An expert in Indian culture and Sanskrit, he has taught various courses in Hindu, Zoroastrian (Parsi), Jain, Buddhist, Christian and Sikh philosophies and religions in the Faculties of Philosophy and Theology (Religion). His publications are on the exegesis of Sanskrit and Pali texts, on Indian religions and on comparative theology and philosophy. His book *The Divinity of Krishna* is mentioned in the prestigious international *Encyclopedia of Religion*, in both the first and second editions. His more than 100 research articles deal with the exegesis of Sanskrit and Pali texts, on Hinduism, on Buddhism and on comparative philosophy and religion. A scholar of international repute, he has received many awards, is a member of various international learned societies and administrative bodies, and on the board of editors of some international journals.

Steven Stolz is a senior lecturer at La Trobe University, Australia. Before becoming an academic, he taught for 10 years as a secondary school teacher in the curriculum areas of mathematics, science, physical education, sport and religious education. Since transferring to the higher education sector, he has received a number of notable academic awards and distinctions, such as the Philosophy of Education Society of Australasia doctoral scholarship in 2011, the Faculty of Education emerging researcher award in 2013 and an invitation to be visiting scholar at the University of Stirling (UK) in 2014. Currently, his primary areas of scholarship are educational philosophy and theory; however, due to his grounding in the Catholic philosophical tradition he gained an interest and commitment to MacIntyre's extensive corpus, which is now in its 10th year. At the moment, he has a particular philosophical interest in Nietzsche's thinking on moral agency, morals and morality, value and values, art and aesthetics, knowledge and truth.

William Sweet is Professor of Philosophy and Director of the Centre for Philosophy, Theology, and Cultural Traditions at St. Francis Xavier University (Canada). A past president of the Canadian Philosophical Association, he is currently Vice President of the Council for Research on Values in Philosophy and a member of the Steering Committee of the Fédération Internationale des Sociétés de Philosophie. He has lectured on six continents and has taught at universities in North America, Asia and Europe. He has published particularly in cross-cultural philosophy of religion, ethics, political philosophy and human rights. He is an editor of the journal *Philosophy, Culture, and Traditions* and is the author and/or editor of some 30 books – among the more recent are *Intercultural Dialogue and Human Rights* (2011); *Migrating Texts and Traditions* (2012); and *Ideas Under Fire* (2013). He is a fellow of the Royal Asiatic Society and the Royal Historical Society and has been named presidente d'onore of the Istituto Internazionale Jacques Maritain.

Władysław Zuziak, from the Pontifical University of John Paul II in Cracow, was born in Lipowa, Poland. He completed his master of theology at the Pontifical Faculty of Theology in Cracow, in 1977, his doctorate at the Catholic University of Louvain-la-Neuve, in 1990 and his postdoctoral studies (habilitation) in 1999. In 1993 he received a scholarship to the Catholic University of America (Washington, D.C.). He has participated in a number of academic conferences, among many others, in Budapest, Louvain, Mexico City, Nijmegen, Paris and Rome. From 1997 to 2000 he was the vice-chair of the Faculty of Philosophy at the Pontifical Academy of Theology in Cracow and chair of this faculty from 2000 to 2006. He has been acting as president of the Pontifical University of John Paul II in Cracow since 2010. He is Vice-President of the Federation of European Catholic Universities (FUCE) and a member of the European Society for the Study of Science and Theology (ESSAT) and the Polish Philosophical Society (PPS). He was from 2003 to 2008 the president of the European section of Conférence Mondiale des Institutions Universitaires Catholiques de Philosophie (COMIUCAP, the World Conference of Catholic University Institutions of Philosophy). His research areas include philosophy of man, ethics, personalism and French contemplative philosophy. His major published works include: *Dojrzewanie świadomości refleksyjnej w filozofii moralnej Georgesa Bastide'a i Jeana Nalberta* (Maturing of Contemplative Consciousness in Moral Philosophy of Georges Bastide and Jean Nalbert, Cracow 1998); *Społeczne perspektywy etyki* (Social Outlook on Ethics, Cracow 2006); and *Wokół tożsamości człowieka* (ed.) (Of Human Identity, Cracow 2006).

Introduction

Jānis (John) Tālivaldis Ozoliņš

Education has been widely criticised in academic circles as being too narrowly focused on skills, capacities and the transference of knowledge that can be used in the workplace. Governments and business, however, are deeply critical of education which does not lead to graduates who are immediately employable and who can contribute to economic growth and national prosperity. Because they provide significant amounts of funding, governments have asserted more and more control over educational institutions, particularly higher education institutions, and these have been forced to provide, not unreasonably, an account of how they have expended the funds they have been allocated. The rhetoric of efficiency and effectiveness, combined with a conception of education as a commercial transaction between a service provider and service user, has seen a shift to the assessment of the education provided and of higher education institutions themselves in terms of measureable outcomes. As well as careful stewardship, governments – and the taxpayers who ultimately provide the funds – are justified in demanding from higher educational institutions (HEIs) an account of how they have been expended. The problem is that the confluence of this obligation together with an impoverished commercial conception of education has led to the exclusion of any other purposes for education except for those which can be measured and which contribute to the employability of graduates. Anything that cannot be reduced to demonstrable behavioural outcomes becomes not only worthless but also well-nigh invisible in the curriculums of universities. The dominance of economic rationalism and neo-liberalism has distorted the nature of education so that it has become a commodity to be packaged, marketed and sold to potential customers. Within the last decade, the language of the marketplace has infiltrated the lexicon of higher education so that students have become consumers of an educational product and academic staff service providers, and education has become an industry.

As Heidegger hypothesised, this has also seen a shift in the organisation of educational institutions so that they are increasingly organised along the lines of an industrial corporation (Thompson, 2001, p. 244). What this means is that in taking education as having a certain kind of use or "handiness", it becomes ontologically defined as having a certain kind of being and reality (Heidegger, 1996, pp. 59–71). As a result, the means of its transmission, the higher education institution, adapts to the form required for its efficient dissemination as a product of a particular kind having a specific use. In its extreme form, this leads to an organisation in which a managerial elite controls the means of production of educational products, develops new products according to what marketing modelling suggests consumers want to buy and discards those that are failing to sell. Tasks are divided amongst product developers and product deliverers. The process is overseen by supervisors whose task is to ensure quality assurance of the product so that consumers receive what they have paid for. The power of technology has been harnessed to help develop products that can be consumed online without the need of any interaction between students and teachers. The phenomenon of Massive Open Online Courses (MOOCs) is the ultimate sign of how far and how deep commodification has become entrenched in education (Deneen, 2013).

The MOOC is ostensibly a free online subject or unit available to anyone who wishes to undertake it and is offered by a prestigious HEI. Those taking it as a free subject, however, do not receive credit towards a degree or a qualification. They may, on payment of a fee, receive a certificate acknowledging their completion of the MOOC should they satisfactorily finish the assessment. The rationale for the MOOC is that it makes accessible, free of charge, the expertise of a great many leading academics, normally only available to the paying students of a particular institution, to the rest of the world. Those taking the online course, therefore, need not miss out on the highest-quality tuition provided by world-renowned experts. It is also a very useful marketing tool since the MOOC can have many thousands of students undertaking it, providing them with a taste of higher education study at a very prestigious institution and at the same time reinforcing its status. Conceived as a means of bringing the work of the very best academics within reach of everyone who is interested in higher education study, but without charging them fees, at first glance seems to be remarkably altruistic. After all, a MOOC offered by Harvard or MIT that costs nothing to the participating student brings higher education within reach of the poorest and most deprived socio-economic groups. The reality, however, is that though many thousands of students may enrol in a MOOC, the drop-out rates are very high, and their impersonal nature makes it impossible for there to be any student-teacher relationship in the learning journey (Haber, 2014, pp. 88–130). The salient point, however, is that MOOCs themselves are a vehicle whereby institutions can advertise their "product," give a free sample of what it is like to study at that institution and spread the advertising message. MOOCs are a remarkable marketing tool and possibly the beginning of a form of massification and standardisation of curriculum.

The obsession with standards and benchmarks, as well as ranking of institutions, observable throughout the world, as institutions strive to demonstrate the quality of their curriculum offerings, is inexorably drawing us towards standardised courses and subjects. The tendency for HEIs to increase in size and develop into multi-campus institutions is another factor in this process. Offering the same course at different sites naturally results in a desire to ensure that the courses offered are of comparable standards, and this means the curriculum that is taught needs to be rigidly controlled. One means of doing this is to have much of the material to be taught available online, including lectures. The course can then be serviced by relatively cheap graduate students and adjuncts who would provide a minimal face-to-face contact and do the assessment (until it can be automated). MOOCs are a brilliant way to increase cost-effectiveness and to standardise courses across different providers. As a final step, there is no need to have different providers either – these can all become franchises of the biggest and most entrepreneurial institutions. The ultimate result of turning HEIs into corporations is that eventually they will begin to behave like other corporations, and the strong will devour the weak as they strive to improve their profitability and climb the rankings.

The process of radically reconstructing HEIs, something already observed as beginning to occur in the post Second World War period in the 20th century, has accelerated in the last decade or so. It has not been accompanied by the adoption of the best corporate models but, rather, the worst of discredited 19th- and 20th-century organisational principles (Chomsky, 2014). HEIs are distinguished by their rigid hierarchical structures where managerialism rules. The vice chancellor is reconceived as a chief executive officer, and the panoply of deputy vice chancellors, provosts, pro vice chancellors, directors, executive deans, associate deans and heads of schools form a managerial pyramid tasked with implementing the latest strategic plan. Professional staff are seen as assisting this process and ensuring its smooth implementation, while academic staff are required to support the institution's strategic plan through their individual agreed annual performance plans. For the workforce to meet the changing requirements of the institution, these performance plans need to be sufficiently flexible to allow for the changing demands of the educational marketplace.[1] A recent example of flexibility and the necessity of a nimble response to changing conditions in the marketplace is the breaking of the traditional nexus between research and teaching. With the creation of academic pathways, academics can choose – or, more often, have chosen for them – a career as a teaching-only academic, one that combines teaching and research, one that is research only, and one that involves administration only. The restructuring of the academic workforce touted as giving academics flexibility in their careers, has the opposite effect, confining them largely to one pathway, especially for teaching-only academics. Another example is provided by the extent to which academic work has become casualised. While the workforce more generally has become casualised, in universities it is not unusual for more than 50 percent of teaching to be done by casual or part-time academics (Barcan, 2013; Gill, 2014). There is much more to be said about the organisation of HEIs in the modern era and the impact that their changing structures have had on the conception of education and the role of academics in its provision (Kwiek, 2012).

Amongst academics, there is profound dissatisfaction with these changes, whether one ascribes them to neo-liberalism, economic rationalism or the massification of education. The clash between the laudable desire by communities to give access to higher education to a wider socio-economic range of individuals and the cost of its provision in a stagnated economic climate is serious, significant and has to be addressed. The difficulty is that in trying to balance competing budgetary pressures, the proposed solution is to turn HEIs into Gradgrindian businesses that squeeze as much productivity out of their employees, the hapless academics, as they possibly can for the least amount of outlay. There is a terrible logic in this since the major cost of running any educational institution is staff salaries. It follows that any means that can be found to minimise this cost will be used. Ironically, squeezing staff salaries does not apply to management as progressively management salary increases have vastly outstripped the salary increases of academic staff (Houghton, 2016). The corporatisation of many institutions has also seen the number of professional staff outnumber academic staff as more and more functions are shifted to lower-paid staff, which itself brings about a shift in the nature of the institution (Larkins, 2012). This also results in the further casualization of the academic workforce, the reduction of tenured positions and a shift of university resources to increasing government-funded student places through bigger and better marketing strategies. These will inevitably focus on marketing those courses which are popular and which will ensure the employability of its graduates. Courses which offer a wide range of humanities subjects, such as history, literature, languages, classics and philosophy, are difficult to market since they are not vocationally oriented. As a result, enrolments in the humanities fall.[2]

Elements of the foregoing discussion will be recognisable to most academics; there is no question that the present corporate model of HEIs is firmly entrenched, and the possibility of any change soon is bleak. In one sense, it is not so much the model of university structure which needs to be challenged but the conception of education which is the means of transmission. What is crucial is that there is resistance to the thought that there is only one understanding of education and to the hegemonic pressure which valorises only that form of education which leads to the development of skills and capacities that an employer will find useful. Conceiving of education in a different way will inevitably lead to a different structure in its transmission.

What is missing in the present model of education is any conception of it as a formation of human persons so that they develop the virtues and values that they need to not only lead successful lives but also be responsible members of their communities, working for the common good and acting to transform them into just societies. The notion of human formation as central to education is a hallmark of not only the Catholic intellectual tradition but also of the Confucian tradition. Religion and culture have crucial roles to play in transmitting the values and beliefs that have underpinned the thought that education is about the initiation of persons into the life of a community, its continuance through the building of just structures and commitment to the common good. It implies a creation of a civil society that can act as a mediator between the power of the state and that of the market. This suggests a much richer notion of education than the neo-liberal model. The essays comprising this volume explore alternative conceptions of education that see it more broadly than the provision of skills and capacities that are marketable in the workplace. It will also be apparent, not so much through the provision of an argument demonstrating its importance but through its deployment in the arguments presented for alternative conceptions of education, that philosophy in fostering a renewed understanding of education as the formation of persons and of civil society has a significant role to play in education.

The first essay, by Jānis (John) Tālivaldis Ozoliņš, reflects on the role that civil society plays in the creation of the democratic state. Most people value democracy and the idea of the democratic state, but there are different conceptions of it. Ozoliņš argues that not all conceptions of democracy are acceptable, and we need to go back to classical formulations to help us identify what its essential elements are. These will include a respect for persons, the rule of law and a concern for the common good. He notes that there is a tension between conceiving democracy as freedom to choose and democracy as the pursuit of justice and the common good. These are not mutually exclusive, however, and it is the responsibility of citizens to make informed and rational decisions where these two crucial values come into conflict. This will only be possible in a democratic civil society that is able to discern, on rational reflection, a way forward. It follows that if we are committed to democracy, then our public institutions, such as schools and universities, must also be committed to the formation of democratic citizens. This means that education cannot be conceived as only concerned with the pursuit of skills and capacities necessary for employment.

William Sweet begins the second chapter acknowledging the many and varied critiques of education that have been made and takes up the challenge to identify those principles of education which will meet some of these criticisms. The root problem, as Sweet sees it, is that a thoughtful understanding of the nature and purpose of education is missing, not only in educational institutions themselves but also within the broader community. Catholic philosophy of education has a venerable history, and Sweet thinks that it provides a useful starting point to begin consideration of what should be the underlying principles of education. The various religious orders that founded educational institutions recognised a number of basic principles of education: (i) a focus on the person; (ii) formation in various religious, social and cultural traditions and (iii) an appreciation of the good, the true and the divine. In elaborating these principles, Sweet draws on a number of sources, including Maritain and Benedict XVI.

In Chapter 3, Alfredo P. Co draws our attention to the great Confucian tradition of education which developed in the Middle Kingdom 500 years before the dawn of the Christian era. He notes that before the development of universities in the West during the Middle Ages, the great centre of learning, called Ji Xia Zhi Xue (稷下之學) or Ji Xia Academy, had been founded in the Chinese state of Qi (齊) in the time of King Xuan (齊宣王) (319–301 BCE). Confucian philosophy, says Co, centres on the nature of human reality and what it is to be a humane person. It is based on five important principles, Ren (仁), Yi (義), Li

(禮), Zhi (智) and Xin (信). The first four, as Co discusses them, are recognisably moral principles that arguably have their counterparts in Western moral virtues. The last, Xin, refers to the commitment of the virtuous person to keep his or her word. Co shows that Confucian education is designed to create a community where people can live in harmony, focussing on the good of human beings and that of society. Missing from Confucian education, however, is a strong sense of the human being as having an immortal soul, and so there is, in the encounter with Christian thought, some disturbing and challenging new ideas to take into account.

Chapter 4, by Peter Roberts, invites us to consider the educational thought of the great Brazilian educationalist, Paulo Freire, who exhorts us to struggle against oppression and the dominance of neo-liberal ideas in social, economic and educational policy. Roberts argues that a key element in Freire's thought is hope, which he regards as a defining feature of human existence. Hope, however, is connected to despair, and it is through reflection on its root causes that we can begin to find a means of overcoming it. Oppression and suffering, however, especially due to an unjust social order as Freire experienced it in Brazil cannot be overcome except through a careful, critical and profound analysis of its origins and the means by which it is maintained so that a radical structural transformation of it can be undertaken. Transformation, however, can only be realised through our becoming more fully human, and this means overcoming those forces which dehumanise us. Roberts shows that out of despair, hope can arise and out of oppression, liberation. It is this which is the core of Freirean education. The broader questions of what makes us human are much more important than merely acquiring skills and capacities which enable us to be employable.

Noel Sheth returns the discussion to the riches of Asian conceptions of education in Chapter 5. The theme, however, remains the same, namely, the kind of education which is needed for human beings to be more fully human. He criticises the largely Western emphasis on rationality, proposing that instead of speaking of education, it is better to speak of formation. This is a much more holistic term in his view and captures what is missing from the education available in most modern educational institutions, namely a sense of the mystery of the world and of the value of intuition. Sheth presents us with three exemplars of the kind of holistic education which he says is needed as an antidote to the lopsided education that is offered in the contemporary world. The three are: (i) the Hindu Mohandas Karamchand Gandhi from India, (ii) the Buddhist Arayatne from Sri Lanka and (iii) the Buddhist Sivaraksa from Thailand. Each of these, in their own way, propose an education which is focussed on what it means to be a human being; Gandhi, for instance, argues for an education which develops character. The soul, he says, cannot be ignored. Ariyaratne advocates an integrated education and stresses the value of personal religious transformation. Sivaraksa proposes that students learn altruism, compassion and peace so that they can fulfil their social responsibilities. These virtues are addressed through the cultivation of wisdom, ethics and meditation.

Steven Stolz turns, in Chapter 6, to an analysis of MacIntyre's critique of the modern university and his argument that philosophy and theology ought to have a central place in both secular and Catholic universities. MacIntyre laments the fact that these two disciplines have become marginalised in modern HEIs. Stolz's central thesis is that MacIntyre's critique should be heeded since he illustrates in a series of works how in the Western world, the lack of consensus about the nature or rationality leads to there being no way of adjudicating between moral traditions. Worse still, there is no consciousness of there being different traditions nor that a secular viewpoint is not value neutral. Stolz argues that MacIntyre's theory of rational vindication, deployed in a dialectical manner, and providing a means of testing the truth claims of rival traditions, needs to be deployed within universities so that they are revitalised and once more become places of independent rational inquiry and wisdom. The key role of universities, therefore, is to develop students who are independent rational inquirers, a far cry from merely having a role in providing skilled workers for the workplace.

The importance of values and of the human person from a phenomenological and Christian personalist perspective is discussed in Chapter 7 by Wladyslaw Zuziak. The focus of the article is on the human person and what follows from an understanding of human nature. That is, it is argued that once we have an understanding of what it means to be a human being, we have an understanding of the values which will enable the human person to flourish. Crucially, education has a central role in developing in students an understanding of the values in the world in which they live and the critical capacity and commitment to improving the world in which they live. Our understanding of ourselves as human beings does not come easily, for we are complex beings, and Zuziak draws on the insights of Maritain and Karol Wojtyla amongst others in providing an account of what it means to be a human person. Such an understanding is essential if human beings are not to be led astray in focussing their attention on themselves and the false goals of materialism. Zuziak also argues that an essential element in our conception of the human person is the recognition of his or her relationship with God. The role of philosophical reflection and analysis is powerfully illustrated in this chapter, demonstrating how alternative conceptions of the nature of persons can provide us with a different perspective on education.

The problematic of secularism and the secularisation of the university as it relates to our conception of what it is to be a human being is taken up in Chapter 8 by Jecko Bello. Secularism as it prevails in the modern world is problematic, for it is destructive in the public arena of traditions and culture since it imposes a form of anonymity on the human subject. There is a tension between the techno-secular assimilation of cultures so that they become uniform, and the impulse is to preserve cultures and traditions. Drawing on the work of Paul Ricoeur, Bello argues that though secularism is problematic, a fruitful way of thinking about the university is as a place where multiple perspectives can come together to be discussed. Bello goes on to discuss Ricoeur's conception of the university as a locus for the inculcation of culture as well as of various skills and capacities.

In Chapter 9 Philip Matthews brings us back to MacIntyre to argue that despite his gloom about moral philosophy, there is consensus about the goods of education. Moreover, the relationship between narrative, practice and tradition that MacIntyre demonstrated can be utilised in a university setting, and this suggests that a MacIntyrean approach to university education can be implemented. Matthews begins his task by firstly considering Macintyre's frustration at the parlous state of moral philosophy and the problem of the incommensurability of rival versions of moral inquiry. He argues that MacIntyre's pessimism about the lack of consensus amongst moral philosophers is overstated, and there is in fact some agreement over thin minimalist moral propositions. This leads to Matthews's argument that it is MacIntyre's method that provides direction to new graduates in the conduct of their professional lives rather than a specific moral theory. That is, it is through narrative, practice and tradition that they learn what is the right thing to do.

Renee Kohler-Ryan and Sandy Lynch continue the discussion of the nature of moral education in Chapter 10, focussing on how students in professional programs can best learn how to make ethical decisions. The formation of students, they remind us, is not simply about the professional skills, knowledge and understanding that they will acquire but also how, within a Catholic university, they can become men and women capable of rational and critical judgement, conscious of the transcendent dignity of the human person. Drawing on Christology, they develop a conception of the human person which highlights the spiritual dimension of human existence. As a consequence, the quest for knowledge is a search for truth, and the ultimate truth is God Himself. Values are only intelligible when they pertain to knowledge and the reality which is God. Kohler-Ryan and Lynch go on to develop a vision of the university very much at odds with the corporate university. Drawing on the seminal Church document, *Ex Corde Ecclesiae*, as they characterise it, the university has an agapeic dimension, which is to say it takes the form of a self-giving community with Christ's self-giving love at its source. Philosophy has a role in elaborating what this means for a university education, and Kohler-Ryan and Lynch focus on discussing the implications a Christological approach to an understanding of the human person has for the teaching of ethics.

Chapter 11 by Ranier Carlo V. Abengaña presents the salient points of Adorno's critique of education, which he does through tracing it back to his critique of culture. Abengaña quite rightly observes that the kind of educational institutions a society gets will be dependent on the kind of society it is. This echoes Ozoliņš, who holds that if we want a democratic society, we need a democratic civil society. Abengaña utilises critical theory to demonstrate that there are three problems that exist in modern education and need to be addressed: (i) education is no longer concerned with developing critical thinking; (ii) education as currently conceived excludes alternative conceptions and (iii) education has become a matter of conformation rather than formation. He then provides an account of Adorno's notion of *Bildung* and *Halbbildung* to show that a key element in education is emancipation, not merely through the gaining of knowledge but through self-understanding of what it means to be a mature and autonomous human person. The philosopher can contribute to the understanding of education as *Bildung* through providing a critique of culture and society.

John G. Quilter in Chapter 12 observes that the neo-liberal conception of higher education reduces it to something transactional like the services provided by a hotel or a car mechanic. There are, however, aspects of higher education which are positive forces of socio-economic change. For instance, expanding the provision of higher education has meant that it is available to a broader socio-economic class, especially those from disadvantaged backgrounds. This is a positive development since enables families to improve their economic and social positions as well as bringing new perspectives to the professions. Despite the positives, Quilter believes that the university is in serious trouble because it is not sure anymore what it is for. He argues this by drawing on examples from his own discipline of philosophy and reflecting on what it means to teach. He provides a strong critique of current practices in teaching and learning and contends that there is much more to learning a discipline than fulfilling learning outcomes. Whatever else a university education is for, it should also develop in students a love of the discipline they are studying.

The final Chapter 13, by Wendyl Luna, following Foucault, contends that the Christian sacrament of confession does not stifle freedom, but produces responsible citizens and is one of the main techniques in the West for producing truth. Foucault is nevertheless critical of the practice of confession, particularly in the context of sex and sexuality. This is because he sees it as connected to various mechanisms of knowledge and power that revolve around sex. According to Foucault, sexuality is constructed, allowing modern power to exercise control and subjecting us to new modes of power. Luna says that understanding the connections between sexuality and confession as linked to modes of power enable us to turn to Foucault's critique of the production of truth. Foucault observes that truth has become the province of the expert, and it is through experts that a politics of truth emerges. Luna then turns to a discussion of *parrēsia*, a way of discussing the truth which binds the speaker in such a way that he or she is committed to the truth despite the risks this might bring. *Parrēsia* is thus not just about truth telling, however, but about proper governance of self and of others. The salient question then is how this can be inculcated in persons.

Each of the essays in this collection has something important to say about education and makes a contribution to thinking about education in a different way. They also illustrate the power of philosophy to provide both the analysis required to elucidate the present parlous state of education and the synthesis of a variety of ideas to propose new ways of conceiving education. Truth be told, they are not all new but revisit older conceptions of education oriented to the formation of persons and the construction of a society that focussed on the common good and with the creation of a just state.

Notes

1 For a discussion of the corporatisation of the American university which chronicles in some detail the resulting changes that have taken place and which criticises the shift to a corporate model of the university, see B. Ginsberg (2011).
2 See, for instance, Armitage et al. (2013), who discuss the decline of the humanities at Harvard over the last 50 years and the reasons for this. Other views, however, suggest that the situation is not quite as bleak as commonly thought, though the closure or amalgamation of classics, history and philosophy departments seems to support the former view. See also Turner and Brass (2014).

References

Armitage, David, Bhabha, Homi, Dench, Emma, Hamburger, Jeffrey, Hamilton, John, Kelly, Sean, Lambert-Beatty, Carrie, McDonald, Christie, Shreffler, Anne, and Simpson, James. (2013). *The Teaching of the Humanities and the Arts at Harvard College: Mapping the Future*. Harvard: Harvard University. Retrieved from: http://artsandhumanities.fas.harvard.edu/files/humanities/files/mapping_the_future_31_may_2013.pdf

Barcan, R. (2013). *Academic Life and Labour in the New University: Hope and Other Choices*. London: Ashgate.

Chomsky, Noam. (2014). Corporate Business Models Are Hurting American Universities. *Salon*, Friday, October 10, 2014. Retrieved from: http://www.salon.com/2014/10/10/noam_chomsky_corporate_business_models_are_hurting_american_universities_partner/

Deneen, Patrick J. (2013). We Are All to Blame for MOOCs. *Chronicle of Higher Education*, June 3, 2013. Retrieved from: http://search.proquest.com.ezproxy1.acu.edu.au/docview/1370714402?accountid=8194&rfr_id=info%3Axri%2Fsid%3Aprimo

Gill, Rosalind. (2014). Academics, Cultural Workers and Critical Labour Studies. *Journal of Cultural Economy*, 7 (1), 12–30.

Ginsberg, Benjamin. (2011). *The Fall of the Faculty: The Rise of the All Administrative University*. Oxford: Oxford University Press.

Haber, Johnathan. (2014). *MOOCs*. Cambridge, MA: MIT Press.

Heidegger, M. (1996). *Being and Time*. Tr. Joan Stambaugh. New York: State University of New York Press.

Houghton, Des. (2016). Opinion: Universities Cry Poor While Vice-Chancellors Make a Motza. *Courier-Mail*, April 15. Retrieved from: http://www.couriermail.com.au/news/opinion/opinion-universities-cry-poor-while-vicechancellors-make-a-motza/news-story/52b8eea62c6a30d9ae5b4faa1426e790

Kwiek, Marek. (2012). *Knowledge Production in European Universities: States, Markets, and Academic Entrepreneurialism*. Frankfurt: Peter Lang GmbH. Retrieved from: http://site.ebrary.com.ezproxy1.acu.edu.au/lib/australiancathu/reader.action?docID=10666127&ppg=107

Larkins, Frank P. (2012). Trends in Non-Academic Staff for Australian Universities 2000 to 2010. *L. H. Martin Institute*. Retrieved from: http://www.lhmartininstitute.edu.au/userfiles/files/HE%20Trends%20-%20Uni%20Gen%20Staff%203_FLarkins_original_updated 270612.pdf

Thompson, I. (2001). Heidegger on Ontological Education or: On How We Become What We Are. *Inquiry*, 44 (3), 243–268.

Turner, Graeme and Brass, Kylie. (2014). *Mapping the Humanities, Arts and Social Sciences in Australia*. Canberra: Australian Academy of the Humanities.

1 Democracy, civil society and education

Jānis (John) Tālivaldis Ozoliņš

Introduction

Many commentators believe that democracy is much eroded, so much so that there is talk of a crisis of democracy. There are various reasons put forward for this, such as dissatisfaction with the political process, lack of trust of politicians and governments, the lack of political literacy, the increasing power of unelected corporations and institutions and the decline in membership of political parties (Campos and André, 2014; Hay and Stoker, 2009; Rapeli, 2014; Vibert, 2007; Whiteley, 2009). Despite this, the central idea that it involves citizens – individuals as members of the state – in decision-making about the responsibilities of the state in effecting the good life for them is highly valued. Arguments rage about what the responsibilities of the state are,[1] but few question the importance and value of democracy.[2] We accept that democracy is important and highly valuable, but it is not always clear what is meant by democracy nor whether it is to be restricted to the political arena or is more generally applicable in wider civil society.

There is extensive literature on democracy, which indicates significant variations in and debate about its nature. As a result, this allows many states to claim to be democratic, so there is a valuing of the notion of democracy, but whether they are actually democratic is another matter. As one extreme example we have states claiming to be democratic, such as the Democratic People's Republic of Korea, with a tyrant, Kim Jong-un, of the kind Plato would readily recognise, in power. North Korea does not fit our intuitive understanding of what is a democratic state. Another example is provided by Zimbabwe, where Robert Mugabe survives as president due to rigged elections.[3] By contrast, neither the United States, United Kingdom nor Australia, amongst Western nations, include democratic in their full names but would represent themselves as democratic states. These three also differ in their political constitutions, but in all three, all citizens are eligible to vote and to stand for election. The extent to which each is a democratic state will depend on what we mean by democracy and the extent to which they deviate from that understanding. To some degree, this will be reliant on our perspective; nevertheless, whatever our view of democracy, we can observe that in a modern state, the ability to influence the direction of government (as the representatives of the people, governing on their behalf) seems diminished. This appears to be related to the size of the state, since as it increases, the locus of decision-making shifts further away from the local level. In addition, much decision-making is undertaken by professional elites who advise government, leaving little opportunity for ordinary citizens to have an input. There are usually good reasons of efficiency and effectiveness why this should be so, but the result of this is that public consultation about issues which affect the ordinary citizen does not take place or does so only in a cursory manner. This causes the interested citizen to become alienated from the processes of government.[4]

Both Plato and Aristotle provide us with an account of the ideal state. Plato develops his ideas about the nature of the state over a number of dialogues, beginning with *The Republic*, in *The Statesman* and finally in *The Laws*. It is only in the latter dialogues that with some reservations, he comes to the view that democracy provides the best form of government. The reasons for this can be well appreciated since Plato believes that the state should be directed towards the common good and justice and not towards the maximisation of freedom. Aristotle in the *Politics*, also considers the question of the ideal state and agrees that the state should be directed to the common good. In Plato's view, concentration on freedom results in individuals pursuing their own selfish ends, and so the possibility of each coming into conflict with the other increases. This leads to a community in which goods are unevenly distributed as well as the need for protection of property by the state. Plato's republic was to be led by someone with the capacity to see what was good and to pursue it on behalf of the citizens. This was not recognisably a democratic state.

Unsurprisingly, Aristotle's account of the state was modelled on the Athenian state. It was democratic in that all citizens were entitled to vote and had the responsibility of holding various offices in turn. Citizens in Aristotle's city-state had to have sufficient leisure to be able to carry out their duties as citizens. This meant that poor citizens were generally unable to take up their responsibilities, and moreover, not everyone could be a citizen. Women were excluded. In addition, Aristotle's ideal state required a large number of slaves. Although there were elements of democracy in Aristotle's state, it too, could not be recognisably a modern democratic state.

In one sense, this is immaterial since it allows us to reflect on the reasons why a democratic state is to be preferred to other forms of state organisation and on the tensions among key elements of a democratic state. It is clear from the foregoing that democracy understood as freedom to determine how to live, that is, as a maximisation of the freedom of the citizen to construct his or her life according to his or her own conceptions of the good life is in tension with a conception of democracy understood as the maximisation of the common good for all citizens. It is evident that polarising around either of these principles leads to different conceptions of society. If the former dominates, then we have a libertarian society where individual rights override the common good, and if the latter dominates, we have a society where the common good overrides individual rights. It seems that the kind of democracy that is possible seems to be much dependent on the type of social and political community in which it arises.

Civil society, we shall argue, is the locus of democracy. Education which takes seriously the formation of citizens so that they accept their responsibilities in a democratic society will only succeed if it is supported both in the basic unit of society, the family, as well as in civil society. Civil society, however, to be democratic, needs to also be formed so that its own structures are democratic and the values it practises are democratic. It is not naturally democratic. Civil society is made up of many different groups, institutions and associations, and it is evident that many associations and businesses are not democratic. Associations have rules about who can join and may be governed by entrenched interests, while businesses can be owned by private individuals to whom employees are beholden. In the former case, membership of the association may be decided by being considered acceptable by a particular group; for example, someone seeking election to a private club might need to demonstrate that he or she has the same values, level of wealth or social standing as other members of the club. He or she may need to be sponsored by existing members who vouch for their acceptability. Thus, membership is conferred through patronage and being acceptable to the most influential group. Continued membership may involve unquestioned loyalty to that group. In the latter case, the business owner is the employer, and so there is an unequal power relation with those who are employees. The employer is not obliged to consult the employees.

It is essential that civil society be democratic, however; otherwise, it is doubtful that the state will be democratic. This is because commitment to democracy is difficult to achieve if citizens have no experience with democratic values and structures in their lives. It is not impossible for a state to be democratic (in having free elections) and civil society lag behind, as appears to have been the case in Pakistan, which interspersed with military dictatorship, has had liberal, democratic government, but its civil society remains closer to feudal society (Waheed and Abbasi, 2013). Given the continuing problems in that country, however, it hardly seems to be an exception to the need for civil society itself to be open and democratic if the state is to be democratic. Hence, while it might be possible, it seems a nation could not be democratic in a full meaning of the term, unless the civil society itself is structured on democratic lines.[5] More particularly, in a democratic civil society, associations and businesses are run in such a way that the views of individuals are taken into account and they are able to participate in the decision-making within those institutions. Democratic citizens are not formed without the support of their families, civil society and the state, but an important condition is that these institutions themselves are democratic. That is, in all the institutions of which they are a part, individuals need to be taught what it means to be democratic and to practise democratic values. It will be argued that schools and universities are the institutions which have a particular responsibility to support the inculcation of the values and virtues required for democracy to flourish.

The concept of democracy

The concept of democracy is contested, and this is due to a number of factors. Firstly, there is the claim that different cultures will have diverse conceptions of democracy so that there is, for example, a Chinese conception of democracy, a Western conception and an African conception. Secondly, there are the two traditions of democracy, both of which can be seen in Plato and Aristotle, that are in tension with one another: democracy as freedom to choose and democracy as concerned with pursuit of the common good and justice. The former tradition in the West is exemplified by Hobbes and Locke and in recent times by Nozick, Rorty and Rawls. The latter tradition is exemplified by the Catholic intellectual tradition but also by Rousseau, Hegel and Marx, amongst others. These are not mutually exclusive, however. Thirdly, different historic, economic and social conditions may also affect the conception of democracy that is held. A society, for example, may be willing to accept certain austerity measures and so a curtailment of freedoms to improve their lives, recognising the value of the common good. From another perspective, they may see that the loss of freedom entailed by a focus on the common good is detrimental to the fulfilment of their individual ambitions.

There are several different ways in which we can characterise some of the main features of democracy. Some of the essential ingredients in democracy will include: (i) membership or citizenship of a particular state or territory; (ii) equality before the law; and (iii) freedom, including of speech, as well as of conscience and of religion. The first element in democracy is perhaps self-evident in that it delineates who is to have a voice and participate in decision-making. For a particular democratic nation or state, this will be its citizens. The question of who is a citizen, however, is not so easily answered, and not everyone who resides in a state will necessarily be a citizen. In Aristotle's Athens, for example, slaves, who made up the majority of those living in the city, were not citizens. In modern states, many resident migrant workers, for example, will not be citizens and so ineligible to participate in the democracy. Equality before the law is an ideal that is also not available to every citizen in equal measure. In many democracies, the high cost of legal representation can mean that ordinary citizens cannot afford to take civil action against large, well-resourced corporations, and indeed, should a large corporation take action against them, they do not have the resources to defend themselves. Equality, just as much as citizenship or membership of a nation, depends on how it is to be interpreted.

In Book VIII of *Republic*, Plato is critical of democracy because it supposes that because all human beings are equal that this means that all opinions are equal, whereas in fact this is not so. He uses the analogy of a pilot who knows how to navigate a ship through dangerous waters – such a person should therefore navigate the ship. It is not a matter of opinion because he or she has the requisite knowledge. Similarly, the state should be guided by those with knowledge who have been educated to know how to rule the state, namely the philosopher-kings. Not all opinions in such a situation are equal. Plato says, when the poor win, the result is democracy (Book VIII, 557a). Although Plato is critical of democracy, it does not mean that he holds that democracy is not a viable form of government. He is much more positive about democracy in the *Laws*, where he holds that the form of government should be such that it encourages liberty, friendship and community spirit in the state (*Laws*, Book III, 697d).

Plato, in support of the first tradition, says that in a democracy, liberty is the finest possession (*Republic*, VIII, 562c-d). Aristotle mentions that democracy is concerned with freedom and sovereignty of the majority (*Politics*, 1310, a30), and in the *Rhetoric*, he says that the end goal of democracy is freedom (1366, a4). In a fuller discussion of the kinds of government, Aristotle adds that the end of oligarchy is wealth, which we can understand him to mean of those who govern, of aristocracy, the maintenance of education and national institutions, of tyranny and the protection of the tyrant. Wealth is the obvious end of oligarchy since membership of an oligarchic government is decided by a property or wealth qualification. Once in power, oligarchs will be motivated by the need to maintain if not increase their wealth. An aristocratic government is one in which membership is determined by having sufficient educational qualifications. Members of such a government will seek to maintain their power by ensuring only those with the right kinds of educational qualifications are able to rule. Hence, education will be an end for such rulers. Monarchical government, where there is a single ruler, can be of two types: one in which the monarch is limited by the constitution and the other, a tyranny, where the monarch has absolute power. In this latter situation, the aim of the government will be to maintain the power of the tyrant. Each of these forms of government become perversions of good government when they are not concerned with the common good (*Politics*, 1279a35). Aristotle, while acknowledging the importance of freedom and sovereignty, holds that the purpose of the state is to enable its citizens to lead happy and fulfilled lives, and this will only be possible when the state is directed to a common end, which is the common good.

There are many forms of democracy, according to Aristotle (*Politics*, Book IV, 1289a27). He also says that it is a form of perversion of constitutional government but is more tolerable than either tyranny or oligarchy (*Politics*, Book IV, 1289a28, 1289a40). By this he means that in constitutional government, there is rule of law, while in some forms of democracy, there is a tyranny of the majority. Democracy has to be combined with a constitution, which is to say a body of laws that regulates the structure of the state so that the tyranny of the majority is obviated. There is in this an important principle of democracy, namely that as is the case in Western democracies, an elected party does not simply rule for its own supporters but for all members of the community, which includes the minority that did not vote for them. Without a constitution to rein in a victorious majority and which directs the government to rule for the good of the entire community, democracy can descend into a form of tyranny.

Democracy can descend into a form of tyranny because no state, democratic or otherwise, is perfect, and so it is unlikely that all sections of the community will be treated equally. A government's supporters will want something in return for their continued support, and this means that they will inevitably be treated differentially than others who are not the government's supporters. In a corrupt society, where a government is not subject to the rule of law, those in power will use it to accrue wealth for themselves and for their supporters. They will use power in their own interests, blocking anything that they oppose. As Aristotle observes, the best form of government is constitutional government, where both citizens and those governing are all subject to the rule of law.[6] Rousseau says that if we identify the rule of law with an ideal system of justice where all citizens are treated equally, then we are bound to be disappointed, for there is no ideal system (Rousseau, 1994). Nevertheless, in a democracy sovereign power resides in the whole community of citizens, and so to that extent each is equal to the other, but it is also obvious that some citizens will enjoy more influence than others. The rich, for example, will wield more influence than the poor. For this reason, the state is ordered via its constitution, which is to say through the rule of law, to moderate the influence of powerful lobby groups. There are significant tensions between the idea of the rule of law as regulating the relationships among citizens and between citizens and the state. This is because the rule of law requires judges to interpret the constitution, and this gives significant power to the judges to override the will of the people. The ruling in relation to gay marriage in the United States is an example where the judiciary made a majority judgement about how the constitution of the United States is to be interpreted. In Ireland, on the other hand, the decision about gay marriage was not made by judges but by the people voting in a referendum.

Aristotle identifies a variety of forms of democracy. Firstly is one where both poor and rich are equal and share in the government and the majority is decisive. In this form of democracy, those who govern, the magistrates, have to have a property qualification but a low one. Those who lose their property lose their rights. A second form of democracy is one in which those who are not disqualified by reason of birth[7] share in government, but the law is supreme. The third form of democracy supposes that if someone is a citizen, he or she shares in the offices of government, but the law is supreme. The difference between this form of democracy and the second seems to be on the basis of how citizenship was acquired. In the second form, citizenship is bestowed by reason of birth, whereas in the third, this is no longer the determinant of citizenship. In the fourth form of democracy, citizens are supreme and can overturn the law. This latter sort of democracy degenerates into tyranny since the majority can make laws which can oppress the minority. It is a form of despotism and is a tyranny because the minority is not equal to the majority as their freedoms are curtailed by the majority (*Politics*, Book IV, 1291b31–1292a37). A salient question is whether Western democracies, under the onslaught of the media, are turning from being democracies based on the rule of law into ones based on the rule of the majority, as expressed through opinion polls. Political parties regularly conduct opinion polls and adjust their views accordingly. Parliaments legislate and so makes law, but it is law which may not be the result of deliberations based on the use of practical reason but on what polling suggests is the most popular opinion.

Constantly driven to act according to popular opinion, this can lead to the kind of tyranny that Aristotle speaks of since a government can overturn legislation made by a previous government.[8] In a celebrated recent case, the incoming Andrews government in the state of Victoria repudiated contracts signed for the building of a new freeway link by the previous government, costing the state somewhere in the vicinity of $500 million dollars.[9] Although it must be acknowledged that there is some complexity here, since incoming governments claim to have been given a mandate by the people to enact certain policies, this does not give them carte blanche. Aristotle appeals to the idea that the laws are part of the constitution of the state and so should not be overturned by appeals to the assembly of people who are entitled to vote since these appeals are open to abuse.

There are also questions about the power of the media – not considered by Aristotle, though he was well aware of the power of demagoguery. The media wield enormous power because people believe what they read in newspapers or hear on television or listen to on the radio. Through relentless advertising, the media are able to mould opinions but without making any appeal to reason or reasoned discussion of issues. Politicians have learned to use the "sound grab", a short sentence that conveys a message but no complexity. There is in this a concentration on conveying, through repetition, a particular policy or particular view but with no attempt to do more than this. A more sinister form of the use of media in this way is through lobby groups making claims about the support that their position has in the community, which leads individuals to want to acquiesce to what they perceive to be the majority view. With the concentration of media ownership in a relatively small number of corporations, the power of the media to shape opinion and hence the law is very significant.[10]

Later in Book VIII of the *Politics*, Aristotle discusses the nature of education, and he argues that education needs to ensure that the individual is able to be a good citizen of the particular kind of society to which he or she belongs (1337a). There are some issues with this since if one lives in a tyranny, then presumably one has to conform to what is required in such a state. There does not seem to be room for critique of the society or state nor for its overthrow. We shall return to the question of education shortly. It suffices to say that in a true democracy, there will be a balance between the rule of law and the rule of the citizens. If citizens are able to exercise practical wisdom, which implies that they also have acquired the other cardinal virtues, then there will be harmony between the rule of law and the rule of the citizens.

We have already indicated some of the main ingredients of a democracy, which included being a member of a specific state or territory and having equality and freedom to live a fulfilled life. Our discussion, however, indicates that there are other requirements that modern democracies need to meet. We can add that in a modern democracy, we also need a political culture which includes competition between political parties, regular parliamentary elections and government by the parliament. Secondly, we need a social structure that is relatively homogenous, with people sharing a common culture, language and history. This is a particular challenge for pluralist and multicultural societies, but as Aristotle points out, a state needs to have some basic common values; otherwise, there will be strife (*Politics*, Book V, 1302a–1303b).[11] Thirdly, an economy is needed which enables people to have a decent standard of living (Keane, 2010, pp. 112–113). This is also not a new thought since Aristotle's analysis of the organisation of the state was premised on citizens having sufficient leisure to attend to their responsibilities as citizens. The attributes of modern democracy will also need to be modified because of indigenisation; that is, cultures and traditions will elaborate how these elements of democracy are to be interpreted (Keane, 2010, p. 113). As we shall argue, culture and traditions are embodied in civil society, and there is a close connection between civil society and the state. As a result, the type of civil society in a particular state will influence the kind of democracy that will be practised in a state.

Democracy manifests through the many interests, lobby groups and activist organisations that compete for the attention of the government and hence hope to affect decision-making. In modern democracies an important question to consider is the relationship between the market and democracy. Some argue that the operation of the market should be left unregulated, while others that argue that it should be regulated through civil society for the common good. Although the connection between the market and democracy is too large a question to consider here, it is worth noting that according to Aristotle, citizens require sufficient leisure time to attend to their responsibilities in a democratic state. Citizens who have to struggle to provide for themselves and their families will hardly have any leisure time at all and so will not be able to engage with their responsibilities in the democratic state. It is clear that where there is a redistribution of wealth to the already wealthy from the poor, that true democracy must inevitably break down.[12]

These reflections lead us to consider the broader conditions that need to exist in a community if it is to foster democracy. Democracy, as Aristotle indicates, involves a community organised according to a particular constitution. This means at its most basic that democracy involves members of a group deciding and being involved in all aspects of the activities of the group, including its relationships with other groups (Marshall, 1950, p. 39), that is, within a state, the organisation of a democratic association operating within civil society. This leads to the thought that it is possible that we can have a democratic civil society but a despotic state. Likewise, it is possible to have an autocratic civil society and democratic state, but as we have already seen, autocratic citizens do not match a democratic state nor democratic citizens a despotic state. Sooner or later, this incompatibility will lead to some form of revolution.[13] A precondition, therefore, for the existence of a democratic state is a democratic civil society. Unless a civil society values democracy and, more importantly, practises in its various structures and arrangements some form of democracy, it is unlikely that the state could be democratic. This, of course, is more complex than is suggested here, and the form of democracy that can be practised in relation to the state will be different from how we might democratically organise an association. In the latter, for example, all members will be able to vote and be part of the decision-making, whereas in the state, citizens elect representatives to make decisions for them. Nevertheless, if a state is constituted for the good, freedom and well-being of its citizens, it follows that the values of its citizens must support and uphold these purposes of the state if it is to achieve these aims. Without being habituated to both virtue, which is necessary to direct citizens to their good, which is happiness, and to the responsibilities of freedom, however, they will not be able to do this.

Habituation to democratic values takes place within a community which itself lives the virtues and values of freedom. No citizens can be formed in these if they are not valued and practised within the society in which they live. Within a democratic community, democratic values will include: (i) respect for individuals and the variations in their needs and aspirations; (ii) providing an equal opportunity to individuals to pursue their interests to realise their potential and their aspirations; (iii) those in power and authority treating them equally; (iv) equality being a recognition of, and respect for, individual differences; and (v) collaboration rather than competition or paternalism as a means of achieving equality, respect and human development (Marshall, 1950, p. 39, quoting Elliott, from *Freedom to be Free*, 1943, p. 84). Given that human beings belong to a variety of different communities and associations, the foremost of which is the family, each of these has a significant role to play in the inculcation of democratic values. While the family is perhaps the most important and educational institutions the next, the attitudes and values in other communities, such as workplaces, to which individuals belong will also be significant in the formation of democratic values.

It is also possible to define organisations and associations in terms of their support for and modelling of democratic values. Organisations themselves can be described as exhibiting certain kinds of human characteristics and personality. Democratic institutions will exhibit personalities that are cooperative, self-respecting and capable of realising their capacities. Those that are not tend to be apathetic, anxious, dependent, antagonistic, repressive and destructive (Marshall, 1950, pp. 40–41). There is a significant difference between democratic institutions and those that are autocratic in their organisation. The autocratic school, autocratic university, autocratic workplace and autocratic state recognise only the will of the leader or of the leadership group as important and acts to suppress all dissent. Individuals are subordinated to aims and purposes to which they have had no input and which are to be achieved irrespective of whether these have any detrimental effects on those who are to carry out these aims and purposes. In the pursuit of wealth, for example, a corporation may ignore the real threats to the health of their workers, or a state instrumentality may ignore the safety of their employees to achieve certain budget savings. In both cases, individuals are sacrificed for what is thought to be more important than human beings. When human beings are unable to find satisfaction in what they do and are frustrated, they will seek outlets for their frustrations, and where this is directed at the state, it can lead to revolution or, at the very least, strike action and civil disobedience. As Dewey says, it is because democratic freedom is the cause of the fullest possible realisation of human potentialities that when they are suppressed and oppressed, they will in time rebel and demand an opportunity for manifestation (Dewey, 1939, p. 129).

The salient point is that the virtue of democracy is that it allows for the development of human beings to their full potential since it provides them with the freedom to act, albeit not unrestricted. It accords them respect and recognition of their creative capacities to contribute to the common good of the community. While this might be somewhat idealistic, the autocratic alternative involves the idea that power is exercised over others to control and to direct them according to the will of those in power. As a consequence, there is a diminution of creative capacity since the only vision which is allowed is that of the autocrat, whoever that may be. The virtue of democracy is that it allows, within some limits, and encourages a freer expression of the creativity of individuals. The stultifying bureaucracy in many institutions, such as some higher education institutions, demands an adherence to a single vision, which their employees are told is the only one possible under existing circumstances. This destroys any capacity for creativity, which after all, tends to be in tension with orderliness and bureaucratically defined performance indicators and outcomes. Alternative visions have to be suppressed, and those who hold them re-educated to conform to what is required. This can be done in a variety of ways: through sanctioning those who fail to conform and through rewarding those that do. In contrast, in a democratic institution in which collegiality is valued, it is realised that the overall aims of an institution can be achieved through multiple pathways.

It is not to be expected that democratic institutions will always be successful in attaining their democratic aims. It is not unreasonable to conjecture that a number will fail to achieve their objectives for no democratic society is perfect. This, however, does not lead us to reject democracy since democratic nations are made up of fallible human beings and will miss their democratic objectives time and again, but it is more important that human beings are able to develop as mature people and that freedom is realised. Democracy as we have characterised it is not just a matter of the organisation of the state along democratic lines. Since it involves human fulfilment, the development of virtue and freedom, it can be understood as a way of life, a complex of human relationships, and not a selection of politico-economic forms (Marshall, 1950, pp. 53–54).

Civil society and democracy

The foregoing discussion leads to a consideration of the characteristics of a democratic civil society. The concept of civil society is complex, and an analysis is well beyond what we are seeking to discuss here; nevertheless, there are some features which we would expect in one that values democracy. Civil society is not just a matter of belonging to particular groupings in society, such as environmentalist associations, gay rights lobby groups, pro-life groups or sporting clubs, but requires the capacity to engage in rational discussion of those issues which they favour with those who might have a different view. In a democratic civil society, an essential ingredient is reasoned argument in the public space. Without reasoned argument, as Habermas has suggested, we fail to respect persons (Habermas, 1998, p. xxxv). A crucial element of democracy is the willingness to listen to the reasoned arguments of all sides to an issue and to build, as far as possible, a consensus about how a matter is to be determined. On some issues, consensus might be impossible, and in such instances, it may be necessary to resort to a vote to decide how to act. This, however, requires some sensitivity to the views of others who do not agree and who are being asked to accept a decision which may be in conflict with their basic values. As we have said, following Aristotle, democracy is not a matter of the tyranny of the majority. If consensus is not possible, then all sides need to come to an agreement to abide by a majority vote, which in all cases, must involve concessions to the consciences of those who disagree. Respect for persons and solidarity with the other demands no less. Decisions which divide a community lead to conflict, and if there are too any instances where a society relies on a majority vote, democracy disappears, and tyranny takes its place.

This is essentially Habermas's approach in discourse ethics. Habermas says, "I call interactions communicative when the participants co-ordinate their plans of action consensually, with the agreement reached at any point being evaluated in terms of the intersubjective recognition of validity claims" (1990, p. 58). There are three validity claims: claims to truth, claims to rightness and claims to truthfulness. What Habermas is referring to is that in laying claim to the validity of a speech act in which a speaker communicates something to another, there are three kinds of claims: the first is a claim where a speaker refers to something in the objective, physical world, that is, to a state of affairs, which is asserted to hold. A second kind of claim refers to something in the shared social world of interpersonal relations and the third to something in the speaker's own subjective world of experiences to which he or she has privileged access. In communicative action, says Habermas, one actor seeks rationally to motivate another by relying on the illocutionary binding or bonding force of the offer contained in his speech act (1990, p. 58) What this means is that though the reasons for the particular claim are not given in the utterance, the hearer, given the relationship between them, accepts what is said by the speaker since there is a tacit guarantee offered that what has been claimed can be supported by reasons. Of course, this will not be the case for every utterance made by a speaker, but the basis for any kind of discourse is that there is a conceptual space created in which agreed fundamental norms of discourse guide the discussion.

Since the idea of a democratic civil society depends on at least shared norms of respect, of communal solidarity, a commitment to truth, reason, justice and the common good, in societies with a plurality of values and traditions, agreement on fundamental norms of discourse is crucial. Differences in values and beliefs already pull people in opposite directions and lead to polarised positions. The difficulty, however, is that the conditions for the existence of a democratic civil society are being eroded, and the public space no longer is one in which reasoned debate can take place. It is, rather, a manipulated space in which perlocutionary force is what matters; that is, the means of persuasion relies on what has an effect on the hearer rather than the validity and soundness of argument. Those who know better, such as media owners, fail to take their responsibilities seriously and instead pursue profit by reducing debate to controversial, simplistic sloganizing. This is perhaps exacerbated by the relative ignorance of those who have taken over the public space. If there is to be a democratic civil society and equal participation in matters of public importance, the parameters of reasoned discourse must be in place, and views of all participants should be respected, provided that they accept the basic values of democratic discourse. Provided that there is a seriousness in addressing the question at hand, no one should be prevented from expressing an opinion. This will include religious perspectives.

Democratic civil society and the values which form its base are indispensable civic values to the modern state. This is because its foundations are communal bonds and public virtue. Unlike Hegel's conception of civil society in which there is a sharp distinction between civil society and the state, what we have suggested, in agreement with Aristotle, is that society cannot be detached from its form of government. Democratic citizens are needed if the state is to be democratic. Those who wish to argue, as Rawls does, for a separation of the public sphere from the private sphere are mistaken if they believe that the values of one can be separated from the other.

Democracy demands its citizens take an active role in the government of the state. This does not mean that every citizen needs to stand for election or to aspire to public office, but given that human fulfilment is tied to the common good, the fate of each citizen is tied to the fate of his or her community. Human beings are born into a civil society and, because they are social animals, will gravitate to one another, forming bonds of friendship. As MacIntyre (1999) says, human beings are dependent rational animals, and the bonds of family and of community are the roots of civil society and of the state. An active role in the government of the state means for citizens that they actively live democratic values in their lives, that they take seriously their responsibilities towards others and contribute to their communities. It does not mean that they embark on a political career. Nevertheless, when individuals act in the service of others, such as looking after the elderly, minding grandchildren and caring for the disabled, they are acting for the common good, and if the democratic state exists for the common good, then they are contributing to the upkeep of the state. Being responsible democratic citizens does not simply mean voting in periodic elections and paying taxes but encompasses all kinds of human activities that support the common good and hence human fulfilment, which is what the state exists to enable and to foster.

It must be recognised, however, that modern societies and states are far from perfect. For example, Iris Marion Young thinks there are limits to what civil society can accomplish. She thinks that citizens must rely on state institutions to take positive action to undermine oppression and promote justice. According to some communitarian views of civil society, state bureaucracy can militate against the fostering of mutual aid and solidarity among members of the community. This is because though various welfare programs support individuals, they also create an "entitlement" mentality that creates a dependency on the state rather than encouraging independence and autonomy. Some Marxists are of the view that state socialism collapses the distinction between state and economy, which helps the lifeworld of civil society to maintain its freedom and autonomy from coercive regulation. The radical anti-capitalist pursuit of justice is better thought of as a project of democratising the state, corporate economy and civil society than bringing all the production and distribution of goods under democratic state direction (Young, 2000, pp. 180–183).

Young stresses the importance of self-development for persons since it means that they can grow and learn (2000, p. 184). This suggests that education is important in providing the right kinds of conditions and opportunities for people to learn how to become fulfilled as persons. We shall turn to a consideration of this shortly. Social justice, she says, requires the mutual limitation of state, economy and civil society. Young argues strongly that profit and market-oriented economic processes impede the ability of many people in most societies to develop and exercise capacities because the aim is always to reduce costs, especially labour costs (Young, 2000, p. 185). What Young does not add is that this is because these processes are directed towards profit only. The logic is then inescapable. If the aim of economic activity is profit, then everything that does not serve to further that aim needs to be eliminated. If labour costs can be reduced, then this is done. If this means mechanising the factory, thus reducing the number of employees required, then this is done. If it means relocating to a country where labour is cheaper, then this done. If something can be outsourced at a cheaper cost, then this is done.

Promoting social justice requires attending to issues of self-development as well as self-determination. Young notes that left to themselves, both the organisation and consequences of capitalist market activity impede the self-development of many people. She believes that authoritative state regulation can limit the harmful effects of economic power. Economic and infrastructure planning, redistributive policies and the direct provision of goods and services by the state can minimise material deprivation and foster the well-being of all members of society (Young, 2000, p. 189).

Civil society, however, does not have access to power in the way in which the state has, and so if its members are to effect any change, they need to use political activism. This is precisely the point made by Adam Ferguson. Wealth, commerce, extent of territory and knowledge of the arts, when properly employed, are the means of preservation and the foundations of power, but these are not the most important thing rather the ability for human beings to be able to exercise their minds and be active (Ferguson, 1995, p. 60). In a democratic state, citizens have some influence over the political process, but they have little influence over the market or the financial institutions and corporations that exist outside the reach of the political process. In a totalitarian state there is potentially less ability to influence the political process and possibly even less opportunity to influence financial institutions and corporations.

One response to this is to suggest that in the marketplace, the solution is the cooperative, in which every individual is shareholder and has an interest in the success of the enterprise. In such an enterprise, every individual has an equal stake and has an equal responsibility for the enterprise. Here, each individual is able to contribute according to his or her abilities, and the economic fortunes of the cooperative depend on each person making his or her contribution. In such a scenario, decision-making is spread, and there is greater opportunity for self-realisation and for fulfilment. Moreover, since the purpose of the cooperative is the common good, rather than profits, it has a very different outlook on how it is to operate. Reducing labour costs by shedding its workforce would not be an option since everyone is a member of the cooperative. If costs are to be trimmed, it will be through more efficient work practices, the adoption of new technologies and other means. Such an arrangement would be consonant with a democratic civil society.

A final question that is important in our discussion of the democratic civil society concerns the question of what we mean by the public space or the public sphere. This is a much more extensive space than in the past when it meant a public debate in a town hall or some actual public space. The public space in the modern world includes social media, the Internet and various other electronic means of communication. Opinions can be expressed in a variety of different ways, none of which take place in any defined space and may also be made asynchronously. Civil society, which we would regard as meeting in the public space, can now do so in cyberspace. Facebook, Twitter, Renren (in China) and various other social networks are now spaces in which individuals can express their opinions. In some cases, collective agreement on some issues can result in powerful changes, revolutions even, within society. What is problematic is that these social media outlets, which act as a kind of electronic public space, do not necessarily encourage reasoned argument, rather a type of unreasoned agreement with the majority. It is a bold individual who disagrees with a majority opinion. Social media can be used to whip up support for a particular cause as well as destroy a person's reputation because of an inappropriate posting.

The existence of flash mobs, for example, is an instance of the power of social media, notably Twitter and Facebook, to enable the organisation of mass protests. The organiser of a flash mob emails, tweets or blogs a particular group of individuals about a particular event that he or she is organising, specifying time and place and other details of the event. Such groups have been organised for quite innocuous activities, such as gathering to eat ice cream, but have also been used for organising political rallies. For example, a flash mob was organised in January 2010 to meet in Tahrir Square in Egypt, with some 50,000 people gathering. It is also possible for flash mobs to be organised to commit crimes. The difficulty in controlling flash mobs has led to governments proposing the limiting of social media tools. Thus far, however, governments have not taken strong action to do this (Kaminski, 2012). Nevertheless, the phenomenon of a flash mob, generated through the use of social media, shows that the medieval witch hunt has moved into modern form.

Other forms of public space could be said to be outgrowths of technology. For example, Adobe Connect, Videoconferencing and Skype are all ways in which the public space is extended into cyberspace. Meetings are held by videoconferencing, for example, with participants in many different places, including in different continents. Webinars where the presenter is in one country and the participants in another are commonplace. The public space is no longer just a three-dimensional location but is much more diffused, and there is now a virtual public space. The question we can ask ourselves concerns the kinds of persons who occupy this virtual public space and the extent to which they too are virtual persons rather than real persons. Space does not permit reflection on this and what it means for interaction among people. The growth of MOOCs is also another example of the expansion of the public space to include a virtual public space. Universities, such as MIT, boast MOOCs with many thousands of students participating. It is a serious question to what extent they represent a decline in the quality of teaching because it replaces the human teacher, present here and now, by a virtual teacher. Podcasts and the like also mean that the teacher need not be present synchronously with the class.

It remains to be seen what effects the extension of the public space into the cyberspace will have on the nature of a democratic civil society. It certainly appears to be a powerful medium, but whether it results in a new versions of lynch mobs or new ways in which citizens can express solidarity with their fellow human beings remains to be seen. It suffices to say that the existence of social media has made communication of a certain kind much more immediate, but whether it allows sustained rational discourse on significant questions is not so certain. Its electronic nature seems to militate against it. It is certainly a rich field for further exploration to see how it can be harnessed for the common good and help the development of a democratic civil society.

Education and the democratic society

In this last section, we turn to the development of the democratic society and the indispensability of education in its advancement. Since a detailed analysis of this would require a volume at least as large as Dewey's celebrated *Democracy and Education* (1915), we can only provide a brief sketch of the connections between the formation of a democratic civil society and state and education. In particular we will restrict our discussion to higher education. From our previous discussion, it becomes evident that democracy requires citizens who value both the freedom that democracy brings and the obligation to be responsible for their fellow citizens. Also required is respect for persons and the moral virtues which accompany the ability to use practical reason. If, as Aristotle says, the purpose of the democratic state is to enable its citizens to lead fulfilled lives and to be happy, there also is a requirement for all citizens to work for the common good and to express solidarity with their fellow citizens. There can be no democratic state, if as Aristotle claims, its citizens are not themselves committed to democracy and to democratic values. These are not *sui generis* but require citizens to be formed in and habituated to the moral virtues and values needed for the creation of a democratic civil society and state. That is to say, the education of the democratic citizen involves the education of character.

In a scathing article, Giroux argues that democracy is on life support in the United States (Giroux, 2014). He contends that what he calls the forces of casino capitalism have steadily dismantled the social provisions of the welfare state, redefined democracy as profit making, increased the role of corporate money in politics, undermined faith in the institutions of democracy and, amongst other things, cut funding to higher education (2014, p. 10). While Giroux is referring to the United States, there is ample evidence that this is a familiar situation within higher education across the globe. In a recent study of Egyptian education, for example, Alshamy argues that though Egyptian education was established with the view to providing a democratic education, and for quite some time was able to achieve an education which supported democratic values, such as social justice, cooperation and social cohesion, the adoption of a free market approach has led to the rise of individualism and profit seeking as values (2014, p. 101). The result has been that what was gained previously has been lost. The steady march of free market ideology into education, repeated in many parts of the world, has eroded the formation of citizens in democratic values.

Giroux argues that what is most feared by neo-liberals is the recognition, as Vaclav Havel remarked, that democracy needs citizens who are concerned with more than just their own interests but are prepared to be active citizens who hold democracy at the deepest levels – at the same level as religion. Giroux says this is where education comes in; children need to be taught that democracy is desirable, possible and can be defended. He argues for a radical democracy, which involves the development of a consciousness of social and economic provisions that enable people to be free of the deprivations of hunger, homelessness, unemployment, inadequate health care and so on (2014, pp. 10–13). There are, apart from these basic needs, however, higher-level needs that are also required. The support by the state of crucial social structures and institutions that enable human beings to be nurtured, such as the traditional family and marriage, which are in the process of being torn down in the Western world in the name of a spurious equality, is vital. The call is for an exercise of a radical consciousness for people to exercise power in all spheres of life where power shapes the conditions of their lives (2014, p. 13).

The problem, as Giroux so eloquently argues, is that much of higher education has been hijacked by a neo-liberal, market-based ideology that has little or no regard for democracy or the ideals of a higher education that is concerned with publicly engaged teaching and scholarship (2009, p. 670). As a result, there is a fading commitment in higher education to the democratic ideal and instead the embracing of corporate power and market values. The only questions being asked in public discourse now about education, such as about knowledge production, the purpose of education and the nature of politics are those framed by the language of market forces (Giroux, 2014, p. 15). This framing is underlined by academics being advised that if they wish to build an academic career to see themselves as business entrepreneurs with an eye for the principles of finance, marketing and management and to build a brand identity, that is, an academic reputation, by marketing high-quality product, that is, publications and presentations (Leopold, 2007). The corporate university regards itself as a profit-making business and adopts not just the language of business and marketing, such as calling students customers or clients and courses products, but also attempts to introduce quality control measures, not just for courses but also academic staff. Performance measures and unit evaluations of teaching are some of the means by which academic staff are reduced to technicians. Alternatively, academics become academic entrepreneurs, valuable only for the grant money they attract and prestige they bring and not for the valuable teaching, research and public service they can provide. Giroux warns that sacrificed in this is any notion of higher education as a crucial public sphere in which democratic citizens are formed (Giroux, 2009, p. 674).

There is much more to be said about the depredations of the neo-liberal model of education which has taken root in our HEIs. It suffices to say that it is an inhumane model because it reduces human beings to human resources to be trained and skilled to serve the capitalist corporation so that it might increase its profits. Society and the state were created to be at the service of human beings, to enable them to be fulfilled, as we have remarked earlier, not to serve an impersonal, infernal market. All is not lost, however, for there is still some vestigial understanding that the role of the university is much broader than just supplying skilled workers. It is the guardian of the search for truth and was established for the pursuit of knowledge through the use of reason. To do this, it must itself be a community of scholars with respect for one another, for reason and truth as well as a deep appreciation of the mystery that is the world. They must also recapture a sense of the holy, that there is much that lies beyond the ability of human beings to know.

Giroux suggests that higher education may be one of few remaining public spheres where knowledge, values and learning offer a glimpse of an education promising the nurturing of public values and critical hope – what Freire calls the practice of freedom. The deepest roots of higher education are philosophical, not commercial (Giroux, 2014, p. 21). While this is largely true, we would add that they are also theological since we cannot know what it is to be human without a sense of awe at the deep enigma that is creation, that is, without a sense of the divine. Theology, which is equally important as philosophy because it deals with the spiritual, is the highest form of wisdom since it is an understanding that we can transcend the boundaries of human reason and come in contact with God, who is beyond our human understanding but from whom all of creation proceeds. God is the absolute ground and source of all human good and value.

It is apparent that an education which will nurture democratic values depends on, firstly, an HEI which itself practises and models democracy. This quite clearly involves a rejection of the corporatisation of the university and returning to structures which support democratic values, such as equality, freedom and respect for persons. It also means looking seriously at how it forms its students. Secondly, this means that a genuine higher education will include the humanities, that is, history, philosophy, the arts, literature, languages, the social sciences and theology. Thirdly, it will mean an HEI with a diverse range of students drawn from every socio-economic class. This is because a democracy consists of a diversity of individuals, and unless we have some encounters with people with different perspectives, experiences of life and points of view, we cannot learn to be tolerant of differences nor learn respect for other points of view. Human beings glimpse reality through a multifaceted prism of experiences, beliefs and values and need to come to the realisation that none see the truth as it really is, but each has something to contribute.

Notes

1 For example, Robert Nozick and John Rawls have different conceptions of the role of the state, with Nozick arguing for a minimalist state, while Rawls sees the state as having a role in redressing the disadvantages of the least well off in society. See Nozick (1974) and Rawls (1999).
2 Plato (2000) argues that democracy can be the source of tyranny since an excess of freedom can bring about the need for control, and this means someone to act as the champion of the people. This leads eventually, according to Plato, to despotic rule. See *The Republic*, Book VIII, 557b-567e.
3 See, for example, the discussion of the parlous state of democracy in Zimbabwe in Moore (2014), who comments that mere elections would do nothing to dislodge the ruling Zimbabwe African National Union-Patriotic Front (ZANU-PF) party. There was ample evidence of considerable vote rigging in the 2013 election, which was not helped by the lack of effort on the part of the opposition parties, especially the Movement for Democratic Change – Morgan Tsvangirai (MDC-MT) party to register and rally eligible voters. A significant question concerns the extent to which Western-style democracy, itself weakened, fits the African context. For another account of the death of democracy in Zimbabwe see Batts (2009).
4 There is the question of whether, realistically, they could have an input. There is a question of expertise, the need to make decisions in a timely manner and the practicalities of not wishing to reveal sensitive state matters publicly, which might also have a bearing on the extent to which the public can be consulted. Despite these provisos, there are very many issues about which the public can and ought to be consulted. Often problems arise when the public are not consulted, and the resulting decisions made are poor and ill-conceived.
5 By structure here is meant having democratic institutions – free press, independent judiciary and freedom of speech.
6 By constitution Aristotle means the organisation of the offices in a state and determines what is to be the governing body and what is the end of each community. Aristotle recognises three forms of constitution, by which he means the laws that govern how the state is set up, how offices are distributed and legislation enacted. It is the constitution which will determine the kinds of laws that need to be enacted to organise a state according to the constitution. The three forms are kingship, aristocracy and constitutional government (*Politics*, 1289a-1289b). He regards constitutional government as the best form of government, and democracy is a deviation from this. Aristotle views the constitutional government itself as established by a rule of law and to guarantee that individual

citizens are not dominated by majority opinion but that all abide by laws arising from practical wisdom. Democracy is a deviation because there are various forms of it, not all of which involve the use of practical reason in determining actions on behalf of the state. See *Politics*, Book IV.
7   Which is to say that they have been born in the state and are entitled to citizenship.
8   Aristotle discusses how in the form of a democratic state where the people have the supreme power, demagogues can persuade the people to overturn the law. In such a state the law has no authority, and, says Aristotle, it is doubtful whether the state has a constitution (*Politics*, 1292a-1292b).
9   Some reports put the amount of money that had to be paid to the consortium contracted to build the freeway as much as $700 million. See AAP General News Wire (2015, March 9).
10 Not everyone agrees that this is the case, but certainly governments are well aware of the effects of the concentration of media ownership in the hands of just a few proprietors. Here one of the issues involves cross-media ownership, where one proprietor controls not just newspapers and print media but also television and radio. See, for example, the discussion on media ownership in Foster (2010, pp. 160–176). For a discussion of why media ownership should be as broad as possible, see Baker (2007, pp. 5–53).
11 Aristotle says there are three main reasons for revolution in the state: (i) the opposition of virtue and vice, which is to say corruption amongst office holders, (ii) disproportionate differences of wealth and poverty and (iii) quarrels among people from different places (*Politics*, 1303b).
12 In his most recent encyclical, Pope Francis blames continuing poverty on the selfish consumerism of developed countries that control the less well-off countries through their foreign debt. See Francis, *Laudato Si'*, sects. 51–52.
13 Here the obvious example is fall of the Soviet Union, where citizens hungering for freedom led to the collapse of the totalitarian Soviet regime. This does not always end well, however.

References

AAP General News Wire. (2015). VIC: East West Link Costs $700m to Axe. March 9, 2015. Retrieved from: http://search.proquest.com/docview/1661262445?accountid=8194

Aristotle. (1952). The Politics. Tr. Benjamin Jowett. In Robert Maynard Hutchins (Ed.). *Great Books of the Western World*. Vol. 9. Aristotle II. (445–548). Chicago: Encyclopedia Britannica.

Aristotle. (1952). Rhetoric. Tr. W. Rhys Roberts. In Robert Maynard Hutchins (Ed.). *Great Books of the Western World*. Vol. 9. Aristotle II. (593–675). Chicago: Encyclopedia Britannica.

Baker, C. Edwin. (2007). *Media Concentration and Democracy: Why Ownership Matters*. Cambridge, UK: Cambridge University Press.

Batts, Callie. (2009). 'In Good Conscience': Andy Flower, Henry Olongo and the Death of Democracy in Zimbabwe. *Sport in Society, 13* (1), 43–58.

Campos, Andre Santos and André, José Gomes. (Eds.). (2014). *Challenges to Democratic Participation: Antipolitics, Deliberative Democracy and Pluralism*. Lanham, MD: Lexington Books.

Dewey, John. (1915/2004). *Democracy and Education: An Introduction to the Philosophy of Education*. New Delhi: Aakar Books.

Dewey, John. (1939). *Freedom and Culture*. New York: G. P. Putnam and Sons.

Ferguson, Adam. (1995). *An Essay on the History of Civil Society*. Tr. Fania Oz-Salzberger. Cambridge, UK: Cambridge University Press.

Foster, Steven. (2010). *Political Communication*. Edinburgh: Edinburgh University Press.

Francis (Pope). (2015). *Laudato Si'*. Papal Encyclical. Vatican City: Vatican Library.

Giroux, Henry A. (2009). Democracy's Nemesis: The Rise of the Corporate University. *Cultural Studies Critical Methodologies, 9* (5), 669–695.

Giroux, Henry A. (2014). The Swindle of Democracy in the Neo-Liberal University and the Responsibility of Intellectuals. *Democratic Theory, 1* (1), 9–37.

Habermas, Jurgen. (1990). *Moral Consciousness and Communicative Action.* Tr. Christian Lenhardt and Shierry Weber Nicholsen. Intro. Thomas McCarthy. Cambridge, MA: MIT Press.

Habermas, Jurgen. (1998). *The Inclusion of the Other: Studies in Political Theory.* Ed. Ciaran Cronin and Pablo De Greiff. Cambridge, MA: MIT Press.

Hay, Colin and Stoker, Gerry. (2009). Revitalising Politics: Have We Lost the Plot? *Representation, 45* (3), 225–236.

Kaminski, Margot. (2012). Flash Mob or Protest Movement: The First Amendment and Regulating Online Calls to Action. Ch. 2. In Reiman Cornelis (Ed.). *Public Interest and Private Rights in Social Media* (3rd edn.). (25–44). Burlington, MA: Elsevier Science.

Keane, John. (2010). Democracy in the Twenty-First Century: Global Questions. In Terrell Carver and Jens Bartelson (Eds.). *Globality, Democracy and Civil Society.* (112–130). London: Routledge.

Leopold, Philip. (2007). The Professorial Entrepreneur. *Chronicle of Higher Education,* August 30. Retrieved from: http://chronicle.com.ezproxy2.acu.edu.au/article/The-Professorial-Entrepreneur/46503/

MacIntyre, Alasdair. (1999). *Dependent Rational Animals: Why Human Beings Need the Virtues.* London: Duckworth.

Marshall, James. (1950). The Nature of Democracy. *Political Science Quarterly, 65* (1), 38–54.

Moore, David. (2014). Death or Dearth of Democracy in Zimbabwe? *African Spectrum, 49* (1), 101–114.

Nozick, Robert. (1974). *Anarchy, State and Utopia.* Oxford: Blackwell Publishing, Ltd.

Plato. (1997). The Laws. Tr. Trevor J. Saunders. In John M. Cooper (Ed., Intro., Notes). *Plato: The Complete Works.* Indianapolis, IN: Hackett Publishing Company, Inc.

Plato. (1997). The Statesman. Tr. C. J. Rowe. In John M. Cooper (Ed., Intro., Notes). *Plato: The Complete Works.* Indianapolis, IN: Hackett Publishing Company, Inc.

Plato. (2000). *The Republic.* Tr. Tom Griffith. Ed. G. R. F. Ferrari. Cambridge, UK: Cambridge University Press.

Rapeli, Lauri. (2014). *The Conception of Citizen Knowledge in Democratic Theory.* London: Palgrave MacMillan.

Rawls, John. (1999). *A Theory of Justice* (Rev. edn.). Cambridge, MA: Harvard University Press.

Rousseau, Jean-Jacques. (1994). *The Social Contract.* Tr. Christopher Betts. Oxford: Oxford University Press.

Vibert, Frank. (2007). *The Rise of the Unelected.* Cambridge, UK: Cambridge University Press.

Waheed, Ahmed Waqas and Abbasi, Javiera Younas. (2013). Rethinking Democracy in Pakistan. *Asian Affairs, 44* (2), 202–214.

Whiteley, Paul. (2009). Where Have All the Party Members Gone? The Dynamics of Party Membership in Britain. *Parliamentary Affairs, 62* (2), 242–257.

Young, Iris Marion. (2000). *Inclusion and Democracy.* Oxford: Oxford University Press.

2 The relevance of a Catholic philosophy of education

William Sweet

Introduction

Educational institutions today, and what goes on within them, are – as we all well know – confronted by a number of critiques. Some critics press for educational institutions to focus on training students for the workplace; there are challenges to pedagogies and, particularly, to the moral and spiritual dimensions of education; and the culture at large ever more emphasizes a thoroughgoing individualism that affects and infects education as well.

In this essay I begin by describing some of what I take to be the major critiques of institution-based education, particularly higher education. To respond to these criticisms, I turn to philosophies of education in the Catholic tradition and identify some of the basic educational principles. I then propose how a (re)focus on those principles might help to address the issues raised in some of the critiques.

Lines of criticism

Education today does not lack for commentators and critics.

In a number of recent books and articles, we find criticisms of and challenges to institutional public education. These criticisms are directed to all levels of education – primary, secondary, and tertiary – but particularly to university undergraduate programs. Several of these studies veer into the polemical, but all the same, they seem to have touched a raw nerve in the public.

I want to begin, then, by identifying three major lines of criticism raised in these books and articles.

Criticism 1: educational institutions fail to prepare students for employment

The first and most common line of criticism comes primarily from *outside* of educational systems and institutions – from parents, business leaders and employers, and the general culture – but also increasingly from students, and its concern is on *outcomes*. Chiefly, it is that public education fails to focus on what it ought to do, namely, train students for the workplace and have them acquire employment-related skills.

One example of this line of criticism can be found in a recent issue of the American magazine *The Atlantic*. The business columnist and author Scott Gerber notes

A degree does not guarantee you or your children a good job anymore. In fact, it doesn't guarantee you a job: last year, one out of two bachelor's degree holders under 25 were jobless or un(der)employed. Since the recession of 2008, millions of high- and mid-wage jobs have been lost – and been replaced with a handful of lower-wage ones. No wonder some young people are giving up entirely – a 16.8 percent unemployment rate plus soaring student loan debt is more than a little discouraging. Yet old-guard academic leaders are still clinging to the status quo – and loudly insisting that a four-year liberal arts degree is a worthy investment in every young American's future (Gerber, 2012).

Many find Gerber's criticism persuasive, and the force of this criticism is supplemented by complaints about the financial (e.g., tuition) and other costs to students – and, eventually, to society. In light of this, an increasing number of people ask whether many programs, particularly in the humanities and social sciences, are worthwhile.

This criticism also gets force from the claim that the workforce needs more skilled workers – that is, that those with needed skills are in short supply and that those with a broader, more humanistic education are either unable, unwilling, or too poorly equipped to fill the positions that need to be filled. Academic programs that contribute to the broader intellectual culture of students – and particularly to their moral and spiritual development – are superfluous or are subjects that can be pursued just as well (if they ought to be pursued at all) on one's personal time.

In some cases, educational institutions have already responded to this critique. In several instances, however, institutions seem simply to have yielded to it and have come to promote education as basically of instrumental value. This is especially evident at the university level, where, increasingly, not only is there little encouragement (and generally few requirements) to take courses in humanistic studies (such as philosophy, literature, and classical and modern languages), but such programmes have increasingly minimal institutional support; we see the closing of philosophy and foreign language and literature departments, or their amalgamation into broader units, in a number of institutions in the UK, the United States, but also beyond.

Admittedly, in a few cases, educational leaders have protested. Martha Nussbaum's recent book *Not for Profit* refers to the 'diminishing place given to the liberal arts in many institutions: their marginalization by technocratic and business-oriented demands' (Brooks, 2011). She looks at examples from the United States and India but also from Europe. She notes that the insights of educational reformers, such as John Dewey and Rabindranath Tagore, 'are neglected, and even scorned,' as parents are 'intent on getting their children filled with testable skills that seem likely to produce financial success' (Nussbaum, 2012, p. 4). Institutions today focus on 'market impact' rather than developing 'critical thinking and empathetic imagining' (Nussbaum, 2012, p. 19).

Still, critics have accused Nussbaum of having an agenda of her own – that the humanities are valuable because of their contribution to a specific social and political ideal of 'liberal progressivism' – and that this is just as instrumental a view of education as the views she challenges.

A second example of this line of criticism focuses on the *quality* of the education that is provided in educational institutions. Critics point to the illiteracy and innumeracy of many graduates. For example, a recent report funded by the Pew Charitable Trusts and conducted by the American Institutes for Research found:

> More than 75 percent of students at two-year colleges and more than 50 percent of students at four-year colleges do not score at the proficient level of literacy. This means that they lack the skills to perform complex literacy tasks, such as comparing credit card offers with different interest rates or summarizing the arguments of newspaper editorials.
> (American Institutes for Research, 2006)

In fact, sociologists of education, Richard Arum (of New York University) and Josipa Roksa (of the University of Virginia) have found that 'students are not studying very hard and not learning very much' (Arum and Roksa, 2011).

A wide range of explanations have been given for this. Some blame universities that, to cover rising costs, admit students with minimal academic competencies; others remark on a 'student body distracted by socializing or working and an institutional culture that puts undergraduate learning close to the bottom of the priority list' (Social Science Research Council, 2014). Others, still, blame faculty who are alleged to give increasingly higher grades to avoid confrontations with students. And there are others, again, who claim that the overall curriculum at colleges and universities is not only unfocussed but tends to centre on the research interests of the professor rather than vice versa. Finally, some invoke the employment of less-qualified staff – for example, teaching assistants and adjunct professors – to teach core courses at universities and colleges (Hacker and Dreifus, 2011).[1]

Critics, therefore, push for more accountability and 'outcomes assessments', whereby not only each program but each course must have a list of predetermined and measureable 'evidence-based' goals or skills to be acquired. This push is also called for in the 2006 report of the US Commission on the Future of Higher Education – a commission led by George W. Bush's secretary of education, Margaret Spellings – titled *A Test of Leadership*. The report claims that at present, there is 'a remarkable absence of accountability mechanisms to ensure that colleges succeed in educating students'. It recommends the creation of a 'searchable, consumer-friendly database that provides access to institutional performance and aggregate student outcomes' and that 'academic programs and institutions must be transformed to serve the changing needs of a knowledge economy' (US Department of Education, 2006).

At some institutions, there is pressure to make *each* course and program identify short-term results that can be tested for after completion. One such model of determining 'outcomes' is the Collegiate Learning Assessment test, promoted by Arum and Roksa (previously referred to) in *Academically Adrift* (2011). Longer-term consequences, not capable of easy assessment and evaluation, seem simply moot. In any event, the focus on outcomes suggests that education is no longer seen as a liberal art but a servile art.

Some attribute this first line of criticism to an increasingly corporatist or neoliberal capitalist character of 'Western' societies, but of course more than one economic system can have this result (e.g., China). What is at root in this line of criticism, regardless of the different economic and social models that adopt it, are utilitarian considerations – that education should focus on a particular kind of product, namely training students for the workplace.

Criticism 2: education is ideological

A second line of criticism of public education focuses on what goes on within educational institutions – particularly within universities – and is found as much within these institutions as outside. Specifically, it has been argued that education has become increasingly politicized and partisan. For some, it is that universities and particular programs simply reinforce existing culture and values; they consciously or unconsciously promote the values and the politics of the *status quo*. Thus Mary R. Jackman and Michael J. Muha of the University of Michigan have argued that 'dominant social groups routinely develop ideologies that legitimize and justify the status quo, and the well-educated members of these dominant groups are the most sophisticated practitioners of the group's ideology' (Jackman and Muha, 1984, pp. 751–769).

For others, it is quite the opposite: that teachers and professors are generally influenced by ideologies that challenge and *undermine* dominant culture and traditions and that this determines what and how they teach, what students learn, but also what ideas are tolerated. For example, in the third edition of his *Tenured Radicals: How Politics Has Corrupted Higher Education*, the American social commentator Roger Kimball (2008) describes 'professors of literature who specialize in the rock videos of Madonna', 'professors who devote their scholarly energies to showing that . . . *The Tempest* is an exposé of Western imperialism,' and scholars 'who maintain that there are no compelling reasons for judging *Middlemarch* to be a greater artistic achievement than the cartoons of Bugs Bunny'. At the root of this, Kimball claims, is what he calls 'the multicultural imperative' that assumes 'that all cultural life is to be explained in political terms, preeminently in terms of gender, race, class, and ethnic origin' (Kimball, 2008; see also Kimball, 1991).

Either way, however, the putative concern is that the educational institutions are operated in a way that does not provide students or society with genuine, reliable, and coherent information – and that does not serve the community, especially the students, in a clear way.

Criticism 3: lack of accountability and social responsibility in education

This latter point leads to a third and related line of criticism: that educational institutions are becoming less and less socially accountable or responsible. It has been claimed that there has been a significant decline in the positive relations between the state or the community (e.g., parents and other 'stakeholders'), on the one hand, and educational institutions (e.g., faculty and administrators), on the other. And in many cases, there seems to be little interest in building healthy and productive relations among these groups.

This feature manifests itself in different ways.

For example, some argue that educational institutions themselves may not want to encourage such relations; one sometimes hears concern from educators and administrators about being accountable to those who do not understand the nature and dynamics of educational institutions, the educational context, and the aims of education or about having teaching and research interfered with by those who are unqualified. (These concerns are frequently expressed at the level of university education.) One also often finds an unease about the level of presence or involvement of outside bodies (e.g., the state, alumni, or the church) within the institution, particularly because of presumed possible negative effects on academic freedom and on hiring.

Others argue that educational institutions are simply reflecting the increasingly individualistic ethos in society – a view expressed in both Western and non-Western countries alike – and that the private interests of the various groups within these institutions have taken priority over social responsibility. While there may be 'positive aspects of this cultural development of an individualist ethos, the "can-do" attitude that is typical of a culture that is shaped by the success of capitalism (de Souza, Durka, Engebretson, Jackson, and McGrady, 2006, p. 873), some have argued that it is increasingly difficult to convince students 'of the value of group-centered learning, of the value of depending on their peers for support and collaboration' (Sleeter, 1991, p. 91), of the value of 'overcoming individualistic self-promotion' and indifference to others, and of the value of 'assisting the weak' and marginalized (Congregation for Catholic Education, 2002). Education, on this view, is primarily about what the individual student or faculty member wants, not about the common good or good of the community.

This individualism is also coupled with a 'social subjectivism' – that there is no overreaching reason or purpose for education and that each may 'take' from the educational system as she or he would like. Appeals to the common good are not infrequently challenged by claims that they restrict the individual rights or (private) goods of the 'stakeholders. It is also widely held that individuals have the right to determine their own good in their own way, so long as it does not harm others,[2] and that the community ought simply accept this.

Educational institutions are criticized, then, because they refuse to recognise, or because they resist, accountability and obligations to the communities from which they draw their material support.

Summary

In short, then, today we find not only many criticisms of education – particularly public education but significant questions concerning how the nature and purpose of education should be understood. What I have described has been directed against a very large number of tertiary, but also primary and secondary, public educational institutions in North America (and perhaps beyond) as well.

Responses and engaging root issues

How might one to respond to these apparently powerful lines of criticism?

One way of responding to many of these criticisms would be to attempt to tackle each with empirical data – to challenge claims about un- or underemployment, or about the needs of the workplace and society, or about the level of skills and abilities of students, or about the ideological orientations of faculty and students.

But such a way of responding, while valuable, does not deal with the root issue. What underlies many of these criticisms, whether the critics realize it or not, is a more general view about the nature and purpose of education and educational institutions – that is, as the theme of this volume asserts, about the meaning of education and what educational institutions should do. At the root of these criticisms, then, is a philosophical issue – an issue in the philosophy of education.

Engaging this root issue is more difficult than one may think because, I would argue, a thoughtful understanding of the nature and purpose of education – a 'philosophy of education' of whatever stripe – is lacking or undeveloped in many public (or state-operated) educational institutions and in a number of private ones as well. While there may be various opinions about the nature and purpose of education in the general culture, ironically, perhaps, there is less and less of a presence of *philosophies* of education.

For example, if one looks at Canadian universities – and they are not alone – there is very little attention paid to the philosophy of education. In the curriculum for the training and education of primary and secondary teachers in Canada, philosophy of education has an increasingly marginal place. (It is well-known that there is very little pedagogical education of faculty at the tertiary level.) Moreover, a review of recent textbooks in the area confirms that while these books provide a survey of some theories and a discussion of some issues, such as curriculum theory, creativity, self-determination, and culture, there is rarely, if ever, a comprehensive theory of what the nature and purpose of education is. Finally, apart from what one may find in education faculties, few Canadian universities regularly offer courses in the philosophy of education.

Second, there is little or no systematic or reflective understanding on the part of the wider community as to what, exactly, it sees as the nature and purpose of education. While there are concerns, they do not coalesce into a positive view of what education is about. From the criticisms noted at the beginning of this article, one might suppose that the purpose of education is to acquire skills required for employment. But should it involve acquiring other skills that may not lead to this? Should it be primarily an intellectual activity, or should it include opportunities for the development of character? Is education to serve individual interests – to promote individual flourishing – or is it to serve a common good as well? Questions such as these are relevant to what educational institutions should do, and the preceding critiques make sense only if the underlying assumptions they make about the nature of the person, the goals of education, and the like, have some justification or foundation.

Finally, and most significantly, I would argue, the notion of a reflective, comprehensive philosophy of education underlying or informing the work of most or all of those who teach, particularly at the tertiary level, is practically absent. While many of those who teach aspire to provide information and skills at a level suited to students that presumably will enable the student to be able to function as a citizen and possibly, enter a profession, what exactly should be taught, how it should be done, whether teachers need to know their students, and so on, are matters often left to individual teachers to determine. Again, how professors understand their professions, how they approach their disciplines and research, what work is involved, what character they should exhibit, and so on – most of these are questions that few take the time to answer explicitly.

It is true that in many educational institutions, one finds mission statements declaring that the institution seeks to help to form good citizens, develop critical thinking skills, promote equity and inclusiveness, and perhaps show a concern for social responsibility. But such mission statements are often marked by vagueness, generality, a desire to be all to all, and a lack of means or commitment to follow up on the statement. Instead of articulating mission statements that at best, entrench existing ideologies and fads, educational institutions (and, specifically, the faculty, administration, and students within them) need to turn – or, rather, return – to what is fundamentally a philosophical question, the question of the meaning and purpose of education.

As a way to respond to the criticisms raised at the beginning of this paper, and as a first step in articulating a philosophy of education, I want to provide a brief outline of some key principles that one finds in Catholic philosophies of education. I do so, first, because such philosophies of education have been long tested and thereby carry some credibility; second, because they arguably do provide a response to many of the preceding criticisms; but, third, because, by focusing on them, we have a place to begin a constructive discussion of the nature and purpose of education in an environment where a genuine philosophy of education seems to be missing.

Catholic philosophies of education

In many countries up until the mid-20th century, a large number of educational institutions had a close connection with religious groups, and many were initially established by religious denominations.

Within Christianity, one finds a range of churches that have established and operated educational institutions. And there have also long been educational institutions established by Jews, Muslims, Hindus, Buddhists, and so on, that exhibit the important connections among religion, culture, and learning. Yet Christian denominations have been particularly influential in establishing schools, colleges, and universities across the globe.[3]

Again, up to the mid-20th century, many educational institutions drew on the values and principles of their founders – and such a 'philosophy of education' was brought to bear in the classroom. In many cases, it was a part of the vocation or charism of those who served as teachers and administrators; it marked how they understood *why* they did *what* they did. In short, whether explicit or implicit, in these institutions – and in their teachers and students – was a theory of education, and this theory provided a common ground and a common source that defined what education was and what its purposes were.

These theories or approaches generally recognized certain basic principles of education: character building; an acquisition of social, cultural, and religious traditions; and seeking knowledge of the good and the true and even of the divine. These principles reflected the inspiration and objectives that lay at basis of the educational institution and, arguably, of education as such.

While for centuries, then, many educational institutions have been informed by an underlying philosophy and inspiration, it is worth noting how far attention to this has been found within the Catholic traditions (Redden and Ryan, 1942; Williams, 2010). Indeed, throughout much of the world, one finds a long-standing engagement of Catholic religious orders in education – the Jesuit, the Dominican, the Benedictine, the Basilian, the Oblate, and the like. Aside from the work of those religious orders, in the past century and a half, one finds major figures who have written influential texts on education, such as John Henry Newman and Jacques Maritain.

I turn now, then, to some of the insights about education found in the Catholic traditions and point out what they regard as the purpose and the basic principles of such an education. This will also, I believe, provide a vision of education that might serve as a response to the lines of criticism noted earlier.

Purpose and principles

Perhaps the key question in a philosophy of education is: what is the purpose of education – and, by extension, what is the objective of educational institutions? While there have been different ways that Catholic philosophers have answered this question, one that encapsulates many of these responses is found in a text on the philosophy of education that was influential in the Catholic traditions of the mid-20th century: *Education at the Crossroads*, by Jacques Maritain. In what follows, I will illustrate a number of the characteristics of Catholic education, referring to the work of Maritain but also to recent documents from the Holy See.

Maritain writes that 'the prime goal of education is the conquest of internal and spiritual freedom to be achieved by the individual person' (Maritain, 1943, p. 11). Unpacking this statement enables one to articulate six basic features or principles – principles that reflect how the Catholic traditions in general have viewed education. While these principles are not exhaustive, they provide, I hold, the basis for a unified philosophy of education.

Six principles

a. Maritain's remark, quoted here, focuses on the person. The *first* principle, then, is that education is person centred. What this means is not that education focuses on what a person wants but on what a person is. It is necessary, of course, to understand what is meant by 'person' here – and Maritain and others would reject the purely materialist or naturalist reductionist view that is so widespread today. The purpose of education – and this is long recognized in Catholic education – is to promote the integrated development of the human person as a being of a moral, intellectual, and spiritual character and as a being of dignity. Thus, education must aim at developing the *whole person* – in a way that promotes an integrity and unity of that person.

While it is true that education for the person and of persons has been a characteristic of many traditions of education, it is fundamental to education in the Catholic traditions. For example, in a 2007 document of the Congregation for Catholic Education of the Holy See, titled 'Educating Together in Catholic Schools', we find the following statement:

> The Catholic school, characterized mainly as an educating community, is a school for the *person and of persons*. In fact, it aims at forming the *person in the integral unity of his being,* using the tools of teaching and learning where "criteria of judgement, determining values, points of interest, lines of thought, sources of inspiration and models of life" are formed.
> (Congregation for Catholic Education, 2007, sec. 13)[4]

We also see this connection between the principles of education and the notion of the person made in several statements of the Holy See in the past decade. In 2007, in an address to Rome's diocesan convention, Benedict XVI declared that 'the essential aim of education . . . is the formation of a person to enable him or her to live to the full and to make his or her own contribution to the common good' (Benedict XVI, 2007). Similarly, at an Ecclesial Convention in Verona in 2006, Benedict said:

> A true education must awaken the courage to make definitive decisions, which today are considered a mortifying bind to our freedom. In reality,

they are indispensable for growth and in order to achieve something great in life, in particular, to cause love to mature in all its beauty: therefore, to give consistency and meaning to freedom itself.

(Benedict XVI, 2006, p. 9)

The development of this courage, this freedom, and this aspiration of 'achieving something great in life' are just part of 'the primary essential aim of [the person-centred] education' that a figure like Maritain saw some 60 years before Benedict (Maritain, 1943, p. 11).

b. What differentiates the account of the person found in many Catholic Christian philosophers from that found in most contemporary Western thinkers is that the person is fundamentally a social being. Thus, a *second* principle of education is that education requires community. Persons exist, grow, and flourish only in community. The school, the university, indeed, any educational institution, is a community. Moreover, educational institutions themselves exist only within a larger community and in relation to other communities.

The key point here is that human beings are not just isolated individuals and that even their identity as individuals is based on society and social relations. Because of these deep relations to – this embeddedness in – the community, one's values, beliefs, and personality are essentially linked to one's social context, and so an individual's good cannot be separated from others. Thus, we have basic obligations or duties to others in our own society – obligations *of* solidarity and loyalty.[5]

This view of the person, then, rejects the claim that persons are 'unencumbered' selves – that is, selves 'understood as prior to and independent of purposes and ends' (Sandel, 1984, p. 86) having as their most important feature their capacity to choose. Rather, individuals are situated within a community, and it is this community that provides them with goals, purposes, and values that serve as, as Charles Taylor puts it, 'authoritative horizons of life' – but also one's very sense of identity (Taylor, 1979, p. 159; see Lundin, 2009).

This, again, is something that we find in some recent texts on education in the Catholic traditions. In 'Educating Together in Catholic Schools', we read:

> Because its aim is to make man more man, education can be carried out authentically only in a relational and community context. . . . Schools, in their turn, take their place beside the family as an educational space that is communitarian, organic and intentional and they sustain their educational commitment, according to a logic of assistance.
>
> (Congregation for Catholic Education, 2007, sec. 12)

The importance of the community applies at all levels of education. According to John Paul II (1990, para. 14), universities are communities, communities of scholars, united by the pursuit of knowledge and of truth. Universities are, of course, a particular kind of educational community – institutions of 'advanced intellectual specialization' – places where (to quote Maritain again) 'a perfected and rational grasping of a particular subject matter' (Maritain, 1943, p. 79) is possible. Still, as communities, they need to reflect a common good as well as have a relation to other communities that support them.

Therefore, the community in which education occurs should not be isolated from the broader community. In June 2015, at the Pontifical University of Ecuador, Pope Francis stated:

> Educational communities play an essential role in the enrichment of civic and cultural life. It is not enough to analyze and describe reality: there is a need to shape environments of creative thinking, discussions which develop alternatives to current problems, especially today.
>
> (Francis, 2015)

c. How is the 'conquest of internal and spiritual freedom,' of which Maritain writes, to be achieved? This leads to a *third* principle. Education involves the pursuit of knowledge.

This may seem an almost banal statement, but reflection shows that it is not.

It is evident that throughout most of what we call the Western world, there is a very high degree of subjectivism – the denial that there is objective truth and, particularly, that there are objectively true values. This is obviously too large a subject to enter into here, but the point is that the effort to achieve the internal and spiritual freedom of which Maritain writes supposes that there is much to learn and that people need to be open to the possibility of new and deeper truths.

Catholic philosophies have long professed the importance of seeking the good and the true – not mere opinion or consensus – and have affirmed that there are matters that are known and that there are truths already known. This principle asserts, then, that while one should be open to the possibility of new and deeper truths, authentic education must reject subjectivism.

d. *Fourth*, then, what is this knowledge that is required for 'the conquest of internal and spiritual freedom' and that education seeks?

It is, in the first place, *knowing the world* in which one lives. But this does not mean knowing just the natural world but, rather, the whole of reality, natural and nonnatural (e.g., spiritual). For many religious traditions, and certainly in the Catholic traditions, it entails knowing the world not simply as a natural phenomenon, but as created, and that one sees the Creator in all things in it. This knowledge includes, in the second place, *knowing oneself* – knowing oneself as a creature of God with a natural orientation to God – and not just as a being of desire, will, and intellect. It is to know one's principles and one's limitations and also to know how to measure up to greater principles. It means developing the discernment that is necessary to judge what one is confronted with in the world; this involves a building up of character. And, in the third place – and again this is especially characteristic of Catholic educational tradition – this knowledge entails *knowing how to serve others*, to be men and women for others, for the community and for the church. And as part of one's knowing the truth, one has to see how these three aspects work together and actively integrate them in the unity of one's life.

This, then, is not mere 'notional' knowledge (to borrow a term from John Henry Newman) but an acquisition of virtue and wisdom.

e. *Fifth*, the conquest and achievement of this internal and spiritual freedom involves the continuous development of one's talents and particularly of the (moral and intellectual) virtues.

The injunction to engage in 'ongoing' or lifelong learning is familiar to many, and writers on Catholic education have insisted on the importance to keep on learning – what the Jesuits have called 'the magis.' While there is no inconsistency here with secular educational ideals, what the Catholic traditions do is emphasize the breadth and the importance of integrating the moral, intellectual, and spiritual.[6]

Education, then, is not simply training for a task; it requires that students take up the activity themselves – that they understand that they must continually seek to develop their moral, intellectual, and spiritual character, so far as they can, and that there is always 'more' that they can do.

f. *Sixth*, to achieve this end – to acquire knowledge, virtue, and wisdom and to live life to the fullest (or, in other words, to be able to know the world, know oneself, and to know how to serve others) – one needs freedom. One needs freedom to be active in learning, to take account of the specifics of situations and of the needs around oneself and to respond thoughtfully. Indeed, human beings not only connaturally tend to freedom, but as Maritain puts it, they have a metaphysical aspiration to 'win' their 'freedom in the order of the spiritual life (Maritain, 1967, p. 166). The Catholic traditions emphasise that this freedom is not license or mere action to do as one wills, without restriction or obligation. Moreover, how this freedom is present within education clearly depends on the kind and the level of education, the capacity of the person, and on the truths already known. Thus, the freedom within an elementary school is obviously narrower than that in a postgraduate programme at a university.

Summary

These features of the nature and purpose of education, found in the Catholic traditions, are basic principles of a Catholic philosophy of education.

In Catholic educational traditions and, no doubt, in most traditions drawing on religious faith, the nature and purpose of education is inseparable from the desire for a relation to the divine. In the Catholic traditions, however, education also has Christ as a model of that truly human life – that life lived fully that is a life of authentic freedom. While this principle may not add additional content, it is the principle that Catholic educators and students have traditionally drawn on when confronted with challenges in living and acting on the preceding principles.

Some may point out, on the one hand, that these principles are characteristic of many comprehensive philosophies of education and that *any* genuine education should reflect them – that they express the conviction that education is a formation of persons, intellectually and physically, but also morally and spiritually, in a way that allows for a genuine integrity. On the other hand, in many environments today, there will be challenges to some – if not all – of them.

I turn, now, to a few, initial rejoinders, listing some of the ways in which such an account of education might be able to address or respond to the three lines of criticism noted.

Rejoinders

A critic may say that even if this sketch of a Catholic philosophy of education were acceptable, in the present context, prospects for implementing such a philosophy are, at best, naïve.

Nevertheless, such a sketch arguably has some credibility because the principles have been tested and have found support, not only in the past but in a number of places in the world today. Moreover, so far as these principles are able to engage, address, or respond to the lines of criticism noted earlier, they may provide at least the basis of a constructive philosophy of education.

Recall the first line of criticism: that the primary purpose of education is to prepare and train students for the workplace or provide employment-related skills – and, therefore, that there must be methods of quality assessment, accountability, and evidence-based goals to ensure that the purpose is achieved.

There is some value in this line of criticism. But to see what the response should be requires, first, asking what is it that persons need, and need to learn, to be able to fulfill their responsibilities, including participating in the workforce. This, then, is to point to the person – to the 'matter' one is working with – but also to the environment in which persons can develop. In other words, to respond to these criticisms, one needs a more comprehensive and sophisticated look at the person in its integrity.

Second, a response requires asking about the purpose of work and employment. It is obviously not just employment for its own sake. It is, rather, contributing to society so far as it reflects a common good (for human beings are social beings) and to develop oneself in a way that allows the person to live a materially adequate life with dignity and to have the means to be a free person and to flourish.

Education for the workplace is important, then, but that workplace ought, ideally, to be one that broadly reflects the needs and dignity of persons. The jobs that are to be filled should reasonably be necessary to human flourishing – not just what a particular person or community desires.

Education, therefore, is not an individualistic activity of simply studying or teaching whatever what one wants but about developing talents and skills and coming to know and understand more about the world in which those skills and abilities come into play.

So, if the well-being and flourishing of the person are part of the purpose of employment, we have a more nuanced view of the claim that education ought to be a place of preparation for the workplace. Recall that the tradition description of *education as a liberal, not a servile, art.*

On the principles outlined, then, there is no fundamental objection to education as a preparation for the workplace, provided that that preparation is placed in the context of broader humanistic principles. What this means, concretely, then, is that education is not just training. Moreover, at the level of late secondary school and university, for example, there may be a need for foundation years or foundation programs before a student continues on to professional programs.

While the critics mentioned might resist this, one must simply reply that this is what 'preparation for the workplace' commits them to.

Now, if there is to be a flourishing or (to use Maritain's words) a conquest of freedom, and given that freedom is not mere license, then education requires pursuing literacy and numeracy. Thus, educators can agree that more effort needs to be made to overcome illiteracy and innumeracy – and this will involve overcoming the view that education is more about social life than the intellectual life and requires attentiveness to the intellectual and cultural needs, and not just the wishes, of students, teachers, administrators, and the wider community.

There must, of course, be accountability.

In some fields, there need to be measures for determining the acquisition of factual knowledge and judgement (e.g., in engineering, law, medicine, and nursing); this is for certification or accreditation by the relevant professional bodies. But mechanisms for accountability must be appropriate. For many disciplines that are not focused on training for a profession, expectations and standards are more difficult to quantify, and the proper measures of accountability might simply be the institution's existing examinations and performance evaluations. After all, what is the 'end' of a degree in literature? Writing ability? Knowing facts? Ability to exercise critical judgement? Or is the end greater and related to the general culture of a person?

In short, while it is important to recognize the significance of the first line of criticism, the solutions of the critics are, arguably, as exaggerated as their account of the problems.

Recall the second criticism: that educational practice is driven by ideologies and increasingly politicized and partisan.

Here, I would suggest, the real problem is not the presence of politics in education – which is unavoidable – but whether educational institutions reflect characteristics such as: respecting the basic value of the person as a whole and especially as a being of dignity with obligations to the larger social community; seeking knowledge and truth in a spirit of intellectual rigour, freedom, and mutual respect; engaging in these activities as communities that are part of a larger community; and doing so in a way that respects the dignity of persons – that is, faculty, staff, and students – and that is attentive to its effects on them and contributing to a common good and the good of society. The constant criterion to have in mind, here, is how do the educational activities serve the good of 'the conquest of freedom' that Maritain encourages people to keep before them? If education serves this end, then the issue of ideology is, arguably, a red herring.

Undoubtedly, there will be resistance to this response from various ideological perspectives — and this leads to the third line of criticism.

Recall the third line of criticism: that institutions and the individuals within them are less and less socially accountable and have increasingly tended to pursue their interests independently of the good of others and of the wider community.

This may seem paradoxical; on the one hand, institutions seek to offer programs of interest to students, parents, governments, and donors. But, on the other hand, this is to be done, as far as possible, on the institutions' own terms.

This paradoxical tendency seems to be motivated, I suggested earlier, by a subjectivism — by an individualistic ethic in the students, faculty, administration, and society as a whole. This affects both how educational institutions identify their interests as institutions and how faculty and students identify *their* interests — that it is primarily a matter of self-concern and not a matter of one's responsibility to the community.

In response, we must recognize that not only many of our abilities, but also our existence and identity (e.g., our language, values, etc.), are the product of our relations to others in society. Thus, we have a responsibility to the wider community that is not determined by the individual alone. As social beings, we have obligations to others and to the community in light of a common good. At the same time, however, we are persons with dignity and rights. Thus, education and educational institutions need to have a relation to that wider community, although that relation is conditioned by the purpose or end of education.

The way to address this matter of accountability — one that is suggested by the principles enumerated — is to return to thinking of educational institutions as communities within larger communities and of the person as a being who has relations to other members of society, nature, and beyond but also who has a right and obligation to develop talents and abilities.

In short, if we can draw on the principles of Catholic education enumerated, we have resources for a robust response to the criticisms against and challenges to educational institutions today.

Conclusion

As I noted at the beginning of this article, education does not lack for commentators and critics. My purpose has been to identify some of the major criticisms of institution-based education today and to see how one might productively respond to them.

One response may be discerned from Catholic philosophies of education, which speak of the formation of persons — persons of virtue and wisdom — and not just the training of future workers.

I have argued that the principles of such a philosophy of education provide us with a means to reply to a number of the major criticisms raised against contemporary education, particularly postsecondary education, and the institutions and activities that constitute it. Going beyond a mere rebuttal of criticisms, these principles challenge, or at least insist on a reframing of, the assumptions on which these criticisms rest.

These principles go further, however, for they offer a further challenge to some elements of current educational practice. Thus, these principles of a Catholic philosophy of education provide us with a starting point to discuss the nature and purpose of education at a time when such a discussion occurs only haphazardly and intermittently in many institutions and in society. Finally, though I have not argued this here, these principles may also serve as more than discussion points but as guidelines for a philosophy of education that can inform not only educational theory and practice in Catholic educational institutions but educational institutions in general.

Notes

1 See also American Council of Trustees and Alumni (2000).
2 This individualist ethos in contemporary culture is examined at length by the American sociologist Robert Bellah in his *Habits of the Heart* (1985), recently reissued in 2008.
3 Catholic colleges and universities are to be found in six continents; similarly, Protestant churches, such as the Free Church of Scotland, operated schools and colleges throughout the Indian subcontinent; there were – and sometimes still are – Presbyterian- and Church of England-affiliated colleges in East Asia and Calvinist institutions in Southern Africa.
4 We find this also in the Code of Canon Law: 'Education must pay regard to the formation of the whole person, so that all may attain their eternal destiny and at the same time promote the common good of society' (Can. 795, 1983).
5 This has been argued at length, in a secular context, by Michael Sandel (see Sandel, 1984, pp. 81–96).
6 The *Code of Canon Law* (1983) emphasizes this development. It states that children and young persons are therefore to be cared for in such a way that their physical, moral, and intellectual talents may develop in a harmonious manner so that they may attain a greater sense of responsibility and a right use of freedom and be formed to take an active part in social life (Can. 795).

References

American Council of Trustees and Alumni. (2000). *Losing America's Memory: Historical Illiteracy in the 21st Century*. Washington, DC. Retrieved from: http://www.sarfoundation.org/res/uploads/LosingAmericasMemory.pdf

American Institutes for Research. (2006). New Study of the Literacy of College Students Finds Some Are Graduating with Only Basic Skills, January 19, 2006. Retrieved from: http://www.air.org/news/press-release/new-study-literacy-college-students-finds-some-are-graduating-only-basic-skills

Arum, R. and Roksa, J. (2011). *Academically Adrift: Limited Learning on College Campuses*. Chicago: University of Chicago Press.

Bellah, R. N., Madsen, R., Sullivan, W. M., Swidler, A., and Tipton, S. M. (2008). *Habits of the Heart: Individualism and Commitment in American Life* (Rev. edn.). Berkeley, CA: University of California Press.

Benedict XVI (Pope). (2006). Address of His Holiness Benedict XVI to the Participants in the Convention, Verona Exhibition Centre, October 19, 2006. Retrieved from http://w2.vatican.va/content/benedict-xvi/en/speeches/2006/october/documents/hf_ben-xvi_spe_20061019_convegno-verona.html.

Benedict XVI (Pope). (2007). Address to Rome's Diocesan Convention on 11 June 2007 at the Basilica of St. John Lateran, 2007. Retrieved from: https://w2.vatican.va/content/benedict-xvi/en/speeches/2007/june/documents/hf_ben-xvi_spe_20070611_convegno-roma.html

Brooks, P. (2011). Our Universities: How Bad? How Good? *New York Review of Books*, March 24, 2011. Retrieved from: http://www.nybooks.com/articles/archives/2011/mar/24/our-universities-how-bad-how-good/

Code of Canon Law. (1983). English translation. Roma: Libreria Editrice Vaticana.

Congregation for Catholic Education. (2002). Consecrated Persons and Their Mission in Schools: Reflections and Guidelines, October 28, 2002. Retrieved from: https://www.ewtn.com/library/CURIA/cceconse.htm

Congregation for Catholic Education (of Seminaries and Educational Institutions). (2007). Educating together in Catholic Schools. Retrieved from: http://www.vatican.va/roman_curia/congregations/ccatheduc/documents/rc_con_ccatheduc_doc_20070908_educare-insieme_en.html

de Souza, M., Durka, G., Engebretson, K., Jackson, R., and McGrady, A. (Eds.). (2006). *International Handbook of the Religious, Moral and Spiritual Dimensions in Education*. New York: Springer.

Francis (Pope). (2015). Address to Educators at the Pontifical Catholic University of Ecuador, Tuesday, July 7, 2015. Retrieved from: https://w2.vatican.va/content/francesco/en/speeches/2015/july/documents/papa-francesco_20150707_ecuador-scuola-universita.html

Gerber, S. (2012). How Liberal Arts Colleges Are Failing America. *The Atlantic*, September 24, 2012. Retrieved from: http://www.theatlantic.com/business/archive/2012/09/how-liberal-arts-colleges-are-failing-america/262711/

Hacker, A. and Dreifus, C. (2011). *Higher Education? How Colleges Are Wasting Our Money and Failing Our Kids: And What We Can Do about It*. New York: St. Martin's Press.

Jackman, M. R. and Muha, M. J. (1984). Education and Intergroup Attitudes: Moral Enlightenment, Superficial Democratic Commitment, or Ideological Refinement? *American Sociological Review*, 49 (6), 751–769.

John Paul II (Pope). (1990). *Ex Corde Ecclesiae, Apostolic Constitution on Catholic Universities*. Washington, DC: United States Catholic Conference.

Kimball, R. (1991). Multiculturalism and the American University. *Quadrant*, July–August, 22–31.

Kimball, R. (2008). *Tenured Radicals: How Politics Has Corrupted Our Higher Education* (3rd edn.). Chicago: Ivan R. Dee Publishers.

Lundin, R. (2009). *Believing again: Doubt and Faith in a Secular Age*. Grand Rapids, MI: Eerdmans.

Maritain, J. (1943). *Education at the Crossroads*. New Haven, CT: Yale University Press; London: H. Milford, Oxford University Press.

Maritain, J. (1967). *The Education of Man: The Educational Philosophy of Jacques Maritain*. Ed. D. Gallagher and I. Gallagher. Notre Dame, IN: University of Notre Dame Press.

Newman, J. H. (1982). *The Idea of a University*. Ed. Martin Svaglic. Notre Dame, IN: University of Notre Dame Press.

Nussbaum, M. C. (2012). *Not for Profit: Why Democracy Needs the Humanities* [with a new afterword by the author]. Princeton, NJ: Princeton University Press.

Redden, J. D. and Ryan, F. A. (1942). *A Catholic Philosophy of Education*. Milwaukee, WI: Bruce Publishing.

Sandel, M. J. (1984). The Procedural Republic and the Unencumbered Self. *Political Theory*, 12 (1), 81–96.

Sleeter, C. E. (Ed.). (1991). *Empowerment through Multicultural Education*. New York: SUNY Press.

Social Science Research Council. (2014). Academically Adrift. Retrieved from: http://highered.ssrc.org/publications/academically-adrift/

Taylor, C. (1979). *Hegel*. Oxford: Oxford University Press.

US Department of Education. (2006). *A Test of Leadership: Charting the Future of U.S. Higher Education*. Washington, DC. Retrieved from: https://www2.ed.gov/about/bdscomm/list/hiedfuture/reports/pre-pub-report.pdf

Williams, K. (2010). Education and the Catholic Tradition. In R. Bailey, R. Barrow, D. Carr, and C. McCarthy (Eds.). *The SAGE Handbook of Philosophy of Education*. (167–180). London: Sage Publications, Ltd.

3 Confucian secular formation and Catholic education

(Or the spiritual education of the *Jun Zi*)

Alfredo P. Co

Introduction

When the English-speaking world talks about the center of learning, we generally gaze at universities, oblivious of the fact that there was a time when centers of learning were hosted by other cultures in another form. Universities have their origin in the higher middle age of Christian Europe (as cited in Burgh, 2010). They started as a form of humble guild, an assembly of merchants and craftsmen, formed for the furtherance and protection of their interests (The Editors of Encyclopedia Britannica, n.d.).[1] These guilds are set against the backdrop of European higher education conducted in cathedrals known as "Monastic Schools." The actualization of the university as a higher learning institution was introduced under the guidance of the Latin Church as continuing promotion of the interest of learning (Johnson, 2000, p. 9). The idea spread across Europe that prompted kings and rulers to create their own universities. The Universitas di Bologna, Universite de Paris, University of Oxford, and Universidad de Salamanca were among the earliest universities.

One of the most important contributions of the idea of a university is its insistence on the value of autonomy in education (Gürüz, 2007). During those days, the pontiff through a papal bull granted autonomy. A teacher admitted to one university was given the right to teach in any university without further examinations, giving rise to the idea of academic freedom (Watson, 2005, p. 373). With its continuous promotion of autonomy and education, the university has become the bastion of learning for its own sake, ideally devoid of personal and political motives.

The unprecedented body of knowledge, innovation, and intellectuals produced by the establishment of universities was greeted with optimism in Europe and became one of the most important driving forces that birthed modern science and the scientific revolution (Huff, 2003, p. 180). With this new academic platform, the university continued to promote its unparalleled relevance through its contribution to research and progress, becoming the model for higher learning up until today.

Ancient Samarkand

Sometime in the second century BC to the end of 14th century AD, there was a formidable trade route that originated in the ancient Chinese capital Chang An (now Xian) that stretched all the way to the Mediterranean edge of the Western world, linking the eastern Chinese empire with the Roman empire. In 1877, the German geographer Ferdinand von Richthofen called it the Silk Road.

The Silk Road became the ancient network of trade and cultural transmission and cultural exchange. It was a busy converging place of traders, merchants, religious pilgrims, monastics, soldiers, and nomads from different ancient civilizations.[2] At the heart of this gigantic Silk Road lay the enormous city of Samarkand, which became the center for the propagation of education and culture in Central Asia.[3] Various religions – Judaism, Manichaeism, Nestorian Christianity, Mahayana Buddhism, and Islam – all interacted with each other in relative peace and harmony. It had the most developed trade market for crafts from all over India, Persia, and China. Merchants were educated not just in the ways of trade but also in the different languages they would need as merchants, which included Arabic, Chinese, Turkic, and even Tibetan (Whitfield, 1999, p. 36).

Samarkand reached its peak of development when it became the capital of a great empire of Amir Timur (also known as Tamerlane), who ordered the construction of an architectural masterpiece that would define his rule. One of these is the famous Registan Square located at the heart of the city.[4] There Tamerlane's grandson Ulugh Beg established one of the most advanced educational institutions of the time, with the largest and finest observatories in the Islamic world, known as Ulugh Beg Observatory.[5] The finest scientists were invited to lecture in the madrassah (which was later adopted in the West, now called a university). Samarkand "attracted many students from all over the Islamic territories, even including the farthest western regions."[6]

Ji Xia Zhi Xue of ancient China

Earlier than that, during the Period of Warring States (475 BC–221 BC) in ancient China was a place called Ji Xia Zhi Xue (稷下之學) or Ji Xia Academy. It was a center of learning where prominent scholars came to discuss, debate, and learn from each other. The place was located in the state of Qi (齊), where King Xuan (齊宣王) (319–301 BCE) styled himself as the great cultural and educational benefactor. He welcomed great scholars[7] across his kingdom to give regular lectures on various topics in the academy. Many great social, political, and moral thoughts flourished, contributing to the frontier of knowledge in the Middle Kingdom. The phenomenon gave birth to the great flowering of hundreds of thoughts known as the Period of Hundred Schools.

The grand historian Sima Qian (司馬遷) recorded that King Xuan of Qi had a fondness for scholars of the classics and advocators/persuaders of statecraft and diplomacy (as cited in Sato, 2003, p. 80). So important was the place these scholars occupied in society that they were held in the highest regard. Their social rank equaled that of great officers of the Ji court, and they received generous stipends and exemption from the daily chores of administrative tasks. The practice of debate raised the intellectual environment that provided "innovation by opposition" (Hartnett, 2011, p. 87).

Education seems to have come to us with distinctive character nourished by the environment in which the idea of learning was born. If the university in medieval Europe was born as a form of *artis liberales*, and Samarkand with science, and Ji Xia with social, political, and moral formation, we have various perspectives on how we have to see the education of humankind.

But my task is the difficult project of introducing a dialogue of two great cultural traditions between Confucian secular formation and Catholic education.

One has to be reminded that the Chinese civilization antedates Catholicism by about 3,000 years. When Carpini, Marco Polo, and Mateo Ricci came to China, China already had met other religions such as Buddhism, Nestorian Christianity, Islam, and Judaism, which had already been to the Middle Kingdom.[8]

An evangelizing Catholic is usually engrossed with the move to bring the good news as a whole package, often oblivious of the host country's culture and civilization. It was the common mistake made by the early missionaries who went to India and China during the colonial period. Entering into an old civilization with the view of supplanting their culture of a well-established civilization is not only suicidal but also downright unsettling.

When Catholicism grew in Europe and ventured its own expansion through evangelization during the colonial age, Christianity was in its prime and went to the rest of the world with a triumphalist mind-set. The colonizers were set to conquer the new world and plant their Western and Christian culture.

Colonization was easy in the underdeveloped world. Western countries, with powerful, dominant cultures, triumphed over these small countries with relative ease. It was a case of a great culture supplanting a developing one. Mexico, the Philippines, and many Latin American countries are examples. But how were they to import politics, culture, and religion to India and China – two civilizations many times their senior? India was the cradle of the Mohenjo-Daro and Harappa civilizations that developed the great religions of Hinduism, Jainism, and Buddhism. China could cite great political and ethical thinkers like Confucius (Kong Zi), Lao Zi, Mencius (Meng Zi), Zhuang Zi and many more.

What did China have at the time of Catholic entry to the Middle Kingdom?

What was Chinese education like when the Christians came to evangelize them? What worldview did they have? An investigation of the philosophical anthropology and the form of indigenous education may be a good point to start.

Confucius and secular education

There was in China, an inspiring father of secular education named Confucius. The man was born in 551 BC and referred to as Kong Zi, the Sage, the Master and the most revered of teachers. British Sinologist Lionel Giles edified Confucius as perhaps the most consummate of sages, the loftiest moralist and the most subtle and penetrating intellect that China has ever seen. He alluded to Confucius as the greatest and noblest representative of the greatest, happiest, and the most highly civilized people on earth (Giles, 1910).

Taking things from a historico-religious and cultural perspective, we see that God revealed Himself to a chosen people, the Jews, gifted them the Ten Commandments, and sent prophets to teach the way to live a meaningful life. The rest of humanity, Chinese civilization included, was left to fend on their own to discover and make sense of their being. The Chinese, without the gift of a pact or a covenant with God, had to discover for themselves how it is to be human and how it is to live a purposeful life.

It was amidst this historical given that the great sage Confucius came to life. Understandably, without God's revelation, his philosophy came to be a secular one. As a philosopher, he focused on the phenomenon of man and proposed a philosophy that centered on the human reality and determined the outstanding characteristics of a philosophy that centered on humanism.

Confucius's teaching is contained in Lun Yu (論語), *The Analects or The Conversations*, a compilation of wise sayings that incorporates the wisdom of the Chinese Sage, acquired from years of intense and sensitive observation of life. At the heart of this conversation is the attempt to educate and cultivate people. Confucian secular education revolves around *Wuchang* (五常) or the Five Constants, consisting of Ren, Yi, Li, Zhi, and Xin.[9]

Ren (仁) and the first moral awakening

Confucius once said that there is but one thread binding his teaching, and this is Ren.[10] Ren (仁) is literally not translatable as it is a term of plurisignification.[11] The pictogram is composed of compound characters; the left character ren (人) means "man" and the right character erh (二), "two" or "second." The compound ideogram literally signifies "man and a second." Ren therefore can be referred to as "consciousness-of-human-others." Ren is the most basic human understanding of human condition, which signifies an existential awakening of a person becoming morally aware of the fact that he or she is not alone, but there is a human other aside from him- or herself.

If we were to rekindle the existential insight in Feudor Dostoyevsky's work, *The Brothers Karamazov*, we find the passage, "Without God, everything is permissible,"[12] and the rest of Western civilization nodded their heads in unison. But the Chinese Sage would seem to tell us otherwise. Without God, a person realizes the existential reality that he or she is not alone, and in this awakening an entire moral and social philosophy emerges.

From this notion of Ren, we realize that it is a substantive principle of human conduct. It speaks of love for humanity in the sense of conscious concern for the well-being of others. Confucius elaborates this idea very appropriately in his anthropocentric articulation of the proverb: "Do unto others what you wish others to do unto you" and "Do not do unto others what you do not want others to do unto you" (Confucius, 1979, 2:12). This was also articulated in the Christian moral dictum some 500 years after.[13]

But the Confucian Golden Rule carries with it two directional articulations known as Zhong (忠) and Shu (恕).

The ideogram Zhong (忠) is a compound ideogram composed of the superior character Zhong (中) "center, central, or middle," while the inferior character is Xin (心), "mind-heart," the unwavering emotion-reason. On the other hand, the character Shu (恕) is a complex ideogram composed of several radicals: Nu (女), "woman;" Kuo (口), "mouth;" and once again Xin (心), "heart-mind." It is a comforting reminder that comes right from the heart of a woman, possibly a mother. Both characters interconnect and relate to Ren (仁) and human reason.

As a teaching, Zhong (忠) signifies the positive aspect of the practice of Ren (仁) in that one must be conscious of others. A person of Ren is one "who, in desiring to sustain himself, sustains others, and in desiring to develop himself, develops others" (Co, 1993, p. 108). All these radiate from the center of one's unwavering mind and unperturbed heart, where his or her whole being becomes the fulcrum of judgment and action. Zhong represents the positive saying of the Golden Rule, "Do unto others as you would like others do unto you" (Confucius, 1979, 2:12). In Zhong Yong or the Doctrine of the Mean (Confucius, 1983a), we find this saying:

> Serve your father as you would require your son serve you. Serve your ruler, as you would require your subordinate serve you. Serve your brother, as you would require your younger brother serve you. Set the example in behaving among your friends as you would require them to behave with you.
>
> (Confucius, 1983a, 8:4)

Shu (恕), on the other hand, signifies cautious and prohibitive advice, a comforting reminder that comes right from the heart of a woman, possibly a mother. In Da Xue (大學), *The Great Learning*, we quote:

> Do not use what you dislike in your superiors in the employment of your inferiors. Do not use what you dislike in your inferior in the service of your superiors. Do not use what you dislike in those who are before you to prove to those who are behind you. Do not use what you dislike at the right to display towards the left. Do not use what you dislike at the left to display towards the right.
>
> (Confucius, 1983b, 10:2)

These twin aspects of the Confucian Golden Rule became known as the "principle of the measuring square."[14] With sensible, serious self-reflection, an individual is able to find the repository of moral understanding of how it is for humankind to proceed interacting with others who is also like him- or herself. This is what the Sage means in saying that Ren is the rule of practice for one's life (Confucius, 1979, 15:24). A person becomes a measure of good or evil; if I want a true answer to true goodness, it just takes serious and honest self-inquiry, and the answer is right there (Confucius, 1979, 7:30).

Confucius on Yi (義)

The internal moral awareness of "the other" however, according to Confucius, must be empowered with a moral élan articulated in the moral teaching of Yi (義).[15] The ideogram Yi (義) is a compound ideogram composed of a superior part and an inferior part. The inferior part of the character is Wo (我) "I, Myself, or the Ego." But the superior part is not as self-evident. There are two schools of thought on this; one says that it is taken from the character Yang (羊) "goat," while the other claims it to be Wang (王) "king." The ideogram Wo (我) placed at the inferior part of the pictogram suggests, "I carry something." But what do I carry?

If we were to assume that the character is taken from "goat," then an analogy should clear the point. "I carry my duty as a mother goat rears her young." But if taken from the character "king," then it signifies "I carry a king." But regardless of carrying "goat" or "king" the ideogram Yi (義) conveys the same idea of a "duty imposed upon me."

Yi therefore signifies "consciousness of one's moral imperative." The moment I become self-conscious of Ren, I also acquire some form of duty imposed upon me by the society into which I am born. Yi becomes a self-moral injunction. Elevating this idea into the social realm, it acquires a heightened social articulation, better understood by looking at two important Confucian teachings of the Rectification of Names and Five Relations.

Yi in the Rectification of Names (正名) and Five Relations (五論)

When Confucius was asked what would be the first thing he would do if he were to become a minister, he replied unequivocally, "The first thing I will do is Zheng Ming (正名)" or the Rectification of Names; "Let the ruler be a ruler, the subject a subject, the father a father, the son a son" (Confucius, 1979, 12:11). For, "if the ruler be not a ruler, the subject not a subject, the father not a father, the son not a son, then even if there be grain, would I get to eat it?" (Confucius, 1979, 12:11).

To further understand and appreciate Confucius discussion on this Rectification of Names, Zheng Ming (正名), we need to also apply it to his teaching on Five Relations or Wu Lun (五論).

No one is ever an island in the Confucian society, for right at the beginning he or she is socially related referred to by Confucius as Wu Lun (五論), Five Relations. Wu Lun consists of Fu-Zi (父子), Father-Son; Fu-Fu (夫妇), Husband-Wife; Xiong-Di (兄弟), Senior Brother-Junior Brother; Peng-You (朋友), Senior friend-Junior friend; Jun-Cheng (君臣), Ruler-Subject.

The first and the most fundamental social bond is called Fu-Zi (父子), Father-Son relations. This paternal relationship is the groundwork of Confucian social philosophy. But what is expected of Fu-Zi, Father-Son relations? The moral teaching of Yi (義) is clear; the father ought to be benevolent to his son, while the son ought to be filial to his father. In the *Analects* we read, "Being good as a son and obedient as a young man is, perhaps, the root of a man's character" (Confucius, 1979, 1:2). Confucius (1979, 4:18) continues,

> Urging the son to behave with care and gentility to his father. In serving your father and mother you ought to dissuade them from doing wrong in the gentlest way. If you see your advice being ignored, you should not become disobedient but should remain reverent. You should not complain even if in so doing you wear yourself out.

For the character you cultivate, as a worthy son will bring you great promise as a public figure, "Simply by being a good son and friendly to his brothers a man can exert an influence on government" (Confucius, 1979, 2:21). Moreover, true respect for one's parent comes with sincere filial responsibility, "Nowadays for a man to be filial means no more than that he is able to provide his parents with food. Even hounds and horses are, in some way, provided with food. If a man shows no reverence (respect), where is the difference?" (Confucius, 1979, 2:7). As one matures in age, he ought to be aware of his parents in their old age, "A man should not be ignorant of the age of his father and mother. It is a matter, on the one hand, for rejoicing and, on the other, for anxiety" (Confucius, 1979, 4:21). Furthermore, a son is reminded, "When your parents are alive, you should not go too far afield in your travels. If you do, your whereabouts should always be known" (Confucius, 1979, 4:19). Finally, when time has come when parents have to go, a filial son is expected to remember them with great love. "If, for three years, a man makes no changes to his father's ways, he can be said to be a good son" (Confucius, 2009, 4:20).

Another familial relation is the matrimonial kind known as Fu-Fu (夫妇), or Husband-Wife relations. In this paradigm, it is said that a husband ought to provide for his wife. But Confucius perceives that there is difficulty in dealing with the wife. "In one's household, it is the women and the small men that are difficult to deal with. If you let them get too close, they become insolent (disrespectful). If you keep them at a distance, they complain" (Confucius, 1979, 17:35). Accordingly, a wife is expected to be submissive to the husband, that she may be able to follow the wish and will of her spouse. As there cannot be two captains sailing one ship to two different directions; there cannot be both father and mother each freely directing the family. They have to operate as one family under the direction of a benevolent father and a submissive wife followed by filial children. This social system hinges on the centrality of social harmony crafted by establishing social norms based on reverential duty to the family.

An ideal Confucian woman (mother) is educated to have San Cong Si De (三从四德), Three Obediences and Four Women Virtues. The Three Obediences are: Wei Jia Cong Fu (未嫁从父), obey her father as a daughter; Ji Jia Cong Fu (既嫁从夫), obey her husband as a wife; Fu Si Cong Zi (夫死从子) obey her sons in widowhood. On the other hand, women are to cultivate the Four Women Virtues: De (德) morality, Fu Yan (妇言), proper speech; Fu Rong (妇容), modest manner; Fu Gong (妇功), diligent work. San Cong Si De are the spiritual fetters of wifely submission and virtues expected of ideal Chinese women. One ought to understand this articulation against the historical reality of the time. Education, or the cultivation of the mind in the ancient world, was mainly for men. Women were kept in the domestic sphere. As such, it was expected that the better-educated partner should take the serious judgment and direction for the family and that power be given to the father.

The third familial relation is called Xiong-Di (兄弟), Senior Brother-Junior Brother. In Confucian society, a senior brother is expected to be protective of his junior brother, while the junior brother is expected to be deferential to his senior brother. Such is the nature of precedence, for one who comes first must ensure that his earlier experience should allow him to protect the younger ones from danger. A deferential attitude of the younger sibling, on the other hand, ensures that his elderly brother will continue to protect him when he is caught in danger. That does not mean that he has only submissive value to cultivate because, in the traditional ancient family circle, it is presumed that he will have someone younger to whom he will have to play the role of a senior brother to. The rules that govern social brotherly conduct provide a healthy blueprint to ensure harmony between brothers. In Lun Yu (論語), the *Analects*, we find this conversation, "What a good son Min Zu Tian is! No one can find fault with what his parents and brothers have to say about him" (Confucius, 1979, 11:5). Another passage reads, "Ru You asked the Master, 'Should one immediately put into practice what one has heard?' 'As your father and elder brothers are still alive, you are hardly in a position immediately to put into practice what you have heard'" (Confucius, 1979, 11:22). While there is a strong temptation to proceed according to one's will, the social norm governing the Brother-Brother relationship provides the opportunity for fraternal harmony.

But even a family is never alone; there are many other families. Extended social relations beyond family life, take the form of Peng-You (朋友), Senior friend-Junior friend relation. At this level, a senior friend must be proper and kind to his junior friend that he may accrue respect from his subordinate, while the junior friend ought to show proper courtesy and respect to someone more senior. These non-familiar relationships may take more work but are essential to cultivating social harmony.

Respectfulness may have the appearance of humility, but the behavior can be of cautiousness that he may not infuriate someone older. In the *Analects*, Confucius cautioned his disciples, saying, "Make it your guiding principle to do your best for others and to be trustworthy in what you say. Do not accept as friend anyone who is not as good as you. When you make a mistake do not be afraid of mending your ways" (Confucius, 1979, 1:18). The Master warned his disciples to be especially careful in cultivating friends, saying,

> He stands to benefit that makes friends with three kinds of people. Equally he stands to lose who makes friends with three other kinds of people. To make friends with the straight, the trustworthy in word and the well informed is to benefit. To make friends with 'flatterer' the ingratiating (flattering in order to gain favor) in action, the pleasant in appearance and the plausible (possible) in speech is to lose.
>
> (Confucius, 1979, 16:4)

Confucius also warned his disciples, "To be importunate (demanding) with one's lord will mean humiliation. To be importunate with one's friends will mean estrangement (distancing)" (Confucius, 1979, 4:26).

The entire social relational network is, however, governed by the relationship known as Jun-Cheng (君臣), or that of Ruler-Subject. In principle, there is little that has not already been said in Fu-Zi (父子), or Father-Son relation, that is not to be found in Jun-Cheng. For Jun-Cheng (君臣), Ruler-Subject, is the model of a paternalistic political system. In a Confucian government, the ruler takes the role of father to the entire community of families. Far from the notion of citizens, the people under heaven are known as members of one big family. As such, the ruler ought to be benevolent to his family, the subjects, and in return, the subjects are to show loyalty and respect to the ruler. This Fu-Zi (父子), Father-Son paradigm, of Confucian society defines the nature of a paternalistic rule. The five relations, including familial and social types, connect and support each other to form a powerful social structure in society; without them society would simply collapse. From the Chinese perspective, such natural social-formal relationships are what make a society a society.

The social names such as Fu (父), Father; Zi (子), Son; Fu (妇), Wife; and Jun (君), Ruler imply two things; the ideal conception Zheng (正), Right, Correct, and the moral imperative of Yi (義). That is to say that there is an ideal notion of a Father, Son, or Ruler and that this ideal is called Zheng (正), "Right," "Correct."

The directive given by Confucius to his students was premised on the idea that he perceived that there was something wrong in society and that it was mainly because people had departed from the duty Yi (義) attached to their names. If one departs from the ideal notion Zheng (正), society becomes chaotic, and the only thing that can solve it is to require people to go back to the responsibility, Yi (義), attached to their social names. When a father refuses to perform his duty to be benevolent, a son might depart from his Xiao (孝), filial piety, and so on until society becomes chaotic. That is why Confucius said, "When names are not correct, what is said will not sound reasonable" (Confucius, 1979, 13:3).

Zheng Ming Rectification of Names (正名) and Yi Righteousness (義) are all interwoven in social purpose, social responsibility, and social accountability. Moreover, there is in these a moral drive that holds them into one social whole. Man is thus told that he is a being with a multifarious Yi (義) duty. He grows with social and moral responsibility as he courses through life. Just as he is son to his father, he will become a father to his future son; just as he is a younger brother to his elder brother, he is an elder brother to his junior brother, and he will be senior or junior to friends in the big family community under heaven.

But how ought a man interact in a Confucian society?

Li (禮) as a social and cultural articulation of Yi (義)

The whole enterprise on how a Confucian social man interacts in a society brings us to another Confucian constant known as Li (禮).

Li (禮) is made up of the left (礻) and the right (豊) characters. The character on the left is taken from the pictogram to worship, and the character to the right is taken from the pictogram of an incense urn with two joss sticks planted on the top. The compound characters of a man prostrating before an urn signify rite, ceremony, decorum, deportment, politeness, good manners, propriety, or civility. It is the decorum of a civilized society. Originally the term was used to refer to religious rites. Confucius used it to include customs and traditions that define proper social interaction. In a society that requires strict social decorum, Li (禮) holds equal importance with the nature of Law, Fa (法).

Li (禮) is distinguished from Law, Fa (法) in that the first was a culturally accepted norm or custom, while the law is enacted according to a legal process. Li commanded positive action, while Fa, Law, was prohibitory. The violation of Fa was punishable by the state, while deviation from Li was visited by social pressure or censure. In a culturally conscious society, Li rises to the countenance of aristocrats, scholars, and Mandarins who were above the law. Fa, meanwhile applied to the rest of Ren Min (人民), or the non-polished multitude. In the Book of Rites, or Li Ji (禮記), we find that "Li does not go down to the common people; punishment does not reach up to the Great Prefects" (as cited in Co, 1993). Li was thus a means of training in virtue and of avoiding evil; it was prophylactic. Fa, on the other hand, was the cure for evil.

Here we see that Confucian society distinguishes two kinds of men, the Da Ren (大人) and the Xiao Ren (小人). Da Ren (literally big man) signifies a superior man: a gentleman, a moral man, a lettered man. This is contrasted to the Xiao Ren (literally small man), who is an inferior man owing to the fact that he is not educated; he is an unpolished human being, a man in the street. In Confucian society, the Da Ren are governed by Li, while the Xiao Ren are governed by Fa. This is the whole meaning of the Li and Fa in this Confucian society. A superior man dreads social pressure and shame caused by social condemnation, while a Xiao Ren fears the severity of the law. Thus, every virtuous social pattern, every virtue-enhancing habit, and every custom that was meant for social happiness and peace is included in Li. On the other hand, every social crime, violent and disruptive to the social order, is punishable by Fa. All moral crimes are classified under Li, while all social and criminal crimes are regulated by Fa.

The demand for cultivation of this civilized character is strong. Confucius said, "When your parents are alive, comply with the rites (Li) in serving them; when they die, comply with the rites (Li) in burying them; comply with the rites (Li) in sacrificing to them" (Confucius, 1979, 2:5). He went further saying, "Unless a man has the spirit of the rites (Li), in being respectful he will wear himself out, in being careful he will become timid, in having courage he will become unruly, and in being forth-right he will become intolerant" (Confucius, 1979, 8:2). It is therefore in Li that one finds the golden mean of civilized life. It is in Li where one finds a perfect balance between the excessive and the deficient conduct of life.

The notion of Zhi (智)

The concept of Zhi is a complex ideogram composed of three radical parts: left, right, and bottom. The left character Zhi (矢) "the act of knowing," Kuo (口) mouth, and yueh (日) "to say" or "to express," or "spoken." This is perhaps the most ancient Chinese ideogram comparable to the combined Greek terms logos + Sophia or of the Indian word Darsana, both of which signify wisdom. The Chinese character Zhi (智) signifies spoken wisdom or transmitted knowledge. While the Chinese used the word Zhi to signify transmitted knowledge in expressing the highest form of rational enlightenment, the Greeks had two separate concepts, logos + Sophia. The Greek concepts "philosophy" and "love of wisdom" convey separation of knowledge and action, as in the case of someone who loves wisdom but may not possess it. But for the Chinese, a person who loves wisdom but does not have it is incapable of conveying wisdom. Zhi implies the necessity of possessing and transmitting wisdom. To live in accordance with one's philosophical conviction is part of man's philosophical activity. To Confucius, moral thinking and moral discourse are intended for action. Finally, Zhi is a virtue attached to the superior gentleman of letters, to the literati, and to the scholar.

Confucius on Xin (信)

Many people seem to give little importance to his parole, and yet Confucius considers language to have moral significance. The Chinese character Xin (信) is composed of the left character is taken from ren (人), "man," and the right character Yan (言), "word" or "logos." As a combined ideogram it means "man before his spoken word." If a man is a moral agent, the language he speaks must carry moral significance. As such, man has moral accountability to what he says. In Ancient China, the term is associated with "keeping promise" or fulfilling what one says. A man must be committed to the spoken word. What else should a moral person do if not to keep vigil over his spoken word, which is an intermediary between thought and action? As we think, so do we speak; as we speak, so do we act. Confucius puts emphasis on the importance of the spoken word, for who keeps vigil to his Xin spoken word gains from others their trust, unity, confidence, and progress.

Jun Zi (君子)

Confucian education is focused on the elevation of man to the level of superior man of moral character that he may gain self-dignity in the noblest form. Put simply Jun Zi (君子) is Confucius's paragon of a moral gentleman. The idea comes from the ancient story of a lord's son that dates back to the Duke Wen of the Zhou Dynasty. A son of a ruler is raised to have a superior ethical and moral position while gaining inner peace through his virtue. He is a paradigmatic man, a moral exemplar, and ideal man akin to Heideggerian Dasein, or a Nietzschean Ubermensch, or the Greek "hoi philakis." In the classical Confucian age, he would be a wise man or a sage. All human moral learning should transform one to become a Jun Zi.

The formation of this gentle man known as Jun Zi is at the apex of human transformation; in him one finds the gentility of manner and the superiority of character. He is the ideal man of letter that rose to the level of nobility in every sense of the word. If Catholicism takes sainthood as an ideal, Hinayana Buddhism takes to an Arahat, and Mahayana to a Bodhisattva, the Confucian ideal is found in a Jun Zi, a perfect secular ideal gentleman of letters.

As Confucianism courses through the history of Chinese civilization, all its teaching were distilled into one great teaching came to be known as the Great Learning or Da Xue (大學).

Da Xue (大學),[16] the Great Learning

Confucian Great Learning provides an insight into the trajectory of a Confucian social-moral agenda. The education of a Confucian man has at its center the creation of a perfect state where people can live in harmony in a community of learned human beings.

It aims at creating a state composed of moral men who have their hearts focused on the good of men and the good of society. The world is for men to discover, reflect on, and find insight into a life of great harmony. This serious reflection of life allows a man to develop a clear mind and calm heart. By setting priorities, his heart becomes focused on what is important for him to cultivate for himself and for society. Men bonding together through socially responsive, harmonizing goals can collectively push the destiny of humanity to a common end that benefits everyone. Man is capable of learning, and with a focused heart and mind, he learns the intricate social system that must be cultivated to achieve balance and harmony in the state. There is no one aspect of learning that can stand independently with the rest. No one can fly with one wing.

Da Xue, or the Great Learning, teaches illustrating virtue, restoring the people, and rising to the highest individual and social moral excellence. The book reads (Confucius, 1983b, pp. 4–7):

> The ancients who wished to illustrate illustrious virtue throughout the world, first ordered well their own States.
>   Wishing to order well their States, they first regulated their families.
>   Wishing to regulate their families, they first cultivated their persons.
>   Wishing to cultivate their persons, they first rectified their hearts.
>   Wishing to rectify their hearts, they first sought to be sincere in their thoughts.
>   Wishing to be sincere in their thoughts, they first extended to the utmost of their knowledge.
>   Such extension of knowledge lay in the investigation of things.
>   Things being investigated, knowledge became complete.
>   Their knowledge being complete, their thoughts were sincere.
>   Their thoughts being sincere, their hearts were then rectified.
>   Their hearts being rectified, their persons were cultivated.
>   Their persons being cultivated, their families were regulated.
>   Their families being regulated, their States were rightly governed.
>   Their States being rightly governed, the entire world was at peace.
>   From the Son of Heaven down to the mass of the people, all must consider the cultivation of the person the root of everything besides.
>   It cannot be, when the root is neglected, that what should spring from it will be well ordered.
>   It never has been the case that what was of great importance has been slightly cared for, and, at the same time, that what was of slight importance has been greatly cared for.

With this encompassing secular Confucian education, we are drawn to ask, what more can Catholic education add to this Confucian Gentleman called Jun Zi?

We recall what early Christians appropriated from Plato, the distinction of the world of ideas and world of senses in his discourse of the theory of ideas or theory of forms: on one hand the nonmaterial, abstract forms (ideas) and the material world of change that we come to know through sensation in the world of senses. Plato asserts the permanence of the world of ideas, which is changeless, compared to the transient reality of the world of the senses, which he perceives as non-real.[17] Augustine appropriated the two-world articulation of Plato into Christianity when he introduced the story of two cities in his work *De Civitate Dei*, where he tells us of the "City of God" and the "City of Man." The idea of creating the notion of two cities was, in fact, complementary to the Christian philosophical anthropology of man being composite of body and soul. As such he tells us that the physical body is a transient reality and is ruled by the physical order, the world of the man living in the City of Man. But he asserts that man has a soul that is immortal and continues on after his death. He tells us that the City of Man is shaped by the love of self, even to the contempt of God, and the City of God is shaped by the love of God, even to the contempt of self. It refers to the secular world of man under the reign of a secular ruler. He tells us that while people live in the City of Man, they do not belong to the City of Man. A man may enjoy the earthly country, enjoying human rights, protection, and preservation of order, but man does not belong to it. Augustine tells us that the City of Man is not our true home. Rather, our true home is in another world called the City of God. The best citizens of the City of Man are those who remember that their true citizenship is in the City of God.

This Christian philosophical anthropology offers a new way of understanding humanity in the Confucian secular world. It comes as a package beginning from the story of creation to Catholic eschatology in the Beatitudes. The issue of entry to a society that has its own way of looking at man and the world becomes the central focus of a mission. For a society with the vision focused on Harmony under Heaven with the entire social fabric defined by the civilization, importing some very politically sensitive matters can be radically disturbing to the Chinese. The City of Man referred to by Augustine needs to be taken with caution, for it relates to the political and social matter that this dear old Chinese civilization held sacred.

But the Christians have a poignant story to tell the Chinese:; the story of a man having a soul, that the soul is immortal, the story of faith, and of hope, and the story of an afterlife, where every man's dream may find its fulfillment. These ideas are new and absent in Chinese civilization. The story that man has in him, not just the physical self but also a spiritual self, is a good entry point. It is absent in Chinese society, and the discourse of a human soul is politically harmless. Immortality of this soul, however, requires a more delicate discussion, especially, because this idea entails how this will be directed as it requires the dynamics of what Augustine distinguishes in the City of Man and the City of God. If it is told in story form, this will give it some power. Storytelling is very much a part of any civilized culture. When told competently by men of good will, ideas can progress. The idea of an afterlife that can be nurtured by hope is a powerful thought. The anticipation of a world where one's unfulfilled dreams in this earthly life may come true has an immense potency to promote a rise to perfection in earthy life. The early Christians entered the Roman culture not because it entered as a religion but as a philosophical idea, and Romans, having been influenced by the Greek cultures, tolerated ideas. Had the Christians entered the Roman civilization as a religion, that could have been completely devastating as it would have challenged the Roman gods and pantheons. But when it entered as an idea, a philosophy, the civilization was ready to listen.

Philosophy taught side by side with religion provided a most potent instrument for Catholic evangelization; that is why Christianity is one religion that requires philosophy be integral part of priestly formation. For religious persuasion requires the potency of reason, though Catholicism retains the primacy of faith, and philosophy is a handmaid of religion. The vision of this interplay of faith and reason for evangelization continues to carry its relevance all the way to our time.

Conclusion

From here, our discussion has shown that the secular Confucius was an ethical-political thinker with a vision for the recreation of an ideal moral society. His goal was to educate men in the family and in society that they might provide significant contributions to the state. He believed this could be done through education. He styled himself as a teacher and gathered young men of his time in the ancient state of Lu to teach them in the cultivation of character through observation, the hard work of study, and reflective thought. At the heart of his education vision was fostering the knowledge and skills that could make a man responsive to the needs of the state so that there could be harmony under heaven. Humanistic thought governed these ideals through a complete secular education that elevated man to the pinnacle of moral challenge. Thus we say that the ideal Confucian gentleman stands astute to learn education from without.

As we proceed to tread the path of education in the 21st century, we have these marvelous reflections to relive, the distinctive character with which humanity nourishes people with the idea of learning will haunt us every now and then. We have easy recall of the long lost days of Ji Xia Zhi Xue in China, madrassah in Samarkand, and the university in medieval Europe to remind us of the beautiful human aspiration for the education of humanity. The contemporary educational vision and liberalism have the advantage of getting their voices heard in the platform people now enjoy. But with a look into history of human civilization, Confucian and Catholic education will continue to enjoy sterling places in the human formation.

The Chinese Confucian man will have some dialoging to do as he meets Catholic education. There will be initial tension, but if man is indeed a universal phenomenon, as we all want to claim he is, then we should only look at him with great hope. Perhaps in the not so distant future, when religions stop condemnation of each other, when cultures stop bias against each other, when science and technology are harnessed to serve and not destroy humankind, when politics are set aside to accommodate the existence of the other, then we can safely say that these human institutions have seriously done their part to educate humanity to keep them in harmony and peace.

Notes

1 It could also be referred to as an organization of scholars and students dedicated professionally to push the frontiers of learning and education under to no authority, either the king or the Church (Hastings, 1895).
2 See (Elisseeff, 2000).
3 Poets and historians of the past also refer to this city as the "[p]recious pearl of the Islamic world," "Eden of the East," "Face of the Earth." See Permanent Mission of the Republic

of Uzbekistan to the United Nations (http://www.un.int). See also the introduction to (Whitfield, 1999).
4 See Permanent Mission of the Republic of Uzbekistan to the United Nations (http://www.un.int).
5 A continuation of the Maragha School tradition established in Iran, which focused on pre-Copernican and non-Ptolemaic systems of explaining the planetary motions. See (UNESCO and WHC, n.d. b). This was also where excellent records of approximate solutions for cubic equations, binomial theorems, tables of sines and tangents correct up to the eighth decimal place, formulas for spherical trigonometry, and most importantly, a stellar catalogue where the position of 992 stars had been recorded were made and kept. (The star catalogue, Zij-i Sultani or Catalogue of the Stars, was one of the first comprehensive stellar catalogues since Ptolemy, and it set the standard for astronomical works until the 17th century.)
6 The result of these scholarly exchanges was a far-ranging influence through a vast area from Transoxiana to the Ottoman empire. When the Timurid dynasty fell and the Safavid dynasty was established, the massive emigration of scholars from the eastern parts of the Islamic territories into the Ottoman empire in the early 16th century remarkably contributed to the development of science in the empire. See UNESCO and WHC (n.d. a).
7 This includes Mencius, Xun Zi, Zou Yan, and Lu Zhonglian.
8 See Co (2015, pp. 107–124).
9 When one enters the Merridian Gate in Forbidden City in Beijing, you see the five bridges representing the Wu Chang (五常), the Five Constants of Confucian Virtues. They are central to the Confucian secular educational formation representing Ren, Yi, Li, Zhi, and Xin.
10 "The Master said, 'Ts'an! There is one single thread binding my way together.' Tseng Tzu assented. After the Master had gone out, the disciples asked, 'What did he mean?' Tseng Tzu said, 'The way of the Master consists in doing one's best and in using oneself as a measure to gauge others. That is all.' " See Confucius (1979, 4:15). Zhong-Su is the articulation of the meaning of Ren as a moral doctrine.
11 James Legge translated it as "Benevolence," Arthur Waley, "Goodness", or a "Human heartedness," or "Goodness," etc.
12 The actual phrase in one translation goes: "*Without God* and the future life? It means *everything is permitted* now." See Dostoevsky (1990, p. 589).
13 "So whatever you wish that others would do to you, do also to them, for this is the Law and the Prophets." See Matthew 7:12 (English Standard Version).
14 It could also be taken to mean as the principle by which a man take his moral awakening as a springboard for the moral understanding of humanity. I am the other, and the other is I in its most fundamental sense.
15 Some Sinologists translate it as "rectitude," "duty," "obligation," "righteousness".
16 The Great Learning as we know it today is the result of multiple revisions and commentaries by a number of Confucian and Neo-Confucian scholars. The Great Learning, along with the Doctrine of the Mean, had their beginnings as chapters within the Book of Rites. Both were removed from the Book of Rites and designated as separate, equally significant works by Zhu Xi (朱熹).
17 Most English translations prefer "theory of Form," but from the time of Cicero all the way to German idealism, they preferred the translation of theory of ideas. W. D. Ross also used the latter in his work Plato's *Theory of Ideas* (1951). But the term was used even by Diogenes Laertius. See "Plato" *Lives of Eminent Philosophers* (Book III Part 15).

References

Burgh, E. (2010). *Medieval Manuscript Production in the Latin West: Global Economic History*. Leiden: Brill.

Co, A. P. (1993). *The Blooming of a Hundred Flowers: Philosophy of Ancient China*. Manila: University of Santo Tomas.

Co, A. P. (2015). Catholicism in Asia: Discoursing the Impacts and Lessons of the Evangelization in China and the Philippines. In *Across the Ancient Philosophical World: Essays in Comparative Philosophy*. (107–124). Manila: University of Santo Tomas.

Confucius. (1979). *The Analects (Lun Yü)*. Tr. D. C. Lau. Harmondsworth: Penguin Books.

Confucius. (1983a). The Doctrine of the Mean. Tr. J. Legge. In *The Four Books*. (41–121). Taipei: Culture Book Co.

Confucius. (1983b). The Great Learning. Tr. J. Legge. In *The Four Books*. (1–40). Taipei: Culture Book Co.

Confucius. (2009). *The Chinese Classic of Family Reverence: A Philosophical Translation of the Xiao Jing*. Tr. R. Ames and H. Rosemont, Jr. Honolulu, HI: University of Hawai'i Press.

Dostoevsky, F. (1990). *The Brothers Karamazov*. Tr. R. Pevear and L. Volokhonsky. San Francisco, CA: North Point Press.

The Editors of Encyclopedia Britannica. (no date). *Guild: Trade Association*. Retrieved from: http://www.britannica.com/EBchecked/topic/248614/guild

Elisseeff, V. (2000). *The Silk Roads: Highways of Culture and Commerce*. New York: Berghahn.

Giles, L. (1910). Introduction. Tr. L. Giles. In *The Sayings of Confucius: A New Translation of the Greater Part of the Confucius Analects* (7–36). Montana: Kessinger.

Gürüz, K. (2007). *Quality Assurance in a Globalized Higher Education Environment: A Historical Perspective*. Istanbul: European Network for Quality Assurance in Higher Education.

Hartnett, R. A. (2011). *The Ji Xia Academy and the Birth of Higher Learning in China: A Comparison of Fourth-Century B.C. Chinese Education with Ancient Greece*. Lewiston, NY: Edwin Mellen Press.

Hastings, R. (1895). *The Universities of Europe in the Middle Ages*. Oxford: Clarendon Press.

Huff, T. (2003). *Rise of Early Modern Science: Islam, China, and the West*. Cambridge, UK: Cambridge University Press.

Johnson, P. (2000). *The Renaissance: A Short History*. New York: Modern Library.

Laertius, Diogenes. (1925). *Lives of Eminent Philosophers*. Tr. Robert Hicks. Books I-V. Cambridge, MA: Harvard University Press.

Permanent Mission of the Republic of Uzbekistan to the United Nations. Retrieved from: http://www.un.int

Ross, W. D. (1951). *Plato's Theory of Ideas*. Oxford: Clarendon Press.

Sato, M. (2003). *The Confucian Quest for Order: The Origin and Formation of the Political Thought of Xun Zi*. Leiden: Brill.

UNESCO and WHC. (no date a). *Short Description (ICOMS-IAU Case Study Format): Maragheh Observatory*. Iran. Retrieved from: http://www2.astronomicalheritage.net/index.php/show-entity?identity=29&idsubentity=1

UNESCO and WHC. (no date b). *Ulugh Beg's Observatory*. Uzbekistan. Retrieved from: http://www2.astronomicalheritage.net/index.php/show-entity?identity=30&idsubentity=1

Watson, P. (2005). *Ideas*. London: Weidenfeld and Nicolson.

Whitfield, S. (1999). *Life along the Silk Road* (2nd edn.). Oakland, CA: University of California Press.

4 Education and human formation
A Freirean perspective

Peter Roberts

Introduction

Paulo Freire has long been regarded as a pedagogue of hope. The link between hope and education has been explored by a number of thinkers over the centuries (see Halpin, 2003). Freire addresses this theme most directly in *Pedagogy of Hope* (Freire, 1994), but references to hope appear frequently in his other writings, from the classic early text *Pedagogy of the Oppressed* (Freire, 1972a) to posthumously published books such as *A Pedagogy of Indignation* (Freire, 2004) and *Daring to Dream* (Freire, 2007). In *Pedagogy of the Oppressed* Freire speaks of hope as one of several fundamental requirements for authentic dialogue, the other prerequisites being love, humility, faith, and critical thinking (1972a, pp. 62–65). At first glance, it might appear as if Freire is trying to inspire rather than theorize here, with a rallying cry based on a set of virtues similar to those found in the Christian Gospels. An appeal to hope in this manner, it might be said, could have rhetorical value but has no place in serious educational scholarship. This chapter suggests that such an interpretation of Freire's intentions would be a mistake. When Freire's work is read holistically, it is clear that he provides a robust philosophical justification for the pedagogical significance of hope, regarding it as not merely a practical necessity but a defining feature of human existence (see further, Mayo, 1999; McLaren, 2000; Roberts, 2000; Morrow and Torres, 2002; Kirylo, 2011; Schugurensky, 2012). Hope for Freire has ontological, epistemological, ethical, and educational dimensions. While it is true that Freire's writing often had an informal and personal register, it is equally true that he wanted to make the case for the importance of hope as rigorous and compelling as possible. Slogans and wishful thinking would not do. Hope as Freire conceived of it is gritty, grounded, and complex. Hope, I shall argue, is intimately connected with Freire's experience, observation, and analysis of *despair*, and both of these notions are essential if we are to understand what makes a Freirean approach to oppression, liberation, and education distinctive and worthwhile.

Freire on despair and hope

In the first chapter of *Pedagogy of Hope*, Freire recalls a time in his life, from the age to 22 to 29, when he would sometimes be "overcome by a sense of despair and sadness" (1994, p. 27). He would, he says, suffer terribly during these periods, often spending two or three days feeling "wounded, bored with the world, as if I were submerged in myself, in the pain whose reason I did not know, and everything around me seemed strange and sudden" (p. 27). He notes that this state of mind could arise without warning in his home or his office or on the street. He would become caught up in a world of his own, oblivious to his surroundings, unable to see friends who were passing by. As these experiences became more frequent, Freire, with the help of his wife Elza, worked hard to place them in their wider contexts. He would try to identify the elements that constituted the experience and understand them:

> When I could see the depression coming, I tried to see what it was that was there around me. I tried to see again, tried to remember, what had happened the day before, tried to hear once more what had been said and to whom it had been said, what I had heard and from whom I had heard it. When you come right down to it, I began to take my depression as an object of curiosity and investigation. I 'stepped back' from it, to learn its 'why.' Basically, I needed to shed some light on the framework in which it was being generated.
>
> (p. 28)

He wondered if his experiences were prompted by the weather or by the visits he would make to schools and families in the social service occupational role he held at that time. He found that while these factors were important in one situation, they would have no impact in another. Upon reflection, he came to see that these influences were significant not in isolation but in connection with each other. He was involved in a process of searching that would leave a powerful mark on his existential experience and play a key part in the development of his educational theory and practice (p. 27). This process was what generated hope:

> At bottom, in seeking for the deepest 'why' of my pain, I was educating my hope. I never expected things to 'be that way.' I worked on things, on facts, on my will. I *invented* the concrete hope in which, one day, I would see myself delivered from my depression.
>
> (p. 29)

Freire was finally able to locate the heart of his despair when the experience of rain and mud was combined with a visit to the home he had grown up in as a child. Memories flooded back to him, including the feeling of deep sorrow his family experienced when Freire's father died. By persistently digging away at his pain, he was able to at last see it more clearly and move beyond it (pp. 29–30).

Following his exhaustive efforts to unearth the contributing factors to the pain he had felt for so many years, and to grasp the relations among these influences, he was now able to pay more careful attention to the forms of suffering experienced by others. He came to see that analysis and self-understanding were not enough (pp. 30–31). His social service work brought him into contact with some of Brazil's poorest citizens. The people with whom he worked endured high rates of malnutrition, infant mortality, and disease with squalid housing conditions, low levels of literacy, and limited access to health care and educational opportunities (see Freire, 1976). They labored for long hours with minimal financial compensation. These realities, Freire came to understand, were no accident; they were reflective of an oppressive social order. Addressing the forms of suffering engendered by this oppression would require both in-depth, careful, critical analysis and radical, long-lasting structural change.

From a Freirean perspective, education and hope are tightly intertwined. Both are necessary, but neither is sufficient in fulfilling our ontological and historical vocation of humanization. Humanization, as discussed at length elsewhere (Roberts, 2000), can be seen as the process of becoming more fully human through critical, dialogical praxis. Praxis in Freirean terms is a synthesis of reflection and action. Its object is social transformation, and this includes self-transformation. As Freire points out, we are never alone, even when physically separated from others. We remain connected to the contexts, the people, and the interactions that have shaped us and continue to work on us as we reflect and act in any situation, any location. Descartes's dictum was "I think, therefore I am," but for Freire this is both inaccurate and incomplete. From a Freirean standpoint, our identity, our distinctive existence as individual human beings, might be better characterized in these terms: "*We* think, and feel, and act; therefore we are." Humanization is an ontological vocation because it is an expression of what and how we are meant to *be* as human beings. It is, however, also an historical vocation, for we can only realize our humanization through action with others in the world – in specific contexts, at given places, with particular purposes.

Dehumanization is the constraining of humanization through the imposition of structural barriers – systems, practices, policies, and laws – or the impeding of critical thought and dialogue. Dehumanization can be evident in the workplace, the home, the school, and many other domains of human interaction. Dehumanizing policies, practices, attitudes, and ideas, and the forms of discrimination that go along with them, often have their origins in prejudice and ignorance in relations with those who differ from us along the lines of class, gender, or ethnicity. Dehumanization, Freire acknowledged, was a reality, but this did not mean there was anything inevitable about it. There is, Freire insisted, nothing in our "natures" that propels us inexorably toward violence or discrimination or exploitation. The propensity some have to engage in these forms of human action is socially constructed. In one sense, *no one* benefits from dehumanization. As Freire makes clear in the first chapter of *Pedagogy of the Oppressed*, when we dehumanize others, we also dehumanize ourselves (Freire, 1972a).

As human beings, we are necessarily incomplete. We become *more* fully human, not *fully* human. It is our unfinishedness that allows us to be hopeful beings, and this is at one and the same time the basis for education. Humanization is not an endpoint to be reached but a lifelong journey, one of constant searching and striving. This might be depicted as an ontology of restlessness; one can, from a Freirean perspective, never quite "sit still." This is in part because the world around us – both what we know as "nature" and the socially constructed world of systems and structures, institutions and workplaces, and policies and people – is undergoing a constant process of change. As beings who reflect upon and act within that world, we cannot remain static. There will always be new problems to face, dilemmas to address, decisions to be made, and actions to be taken. As Freire sees it, we cannot "step aside" from this entanglement with the world. To attempt to do so – to maintain a "neutral" posture – is either disingenuous or naïve. There are no neutral positions to occupy in existing as human beings; we are, from the moment we are capable of exercising reflective consciousness, *ethical* beings. Freire explains:

> [M]ore than beings in the world, human beings become a *presence* in the world, with the world, and with others. Recognizing *the other's* presence as a 'non-self,' this presence recognizes itself as 'its own self.' It is a presence that thinks itself, that knows itself as presence, that intervenes, that transforms, that speaks of what it does and also of what it dreams, that apprehends, compares, evaluates, valuates, that decides, that breaks away. It is precisely in the domain of decision, of evaluation, of freedom, of rupture, of option, that ethics emerges as a necessity and imposes responsibility. Ethics becomes inevitable and the possible transgression of it an antivalue, never a virtue.
>
> (Freire, 2004, pp. 98–99)

In Freirean theory, oppression and liberation can be seen as the concrete manifestation of dehumanization and humanization, respectively. Oppression, Freire argued, stands as one of the dominant "epochal themes" of the 20th century (Freire, 1976). We humanize ourselves, and thereby affirm our existence as hopeful, ethical beings through the epochal *task* of liberation. Despair from a Freirean perspective can be seen as both a state of mind (e.g., the depression Freire himself experienced in his 20s) and a *situation*. It is possible to describe the conditions Freire observed among the impoverished Brazilians with whom he worked in exactly this light: their circumstances constituted a situation that we should *all*, as fellow human beings, find troubling. Simone Weil (1997) talked about affliction, the dire conditions experienced by those who were desperately poor, in a similar way. The Dostoevskian principle of each of us being responsible for all, conveyed in *The Brothers Karamazov* (Dostoevsky, 1991) and taken up by one of the 20th century's most influential ethical thinkers, Emmanuel Levinas (1969, 1998), is helpful here. The affliction and desperation experienced by some is simultaneously a call to us *all* to respond. As Weil (1997) observes, "We have to say like Ivan Karamazov that nothing can make up for a single tear from a single child, and yet to accept all tears and the nameless horrors which are beyond tears" (p. 131). Weil adds, "We have to accept these things, not in so far as they bring compensations with them, but in themselves. We have to accept the fact that they exist simply because they do exist" (p. 131). Acceptance here is neither advocacy nor acquiescence but rather acknowledgement. For Freire, acknowledgement is a necessary, though not sufficient, condition for engagement – for responding to the suffering of the other, who's suffering is also our own, whether we recognize it as such or not. The idea of "responding" implies that this *matters* in an ethical sense; to respond means, in one way or another, we *care*. Thus, to say that despair debilitates and traumatizes and terrifies does not mean nothing good can come of it. A situation of despair can be dehumanizing but the manner in which we respond to it can be humanizing. What cannot be defended from a Freirean point of view – and in this sense Freire is very much like Miguel de Unamuno (1972) and Elie Wiesel (Aronson, 2007) – is *indifference*.

Despair sometimes seems to be an individual "problem" that can be "fixed" with appropriate therapy or drugs, but Freire's work suggests otherwise. Both the experience of despair and the manner in which it is addressed will always be social in nature. In Freire's case, it was not just a process of deep self-reflection and analysis but also the involvement of Elza and the feedback he received from the workers he encountered in his educational efforts that proved pivotal in allowing him to gain something productive from his experience of despair. His despair was never merely "personal"; it was always, in one way or another, shared with others. Despair proved to be *educative* for Freire; he learned from it, developing a deeper understanding of himself, his past, and priorities in the present and future. Despair played an important role in shaping Freire's pedagogical theory and practice, sharpening his sense of to whom and what he was committed and why. Freire's analysis of his own despair helped him to acquire a better grasp of the limits and possibilities of education. While it is true that Freire felt he could "bury" the depression he experienced as a young man, having finally put the pieces of the puzzle together, this does not mean the process of addressing despair was over for him. For what he learned in analyzing his own situation opened up other, wider problems demanding attention – problems that would occupy him as an educator for the rest of his life.

Freire's case is instructive in allowing us to see that despair isn't a condition – a state of mind or a situation – that lends itself to quick and easy "solutions." *Addressing* a situation is not the same as solving it. This distinction is important in Freire's educational theory. In his famous critique of banking education, Freire (1972a) offers as an alternative, not problem-solving education but problem-*posing* education. He does so for at least two reasons. First, the notion of posing problems accords with our vocation of humanization. We are, when granted appropriate opportunities, curious, probing, questioning beings. Rendering the world problematic is consistent with our wish to know more – to not simply accept that which has been given, either by our prior experience and understanding, or by others via political speeches, policy documents, television broadcasts, newspaper stories, and so on. The act of posing problems awakens and extends our capacities as reflective, critical beings. Second, the problems faced by those with whom Freire worked – the extreme conditions of impoverishment described earlier – were not of a kind that lent themselves to simple, single, quick answers. Addressing these problems would be complex, time-consuming, and difficult – but no less worthy of attention for that. Freire would remind us, however, that as we reflect and act, with others, to address complex problems, the results of our transformative activity frequently throw up new problems to be addressed. This is a process that is never complete but that should, from a Freirean perspective, not serve as a deterrent; if anything, it should heighten our sense of commitment and strengthen our resolve to continue our educative efforts.

The same point holds when we think about the ways in which we might respond to despair. Our eagerness in seeking to escape from it is indicative of both the trauma it creates, inwardly and outwardly, and the significance of the problem with which we are dealing. We don't want to experience despair because it is unpleasant, difficult, and uncomfortable. It can fill us with a sense of dread (as Kierkegaard understood), perhaps even terror. Being immersed in a state of despair can leave us feeling immobilized, humiliated, and unable to interact effectively with others. Despair disrupts, demoralizes, and sometimes destroys. Cast in this light, it is not difficult to see why despair might seem entirely negative. Nor is it difficult to understand why many of us attempt to ignore it, or suppress it, or run from it, or "fix" it (as quickly and painlessly as possible). Yet in acknowledging the intensity of the experience of despair in this manner, there is also an implicit recognition of its potential importance in realizing our humanity. In *addressing* despair, rather than trying to "solve" it, we can learn from it; we can come to more deeply understands ourselves as human beings and acquire a keener sense of what, when poised on the very edge of destruction, matters most to us.

Despair is not infrequently defined as a state or condition in which we are "without hope." From a Freirean perspective, however, if we are without hope, we are no longer human. In a world populated by human beings, then, there are no situations that are without hope. To exist as a human being is to always retain the hope that conditions could be otherwise. (There is, indeed, some evidence of a biological basis to this; hope has played an important role in our evolution as a species: see Tiger, 1999.) As noted elsewhere (Roberts, 2003a, 2003b), it is precisely when circumstances are most desperate, when despair seems most complete, that hope comes most fully into being. Hope is given life, meaning, and significance in those very times when it seems most distant. We speak of "throwing our arms up in despair" when facing the most complicated, difficult, traumatic situations, as if all is lost and nothing can be done. Placed in broader perspective, there are no problems that cannot be addressed in some way. Despair does not cancel out hope; it *invites* it (cf. Nesse, 1999, p. 431). When all appears well, when a situation seems least problematic, hope has no reason to spring to life. Kierkegaard (1989) recognized that even when serenity and happiness seem to prevail, despair can lurk beneath the surface. Despair need not be identified or understood to be present, and to be working on us, shaping how we construct our lives, how we conceive of happiness, how we interact with others in the world. Similarly, it might be said that we can have hope without realizing how or why or when this might be so. The possibility of hope sits waiting for situations that will allow it to do its work, fueling commitment, enabling us to rethink the problems we face and to act, with others, in transforming the world.

If we are to understand why hope was so important to Freire, we must probe further in exploring his theory of oppression and liberation. We must recall the contexts in which Freire worked. Freire's concept of hope is grounded in his ontology – his theory of humanization and dehumanization – but in his work as an educator, it was also a practical necessity. Freire's interest is not in an empty, blind or naïve hope that ignores the brutal realities of oppression. Oppression must, if we are to pursue our vocation of humanization, be highlighted, confronted, and contested. Of course, as subsequent discussion will show, Freire's theory of oppression is not without its shortcomings and critics. Oppression is a complex, multilayered phenomenon, worthy of careful, in-depth philosophical investigation. Freire took this philosophical task seriously, and he responded to some of his critics but did not satisfy all in doing so. One idea that binds most theories of oppression is *suffering*, and this notion is important given the focus of the present chapter. From a Freirean standpoint, the capacity to face the suffering that oppression brings is an expression of hope. Liberation for Freire is to be found not when suffering is "resolved" but in the process of struggle itself. This is both a struggle *against* oppression and a struggle *for* the development of certain human virtues, as the next section suggests.

Oppression, liberation, and education

Over the last two to three decades, Freire has often been criticized for the "universalist" nature of his theory of oppression and liberation. Freire's references to "the oppressed" and "the oppressors" in *Pedagogy of the Oppressed* (Freire, 1972a), it has been suggested, gloss over the multilayered, often conflicting forms of oppression experienced by people of different ethnicities, genders, and classes. Freire is seen to pay insufficient attention to questions of difference and to the specificities of particular forms of oppression. It needs to be acknowledged, for example, that a peasant man may be oppressed by his landlord but also act in an oppressive way toward his wife or children (cf. Weiler, 2001). These criticisms suggest the need for a more complex theory of liberation: one that will take into account the tensions between different oppressor/oppressed discourses and identities and avoid what some see as the disempowering effects of universalist prescriptions (cf. Ellsworth, 1989).

Freire has responded at some length to these criticisms (Freire, 1996, 1997b; Freire and Macedo, 1993). In *Mentoring the Mentor*, for example, Freire claims that questions relating to layered and multiple identities had always preoccupied him (Freire, 1997b, p. 311). He draws attention to ambiguities and contradictions he often encountered in his political and pedagogical work between different levels of oppression. He provides the example of a woman who was illiterate, suffering, as her husband and eldest son did, from an oppressive social system. She had to face an additional struggle, however, against the oppressive machista attitudes of her husband and son, who tried to prevent her from becoming literate. Freire also encountered many teachers who "while being oppressed by the political system in which they operated, were in turn oppressors of their students" (p. 311).

Freire urges readers to recognize that his work is not confined to *Pedagogy of the Oppressed*. He notes that it would be unacceptable for him to attempt to provide "teacher-proof" answers to educational problems in contexts other than those with which he is familiar. In *Mentoring the Mentor* he refuses, as he has always done, to provide universal pedagogical recipes. In answer to the charge that his work does not address the specificities of race and gender in the US context, Freire admits that he could not possibly do this without knowing that context. What he does provide, however, is "a general framework that calls for a deep respect for the Other along the lines of race and gender" (p. 309).

Freire argues that while he was always sensitive to examples of racial oppression, his primary focus in *Pedagogy of the Oppressed* was class oppression. It was, Freire says, precisely because of his growing awareness of the specificities of different forms of oppression (along the lines of language, gender, and ethnicity, among others) that he defended the thesis of "unity in diversity." Freire's concern in his later years was that while groups on the political right were able to forge a pragmatic unity despite tensions and differences (e.g., between economic liberalism and moral conservatism), intellectuals and activists on the left had spent much of their time fighting each other, with often bitter theoretical wars over questions of class, gender, ethnicity, and politics (cf. Freire, 1997a). Freire maintains that what is needed is a collective struggle against all forms of oppression. In *Letters to Cristina,* he writes:

> Our struggle as women, men, blacks, workers, Brazilians, North Americans, French, or Bolivians, is influenced by our gender, race, class, culture, and history, conditionings that mark us. Our struggle, nevertheless, departs from these conditionings and converges in the direction of being more, in the direction of universal objectives. Or else, for me at least, the fight would make no sense.
>
> (Freire, 1996, pp. 164–165)

There is, as has been discussed elsewhere (Roberts, 2003a), a complex relationship between universals and particulars in Freire's work. Freire's support for a position of unity in diversity (Freire, 1994, 1996, 1997a), in which differences would become a source of strength rather than fragmentation and divisiveness, has not satisfied all of his critics. By holding on, in *Pedagogy of Freedom* (Freire, 1998a) and *Pedagogy of Indignation* (2004, p. 92), to the idea of a universal human ethic, Freire retained what some see as an unhelpful and naïve modernist optimism.

Yet what binds Freire and many of his critics is the idea that liberation is tied, both theoretically and practically, to the notion of oppression. Liberation is conceived as a process of struggle against oppression – however that might be defined.

This is, in part, a recognition of the contexts in which Freire's ideas emerged. Freire's work as an adult educator was primarily in Latin American and African countries, from his original literacy programs in Brazil to his efforts in Chile, Guinea Bissau, and other countries (see Freire, 1972b, 1976, 1978). In Brazil in the 1950s and 1960s, the disparities between different social groups were substantial, and Freire was, as an educator, confronted with extreme poverty among both the urban and rural groups with whom he worked. These extremes were still evident in Brazil near the end of the century, and in his later works Freire writes passionately about the destructive impact of neoliberalism in perpetuating such inequities. As noted previously, for Freire, oppression had become a dominant theme of the 20th century, and he was supportive, though not blindly so, of many liberation movements that emerged across different parts of the globe in response to this.

But when we pause to ask, hypothetically, what might become of liberation if oppression was removed, Freirean theory provides only some of the answers. Would liberation be necessary, or indeed have any meaning as a concept, in a world without oppression? In some respects, the question is of limited value, for we have to live in and work with the world as it is now, not as it might be in an abstract, imaginary, ideal reality. The world we have now is, as Freire and others have demonstrated, clearly one characterized by widespread oppression. Freire did not argue explicitly that oppression of one kind or another would always be with us, but neither did he suggest that a "solution" to problems of mass starvation, gross exploitation, the child sex slavery industry, and the like could be found quickly and easily. He spoke passionately about the need to address these problems and to replace the ethics of the market with an attitude more respectful of the consequences of economic and social policies for human lives and the environment. This message comes through very strongly in later works such as *Pedagogy of Indignation* (Freire, 2004). Freire was aware, however, that there were deep structural impediments to rapid change. He remained convinced that capitalism was an "evil" – that is, *necessarily* oppressive – system (see Freire, 1996, 1998a, 2004) and that any attempt to overcome problems such as exploitation and hunger while retaining the capitalist mode of production would ultimately be doomed to failure.

Thus, to talk of liberation in a world without oppression would be to engage in a process of speculative theorizing, ignoring the fact that we are shaped by social structures, policies, and systems. We are, Freire reminded us, beings of history and culture, influenced in ways we often cannot recognize by the traditions, practices, and beliefs of our past. We are, importantly, never fully *determined* by dominant structures, ideas, and practices, past or present. But if we are to bring about change, we must do so in this world, with all of its complexities and problems. Liberation thus becomes a matter both of recognizing limits and of understanding possibilities *given* those limits. This is consistent with Freire's approach to the question of utopia. The utopian element in Freire's thought is evident from his earliest writings and persists across his corpus of published works. Utopia for Freire arises from our unfinishedness as human beings and the hope that comes with this. Hope is not enough on its own; utopia can only come into being through searching, striving, and struggling. It demands of us that we exercise our abilities to reflect, to act, to engage in dialogue with others, and to transform ourselves and the world. Freire was concerned with building *better* worlds, not perfect worlds; he was interested not in fantasies but in *possible* dreams (Roberts and Freeman-Moir, 2013; Torres and Noguera, 2008).

Rather than focusing on the possibility of liberation in a world without oppression, it is perhaps more productive to consider whether the Freirean notion of liberation is *merely* the process of struggling against oppression. We might accept, with Freire, that the world as it is currently structured is oppressive, in multiple ways, with different consequences for different oppressed groups. It might also be acknowledged that any robust theory of liberation must at the very least take into account the reality of oppression – in its myriad different forms. This does not compel us to make the struggle against oppression *the* defining feature of such a theory. In Freire's case, clearly this kind of human struggle is a key theme, but it is arguably not the only form of human struggling and striving Freire wants to consider and not the only key element in his theory of liberation.

As noted at the beginning of the chapter, from his earliest writings, Freire has emphasized the importance of human virtues such as love, hope, trust, faith, and critical thinking (see Freire, 1972a). In later works, these virtues occupy a more prominent place in Freire's discussion of education, ethics, and politics. Freire identifies a set of what might be called epistemological virtues – scholarly or intellectual dispositions – of value in the educational process. These include an investigative and probing frame of mind, curiosity, humility, openness, reflectiveness, a willingness to question and to be questioned, a dialogical and collegial spirit of inquiry, and a desire to know (Freire, 1985, 1996, 1998b; Freire and Faundez, 1989). These intellectual dispositions complement (and overlap with) a wider set of educational virtues. Freire's later books are replete with examples of the qualities teachers should bring to bear in their work with students. He speaks in this context of tolerance, honesty, clarity, knowledge of one's subject, thoroughness, commitment, and a willingness to listen and learn from other participants in an educational setting (Freire, 1994, 1996, 1998a, 1998b, 1998c; Freire and Shor, 1987; Horton and Freire, 1990). In his later publications, Freire stressed the importance of structure, direction, and rigor in liberating education (Roberts, 2000). He also emphasized the importance of emotion as well as reason in education and human development (Roberts, 2008). Love – of one's fellow human beings, of the process of study, and of the students with whom one works – became a key motif in his later books (see further, Darder, 2002; Fraser, 1997).

From these works, it is possible to construct a view of a certain ideal – a mode of being in and with the world and with others – that might be said to underpin Freire's ethic and educational theory. There is what could be called a "shadow" theory of liberation underlying his work and particularly his later writings: a virtue-based account of human striving suggestive of criteria to which the struggle against oppression (in all of its forms) must conform if it is to be characterized as liberating. The struggle against oppression remains the dominant feature of Freire's ideal, but it does not *in itself* define that ideal.

There can, then, be struggles against oppression that are profoundly at odds with the Freirean notion of liberation: they may be anti-dialogical, unreflective, lacking in love and care for others, closed to criticism and questioning, and so on. Similarly, it becomes possible to conceive of individuals and groups striving to realize the ideal – embrace and practice the virtues articulated by Freire – without self-consciously engaging in a struggle against oppression. This would not mean, however, that such people may not *be* so engaged. For, from a Freirean perspective, being dialogical, open-minded, tolerant, and so on can be seen as a form of indirect resistance against oppression.

Freire never published a book specifically devoted to this subject, nor did he refer explicitly to other bodies of work (e.g., virtue ethics, the ethics of care, and work on the philosophy of emotion) that might have been helpful in developing his ideas. Instead, as is true of many key Freirean themes, his philosophy of liberation must be drawn from a holistic, contextualized, and critical reading of his work (Mayo, 1999; Roberts, 2000, 2010; Schugurensky, 2012). Such a reading suggests a richer, more complex and multilayered theory of liberation than some commentators have conveyed in their discussions of Freirean ideas.

Nevertheless, some significant gaps remain. In particular, Freire has little to say about the spiritual dimension of liberation and the role of practices such as meditation in the pursuit of this. In the next section I develop this theme further, with reference to the idea of a "pedagogy of great convergences." A focus on "great convergences" also allows us to consider afresh the meaning and significance of hope, and its connection with despair, in Freire's work. Such an approach, moreover, has important practical implications for contemporary education and intellectual life, as noted in the following section.

Freire and a "pedagogy of great convergences"

The posthumously published work *A Pedagogy of Indignation* (Freire, 2004) includes a letter from Balduino Andreola to Freire. In his letter, Andreola (2004, p. xliii) aligns Freire with other intellectuals, activists, and spiritual leaders who advanced a "pedagogy of great convergences." The people he names as examples are as follows:

> Gandhi, Pope John XXIII, Martin Luther King Jr., Simone Weil, Lebret, Frantz Fanon, Che Guevara, Teresa of Calcutta, Don Helder, Mounier, Teilhard de Chardin, Nelson Mandela, Roger Garaudy, the Dalai Lama, Teovedjre, Betinho, Paramahansa Yogananda, Michel Duclerq, Fritjof Capra, Pierre Weil, Leonardo Boff, Paul Ricoeur, and others.
>
> (pp. xliii–xliv)

This appears to be a rather eclectic mix, but what unites these thinkers and leaders, Andreola says, is their commitment to a "more human, fraternal, and solidarity-based vision for the world" (p. xliii). Andreola sees in Freire's later written work a shift "from the West toward the East and the South" (p. xliii). He suggests that while Freire embraces the "the rigor of science and philosophy," he is "much closer to the thinking and the vision for the world of the great Eastern masters, as well to the cosmic, mystical, and welcoming spirit of the African peoples" (p. xliii).

As has been noted elsewhere (Roberts, 2010), care needs to be taken in the way Andreola's comments are interpreted. Freire had little to say *directly* about Eastern thought and spiritual traditions; nor did he discuss, overtly or in any detail, mysticism or meditation in either the West or the East. It is also important to stress that there is, of course, no single, homogeneous mode of thinking, being, or acting within either Western or Eastern traditions. Any attempt to reduce the myriad, heterogeneous ways of thinking in the West to "*the* Western mindset" (Bowers, 1983) is deeply problematic (Roberts, 2000, 2003b). The same is true of the multiplicity of different Eastern traditions.

Andreola is right, in my view, to see something deeper in Freire's work that binds him with many Eastern thinkers. At first glance, however, the connections are not obvious. The key is to recognize points of theoretical kinship while also acknowledging some tensions and being willing to extend ideas worthy of further development in Freire's work. Toward that end, let me offer a few thoughts on possibilities for ongoing reflection and research.

First, we might want to ask what it is that would make this a *pedagogy* of great convergences. Not all of the people named by Andreola are, in the usual sense of the term, educationists. This does not mean their work is not *educational*. There is much that might be gained by asking what and how we learn from these "great masters of humanity," as Andreola calls them (2004, p. xliii). Do they teach us by their actions, their words, or in some other way? It is also helpful to consider how learning from the examples provided by such lives might differ from one context to another. What might we gain from Gandhi now, in a country of the so-called First World, that is distinctive when compared with an encounter in earlier times and in other places? Where do ideas converge, and where do they break apart?

The danger of "heroizing" such leaders needs to be kept in mind. This has, as Boler (1999) notes, been a problem in some readings of Freire's work. The influence of the activists and thinkers identified by Andreola mustn't blind us to their faults and weaknesses. The rigor in Freire's work to which Andreola refers must be applied to Freire himself and to all of the others named. This is, in part, what makes this a pedagogical convergence: the very process of engaging the ideas, and of reflecting critically on the actions, of people of influence is a learning exercise. One of the first ways in which this can be done is to problematize the notion of "greatness" itself. What does it mean to be a "great thinker" or a "great leader"? What politics are at work in the elevation of some people to this status, while others – often toiling away quietly but nonetheless making a profound difference in peoples' lives – achieve very little public recognition for their efforts? How can the voices of those who have been invisiblized be made more prominent?

Feminist and indigenous scholars have taken a lead in this area in a variety of fields within the humanities and social sciences over the past 30 or 40 years, and work of this kind continues to be necessary and important in the 21st century. New forms of suppression under the guise of a "war against terror" have been developed, inhibiting freedom of speech and action. Universities, supposedly the protectors of academic freedom and critical thought, have not been immune from these forms of suppression. Taking the idea of a pedagogy of great convergences seriously means, among other things, respecting the value of constructive critique. The people named by Andreola have all, in different ways, made their mark on the world by being prepared to question received wisdom, prevailing attitudes, and existing social structures. Subjecting their own work to careful critique pays homage to that work and continues the "great conversation" to which they have contributed.

One of the hallmarks of the work undertaken by many of the people named in Andreola's list is the coherence between their words and their deeds. Freire refers to this as a form of coherence – an ethical consistency between theory and practice, often easy to espouse but much harder to enact (Freire, 1998a, 2004). Freire's conviction in this area was put to the test during the period in which he served as secretary of education in the municipality of São Paulo (1989–1991) (see Freire, 1993). He faced enormous challenges in this role, with run-down schools, overwhelming poverty, and a pervasive attitude of fatalism and hopelessness among some of the people with whom he was working. That he was able to effect worthwhile changes in the administration of schooling in this vastly populated area was testament to his commitment and abilities as an educator (see O'Cadiz, Wong, and Torres, 1998), but his tenure in the role was limited, and at the time at which he left there much work still to be done.

One of the ongoing tasks in building a pedagogy of great convergences will be to recognize ways in which the past converges with the present and the imagined future. As we have seen earlier in the chapter, our work as human beings is, from a Freirean point of view, never finished. There is never a time at which we can declare ourselves, or the process of education and social change, complete. Further reflection and action will always be necessary. Holding on to a "possible dream" remains more vital than ever in times of desperation and despair. The era of neoliberal reform is, for Freire, a period in human history of exactly this kind. Freire reserves his most vigorous criticism in later works (Freire, 1998a, 2004, 2007), for the politics of neoliberal global capitalism, and some of the changes he observed in the last years of his life have now become an entrenched feature of economic and social policy in many parts of the world (see further, Roberts and Peters, 2008).

This, I think, is where Andreola's list has particular contemporary significance. There is a certain orientation to ethical, political, and pedagogical questions that distinguishes Freire and a diverse range of other thinkers, East and West, from some of the ideas that have become dominant across the globe over the past few decades. The neoliberal focus on self-interest, consumption, choice, competition, and the commodification of knowledge and education stands opposed the ideas and practices of all of the thinkers, spiritual leaders, and social activists named by Andreola. The emphasis on love, dialogue, tolerance, honesty, curiosity,

Education and human formation 79

open-mindedness, rigor, and political commitment in Freire's work is shared by others on Andreola's list. Acknowledging, respecting, and attempting to understand different traditions and cultures, while not necessarily accepting all beliefs or practices within them, is another point in common. These are the "great convergences" in the work of the people identified by Andreola.

What of the spiritual connections to which Andreola refers? (For the purposes of this discussion, the term "spirituality" will be used as inclusive of "religion." It is accepted, however, that this way of employing the two terms is by no means unproblematic.) Freire has, on occasion (e.g., Freire, 1985, 1997a), commented on his religious beliefs and his relationship with the Christian Gospels. He has confessed to feeling a certain discomfort in doing so (see Freire, 1997a), but certain features of his orientation to Christianity have become clear over the years. Freire interpreted the Gospels as a call to social action. He did not ignore the notion of personal salvation altogether, but he was adamant from his earliest work as an educator in Brazil that this should be coupled with – indeed, *forged through* – the process of struggling against oppression. He spoke of love in a manner that was consistent with Christ's call to love one's neighbor as oneself. This, for Freire, implied not merely treating others as one would like to be treated oneself but acknowledging that one's neighbor *is* oneself. We are, Freire argued, always social beings, and our actions, attitudes, and beliefs are, in this sense, not merely our own but also those of others. It is, from a Freirean point of view, impossible for a human being to act, think, or *be* alone (see further, Roberts, 2000). This interpretation of the Christian Gospels placed Freire at odds with the conservative wing of the Catholic Church in his native Brazil (see Mackie, 1980), but he was later to find kindred spirits among those who became known as liberation theologians.

Beyond these fairly sparse references to Christ, the Gospels, and the Catholic Church, Freire has little to say about matters of spirituality. This does not mean he has nothing to offer in this area. While a fragmented reading of Freire's work may suggest irreconcilable differences, there are arguably important connections that might be made among some traditions of meditative practice and elements of Freire's epistemology, ethic, and educational theory. For example, productive links might be made between certain forms of concentrative meditation and the process of "epistemological encircling" described by Freire in *Pedagogy of Indignation* (Freire, 2004, p. 84) and other later publications. Other quite unexpected connections can sometimes be made, as Fraser (1997) demonstrates in drawing a comparison between Freire and Taoism on the themes of love and history. Fraser shows, for instance, that there is considerable agreement between Freire and the *Tao Te Ching* on the nature of leadership and that this has significant implications for education. The comparisons can cross barriers often erected between different genres of written work. Freire's emphasis on dialogue, uncertainty, the process of struggle, and transformation, for example, is also evident in the work of novelists such as Dostoevsky and Hesse, both of whom thought deeply about philosophical and spiritual questions (see Roberts, 2005, 2007, 2010, 2012).

Freire's occasional explicit references to spirituality in his later writings pose some intriguing questions about where his thought would have taken him had he been granted another 10 years of life. For instance, in *Pedagogy of Indignation* he proclaims:

> The philosophies that will help us the most will be those that, without ignoring materiality or minimizing its weight, will not timidly shy away from historical analysis and from comprehending the role that spirituality, not necessarily in a religious sense, [but] feelings, dreams, and utopias play in the changing of reality.
>
> (p. 76)

These comments beg further questions. Freire does not elaborate on precisely why and how feelings, dreams, and utopias might be considered part of the "spiritual" domain. Nor does he say a great deal about others who have thought about spirituality in this way. The relationship between the "material" and the "spiritual" could also benefit from further exploration.

There are, then, limits to what we can gain from Freire alone. If the possibilities in Freire's work for a fruitful exploration of questions of spirituality and meditation are to be realized, Freire's ideas need to be put into critical conversation with those from other writers and traditions. The thinkers named by Andreola provide a helpful starting point in pursuing this agenda further, to which can be added many others. A pedagogy of convergences is also a pedagogy of *conversations* – across cultures, spiritual traditions, disciplinary boundaries, and time – and continuing those conversations, by expanding the list of thinkers and activists considered, is an important task for the future.

Concluding comments

Paulo Freire, like Miguel de Unamuno (1972), never stopped struggling. The passion with which he expressed his opposition to neoliberalism in later works was an extension of the political commitment so evident in classic early texts such as *Pedagogy of the Oppressed* (Freire, 1972a). The title for one of his posthumously published books *Pedagogy of Indignation* was apt: in his last years, Freire continued to feel real anger, tempered with reason, at the violence done to the human body, soul, and spirit by oppressive structures, policies, and practices. He acknowledged the despair associated with the forms of oppression engendered by neoliberalism but could see something of profound educational value in trying to understand and address this despair. Across his corpus of published writings, the struggle against oppression remained one of the key features of Freire's theory of liberation. This struggle only makes sense, however, only becomes humanizing for Freire, when it is simultaneously an expression of key virtues such as love and hope.

In the last decade of his life, Freire was a prolific writer. This productivity had its weaknesses as well as strengths. In his effort to say as much as possible while facing a hectic schedule of other commitments, the quality of his writing sometimes suffered, and some of his ideas warranted further analysis and development. He was always clear, however, that he was just one part of a bigger pedagogical picture. He knew the limits of his own work, just as he was aware of the limits of education. Freire saw himself as an incomplete and imperfect human being. He was a teacher, not a preacher; he never regarded himself as a guru or a savior; and he did not want the ideas he conveyed in his books to be seen as recipes or methods to be followed slavishly, regardless of the particulars of a given pedagogical context. His voice is but one among many in the ongoing struggle to build a pedagogy of great convergences – and of hope. Almost two decades on from Freire's death, the need to continue that legacy, through hard intellectual and practical work with others has never been greater.

Acknowledgements

A version of this chapter appears in Roberts (2015). *Happiness, Hope, and Despair: Rethinking the Role of Education.* New York: Peter Lang. Parts of the chapter were first published as Roberts (2008). Liberation, Oppression and Education: Extending Freirean Ideas. *Journal of Educational Thought, 42*(1), 83–97. I am grateful for permission to reproduce material here.

References

Andreola, B. A. (2004). Letter to Paulo Freire. In P. Freire (Ed.). *Pedagogy of Indignation.* (xxxiii–xlv). Boulder, CO and London: Paradigm.
Aronson, D. (2007). Elie Wiesel: Indifference is Not an Option. Originally published in the *Council Chronicle*, National Council of Teachers of English, June, 2007. Retrieved from: http://www.debaronson.com/profiles/elie_wiesel_indifference_is_not_an_option/.
Boler, M. (1999). Posing Feminist Queries to Freire. In P. Roberts (Ed.) Paulo Freire, *Politics and Pedagogy: Reflections from Aotearoa-New Zealand.* (pp. 61–69). Palmerston North: Dunmore Press.
Bowers, C. A. (1983). Linguistic Roots of Cultural Invasion in Paulo Freire's Pedagogy. *Teachers College Record, 84* (4), 935–953.
Darder, A. (2002). *Reinventing Paulo Freire: A Pedagogy of Love.* Boulder, CO: Westview Press.
de Unamuno, M. (1972). *The Tragic Sense of Life in Men and Nations.* Tr. A. Kerrigan. Princeton, NJ: Princeton University Press.
Dostoevsky, F. (1991). *The Brothers Karamazov.* Tr. R. Pevear and L. Volokhonsky. New York: Vintage Books.
Ellsworth, E. (1989). Why Doesn't This Feel Empowering? Working Through the Repressive Myths of Critical Pedagogy. *Harvard Educational Review, 59* (3), 297–324.
Fraser, J. W. (1997). Love and History in the Work of Paulo Freire. In P. Freire, J. W. Fraser, D. Macedo, T. McKinnon, and W. T. Stokes (Eds.). *Mentoring the Mentor: A Critical Dialogue with Paulo Freire.* (175–199). New York: Peter Lang.
Freire, P. (1972a). *Pedagogy of the Oppressed.* Harmondsworth: Penguin Books.
Freire, P. (1972b). *Cultural Action for Freedom.* Harmondsworth: Penguin Books.
Freire, P. (1976). *Education: The Practice of Freedom.* London: Writers and Readers.

Freire, P. (1978). *Pedagogy in Process: The Letters to Guinea-Bissau*. London: Writers and Readers.
Freire, P. (1985). *The Politics of Education*. London: Palgrave MacMillan.
Freire, P. (1993). *Pedagogy of the City*. New York: Continuum.
Freire, P. (1994). *Pedagogy of Hope*. New York: Continuum.
Freire, P. (1996). *Letters to Cristina: Reflections on My Life and Work*. London: Routledge.
Freire, P. (1997a). *Pedagogy of the Heart*. New York: Continuum.
Freire, P. (1997b). A Response. In P. Freire, J. W. Fraser, D. Macedo, T. McKinnon, and W. T. Stokes (Eds.). *Mentoring the Mentor: A Critical Dialogue with Paulo Freire*. (303–329). New York: Peter Lang.
Freire, P. (1998a). *Pedagogy of Freedom: Ethics, Democracy, and Civic Courage*. Lanham, MD: Rowman & Littlefield.
Freire, P. (1998b). *Teachers as Cultural Workers: Letters to Those Who Dare Teach*. Boulder, CO: Westview Press.
Freire, P. (1998c). *Politics and Education*. Los Angeles, CA: UCLA Latin American Center Publications.
Freire, P. (2004). *Pedagogy of Indignation*. Boulder, CO: Paradigm.
Freire, P. (2007). *Daring to Dream*. Boulder, CO: Paradigm.
Freire, P. and Faundez, A. (1989). *Learning to Question: A Pedagogy of Liberation*. Geneva: World Council of Churches.
Freire, P. and Macedo, D. (1993). A Dialogue with Paulo Freire. In P. McLaren and P. Leonard (Eds.). *Paulo Freire: A Critical Encounter*. (169–176). London: Routledge.
Freire, P. and Shor, I. (1987). *A Pedagogy for Liberation*. London: Palgrave MacMillan.
Halpin, D. (2003). *Hope and Education*. London: RoutledgeFalmer.
Horton, M. and Freire, P. (1990). *We Make the Road by Walking: Conversations on Education and Social Change*. Philadelphia, PA: Temple University Press.
Kierkegaard, S. (1989). *The Sickness unto Death*. Tr. A. Hannay. London: Penguin.
Kirylo, J. D. (2011). *Paulo Freire: The Man from Recife*. New York: Peter Lang.
Levinas, E. (1969). *Totality and Infinity*. Tr. A. Lingis. Pittsburgh, PA: Duquesne University Press.
Levinas, E. (1998). *Otherwise Than Being or Beyond Essence*. Tr. A. Lingis. Pittsburgh, PA: Duquesne University Press.
Mackie, R. (1980). Contributions to the Thought of Paulo Freire. In R. Mackie (Ed.). *Literacy and Revolution: The Pedagogy of Paulo Freire*. (93–119). London: Pluto Press.
McLaren, P. (2000). *Che Guevara, Paulo Freire, and the Pedagogy of Revolution*. Lanham, MD: Rowman & Littlefield.
Mayo, P. (1999). *Gramsci, Freire and Adult Education: Possibilities for Transformative Action*. London: Zed Books.
Morrow, R. and Torres, C. A. (2002). *Reading Freire and Habermas: Critical Pedagogy and Transformative Social Change*. New York: Teachers College Press.
Nesse, R. M. (1999). The Evolution of Hope and Despair. *Social Research, 66* (2), 429–469.
O'Cadiz, M. D. P., Wong, L., and Torres, C. A. (1998). *Education and Democracy: Paulo Freire, Social Movements and Educational Reform in Sao Paulo*. Boulder, CO: Westview Press.
Roberts, P. (2000). *Education, Literacy and Humanization: Exploring the Work of Paulo Freire*. Westport, CT: Bergin and Garvey.
Roberts, P. (2003a). Pedagogy, Neoliberalism and Postmodernity: Reflections on Freire's Later Work. *Educational Philosophy and Theory, 35* (4), 451–465.
Roberts, P. (2003b). Epistemology, Ethics and Education: Addressing Dilemmas of Difference in the Work of Paulo Freire. *Studies in Philosophy of Education, 22* (2), 157–173.

Roberts, P. (2005). Freire and Dostoevsky: Uncertainty, Dialogue and Transformation. *Journal of Transformative Education, 3* (1), 126–139.

Roberts, P. (2007). Conscientisation in Castalia: A Freirian Reading of Hermann Hesse's *The Glass Bead Game*. Studies in Philosophy and Education, 26 (6), 509–523.

Roberts, P. (2008). Liberation, Oppression and Education: Extending Freirean Ideas. *Journal of Educational Thought, 42* (1), 83–97.

Roberts, P. (2010). *Paulo Freire in the 21st Century: Education, Dialogue and Transformation.* Boulder, CO: Paradigm Publishers.

Roberts, P. (2012). *From West to East and Back again: An Educational Reading of Hermann Hesse's Later Work.* Rotterdam: Sense Publishers.

Roberts, P. (2015). *Happiness, Hope, and Despair: Rethinking the Role of Education.* New York: Peter Lang.

Roberts, P. and Freeman-Moir, J. (2013). *Better Worlds: Education, Art, and Utopia.* Lanham, MD: Lexington Books.

Roberts, P. and Peters, M. A. (2008). *Neoliberalism, Higher Education and Research.* Rotterdam: Sense Publishers.

Schugurensky, D. (2012). *Paulo Freire.* London: Continuum.

Tiger, L. (1999). Hope Springs Internal. *Social Research, 66* (2), 611–623.

Torres, C. A. and Noguera, P. (Eds.). (2008). *Social Justice Education for Teachers: Paulo Freire and the Possible Dream.* Rotterdam: Sense Publishers.

Weil, S. (1997). *Gravity and Grace.* Tr. A. Wills. Lincoln, NE: Bison Books.

Weiler, K. (1991). Paulo Freire and a Feminist Pedagogy of Difference. *Harvard Educational Review, 61* (4), 449–474.

5 Holistic formation in Asia

Noel Sheth, S. J.

Introduction

In my title, I have deliberately chosen the term 'formation' instead of 'education'. The way education has developed in modern times, it has become very much one-sided or lopsided. The word 'formation' evokes the sense of an all-round moulding that gives priority to values, ethics, and character building. Formation conveys the sense of holistic education.

Modern educational institutions, by and large, focus on rationality that forgets intuition and mystery, on technology rather than values, on quantity instead of quality, on consumerism rather than morality, on profits rather than human beings, on economic growth rather than sustainability, and on a monoculture rather than diversity of cultures.

Recently the International Federation of Catholic Universities (IFCU) conducted a worldwide survey of students in Catholic universities. The survey confirms some aspects of what I have said about present-day education. For example, to the question about their main project for the next 15 years, the majority of the students responded by stating that their main aim would be a good job (62.4 percent), and that, too, one that offered a good salary (51.8 percent) – and a third of the respondents did not mind even if the company discriminated against women, employed child labor, and was racially or ethnically prejudiced; or the students would start a family (45.5 percent), and this figure can be augmented by another 13.5 percent who said they wanted children, bringing it to a total of 59 percent; or that they would make plenty of money (30.3 percent). But an extremely small percentage said that they would work towards a more just society (8 percent) or participate in social justice movements (4.8 percent), or get involved in a religious group (2.6 percent) (Gomez and Cubillo, 2014, pp. 73–74, 77–79).

Against the backdrop of such a sorry state of affairs, I present the voices of the Hindu Mahatma Gandhi of India, and the Buddhists Ariyaratne of Sri Lanka, and Sivaraksa of Siam (Thailand),[1] who not only spoke and wrote about holistic formation but also actually implemented such holistic, alternative forms of education.

Mohandas Karamchand Gandhi

Gandhi's holistic formation in South Africa and India

Although Gandhi (born in 1869, died in 1948) is not against literary education in itself, which has its place and function, but what is paramount is the formation of character. Literary education does not necessarily lead to ethical behavior and dutifulness, and is not even necessary for cultivating self-control (Gandhi, 1958–1984, 1988, vol. 10, p. 55). He lists a number of characteristics of character, which include chastity, honesty, nonviolence, contentment, simplicity, a strong sense of duty, time management, and freedom from greed, thieving, and fear. This is the purpose of true education; it should not be merely to get a job (Gandhi, 1958–1984, 1988, vol. 14, pp. 134–135). One should not make literary education an obsession; he is convinced 'that literary training by itself adds not an inch to one's moral height and that character-building is independent of literary training'. British literary education merely made Indians 'clerks and interpreters' (Gandhi, 1958–1984, 1988, vol. 20, p. 162). It did not help them to cope with life and did not make them contented and happy (Gandhi, 1958–1984, 1988, vol. 29, pp. 421–422).

The three Rs, reading, writing, and arithmetic, are essential, but they are taught in a manner that has no relevance to the local existential circumstances. What the students learn in school is quickly forgotten because it has no bearing on their village milieus (Gandhi, 1958–1984, 1988, vol. 41, p. 174). Furthermore, these subjects, by themselves, do not produce purity of heart, which is essential for a proper education. The knowledge and recitation of the Vedas, expertise in Sanskrit, Greek, or Latin and other subjects are all useless if they do not help us to nurture purity of heart (Gandhi, 1958–1984, 1988, vol. 34, pp. 422–423).

Gandhi does not devalue the sciences either. He says, for instance, 'Our children cannot have too much of chemistry and physics'. However, he thinks that education has been lopsided, concentrating solely on developing the intellect. Since manual labour is neglected, 'the hands have almost atrophied'. In addition, 'the soul has been altogether ignored' (Gandhi, 1958–1984, 1988, vol. 26, pp. 275–276). The mental, physical, and spiritual aptitudes cannot be developed separately. All three are, in fact, interrelated and form one composite whole; all three blend together to form the whole person. For example, if students, who are simultaneously helped to cultivate the heart, are taught a craft, not merely mechanically but with a theoretical knowledge of how the craft takes shape; that is, with a deep knowledge of the process, which would involve the understanding of mathematics and other sciences, they would not only develop their physiques but also their intellectual acumen, which would be born of concrete life experience and is not mere bookish knowledge (Gandhi, 1958–1984, 1988, vol. 65, pp. 73–74). In other words, for Gandhi the emphasis is not on the three Rs but on the three Hs: the head, the heart and the hand (Cenkner, 1976, p. 102).

Unfortunately, many Indians look down on manual labor as something despicable; they do not understand the dignity of labor. Especially in India where more than 80 percent of the people live in rural areas, it is absurd to concentrate only on literary education and render the students incapable of doing physical work. In a poverty-stricken country like India, guidance in manual work will enable students to pay for their training as well as equip them with a skill that they can rely on in later life (Gandhi, 1958–1984, 1988, vol. 21, pp. 38–39). Intellectual work and gainful manual labor are not two separate things; they are intrinsically connected. They are of equal value; indeed, in a sense, manual work is more important because children use their limbs first and then their intellect. Games and sports have their place, but their purpose is primarily relaxation and not health; this latter need is to be served more by work, which will also help the students make a certain amount of money (Gandhi, 1958–1984, 1988, vol. 34, pp. 98–99). Gandhi has a special preference for hand spinning of yarn and handweaving of cloth since he considers it as the ideal and universal way of self-financing, making students self-reliant, and providing clothing for the poor, thus leading to embargoing of imported (British) yarn and cloth, and at the same time a fine way of exercising the body and the mind. Everyone needs food and clothing; hence, hand spinning can be a work common to all in India (Gandhi, 1958–1984, 1988, vol. 19, p. 481; vol. 20, p. 225).

Another important aspect of education is social service. Students who do social service, for example, relief work, will benefit immensely even when education is temporarily interrupted. Actually, such service is in fact a complement to the students' education, since after all, the purpose of all education is service (Gandhi, 1958–1984, 1988, vol. 35, pp. 120–121). Indeed, the service of society also leads to one's spiritual progress. Service to society is as valuable as offering ritual sacrifice (*yajna*) to God (Gandhi, 1958–1984, 1988, vol. 34, p. 97).

Gandhi strongly reacts against studying in the English language in India instead of in one's mother tongue. It has made Indians slavish imitators of the British, who considered the native languages and cultures of India to be 'worse than useless'. English education has 'the tendency to dwarf the Indian body, mind and soul' (Gandhi, 1958–1984, 1988, vol. 20, pp. 42–43). Nevertheless, the real blame is on the English-speaking Indians who have enslaved India: they have increased the extent of duplicity, oppression, and corruption (Gandhi, 1958–1984, 1988, vol. 10, p. 56). Gandhi is also against going abroad for one's education, although he himself did so. Such students do not fit into their Indian culture. One's native land promotes a flourishing growth (Gandhi, 1958–1984, 1988, vol. 85, p. 238).

English is a global language and can give Indians 'the best of Western literature, thought, and science' as well as open up a window to international trade and diplomacy, but it should not replace the Indian mother tongues. It should be possible to cultivate the mind without English (Gandhi, 1958–1984, 1988, vol. 19, pp. 314–315; vol. 75, p. 265). It is utter delusion to imagine that we cannot manage without English. The Japanese do not experience such vulnerability as Indians do without English (Gandhi, 1958–1984, 1988, vol. 67, p. 162), and Russia accomplished all its scientific development without the use of English (Gandhi, 1958–1984, 1988, vol. 85, p. 88). It may be a language of urban India, but it cannot reach the millions in rural India (Gandhi, 1958–1984, 1988, vol. 56, p. 204). It is noteworthy that in spite of all his insistence on the importance of one's mother tongue, Gandhi frankly and humbly confesses that his knowledge of his own mother tongue, Gujarati, is far from perfect: he admits that he made mistakes in Gujarati spelling and grammar in his own newspaper (Gandhi, 1958–1984, 1988, vol. 23, p. 496).

Education must be based on the culture and life of people. Many of the Indian students who study in English-speaking schools are alienated from their own culture and values and lose their faith in God and their trust in God's providence as well as their respect for parents and love for the family. Worse still, they become convinced that their own traditional culture and values are worthless, foolish, delusory, and uncivilized (Gandhi, 1958–1984, 1988, vol. 21, p. 38). On the other hand, while Gandhi severely criticizes the British in different domains, including indulging in alcoholic drinks and gambling at horse races, he also exhorts Indians to emulate their virtues, such as English nobles in England treating their servants as members of the family, without any discrimination, leave alone caste prejudice, which is so characteristic of India, and their mingling with common folk, for example, royalty working and rubbing shoulders with ordinary sailors. He tells fellow Indians that all their erudite education would be worthless if it did not teach them 'the art of feeling one with the poorest in the land' (Gandhi, 1958–1984, 1988, vol. 56, pp. 289–290). He also points out that Indians can learn from the British to keep places spick and span and neat and tidy (Gandhi, 1958–1984, 1988, vol. 85, p. 255).

Gandhi accuses Indians of mindlessly accepting British views and interpretations without realizing that there are divergent perspectives. British economics cannot be the same as Indian economics, just as economics explained in German and French languages differs. The interpretation of historical events by the English and the French, for instance, would depend on the varying British and French viewpoints. Even the teaching of mathematics in India should not be based on British illustrations. For instance, the teacher should not teach arithmetic by referring to the distance between Manchester and Liverpool. Instead, the teacher should use examples from India; in this way, students will learn Indian geography and history too (Gandhi, 1958–1984, 1988, vol. 36, pp. 394–395).

For Gandhi, religion is an integral part of education. Truth is found in the scriptures of all religions (Gandhi, 1958–1984, 1988, vol. 13, p. 23). Besides introducing the students to the common fundamentals of religion, the syllabus for religious studies should include the reverential and respectful study of the doctrines and practices of different religions (Gandhi, 1958–1984, 1988, vol. 37, pp. 254–255). This will lead to tolerance and love for other religions (Gandhi, 1958–1984, 1988, vol. 36, p. 421) in addition to the deepening of one's own faith (Gandhi, 1958–1984, 1988, vol. 35, p. 343). For him, religious education is not mere academic study of religion but, even more, the practice of religion

(Gandhi, 1958–1984, 1988, vol. 41, p. 291). While books are helpful, they will be ineffective if the teachers do not practice religion: students learn more from the living example of their teachers (Gandhi, 1958–1984, 1988, vol. 35, p. 306).

Real education enables us to discover our true self, God, and truth. Hence the purpose of all disciplines, whether physical sciences or art, is not to earn a living but to help us realize our true self (Gandhi, 1958–1984, 1988, vol. 50, p. 182).

Adult education, particularly in villages, is sorely lacking in India. Adult education, too, has to be holistic. It is not enough to teach adults the three Rs; in fact, it is not so necessary. They must be helped to become good citizens. Adults, like children, have to be taught crafts, especially agriculture. Majority and minority groups need to learn how to relate to each other. They need to learn how to be good neighbours and live in harmony with all castes and outcastes. They should be helped to overcome their being discriminated against on the basis of caste. Adult education, imparted in the mother tongues of the adults, is meant to help them live productive social lives, enabling them to be self-supportive and self-reliant (Gandhi, 1958–1984, 1988, vol. 78, pp. 237–238; vol. 82, pp. 143–144).

Alternative forms of education

The Tolstoy Farm in South Africa

Gandhi was not content to merely theorize about education, but he started alternative forms of education. For instance, when he was in South Africa, he began the Tolstoy Farm for some Indian families, that is, the parents and their children. He started a school for the children who belonged to various religions. He coaxed them to celebrate their different rites and practices in accordance with their respective religions. Even though they had different cultures and backgrounds, he wanted the students to live together as one family, and he lived with them as their paterfamilias.

All were required to do manual work in the kitchen and in the garden and to pick up skills like cooking, footwear manufacturing, and carpentry. Mr. Kallenbach, one of the teachers, went to a Trappist monastery and returned with the art of shoe making, which Gandhi then picked up and also taught the others. The students were not made to work on their own. The teachers also joined them in doing the same work.

He gave them basic literary education, mainly teaching different Indian languages as well as English. He depended on the parents to help in the teaching. There were few textbooks. Most of the time he imparted to them the wisdom he had culled from reading different books. This saved them from the drudgery of reading books, and the classes were thus more interesting.

Gandhi gave top priority to developing moral fiber and the spiritual life. The students were instructed on the basics of their different religions and scriptures. He concentrated on forming character and helping them to grow in the spirit, to experience God, and to progress towards self-realization. He generated in them the desire for self-control and trained them in self-denial by urging them to follow his example of vegetarianism and periodic fasts. He once resorted to corporal punishment, but he repented this act of violence. Later, he did penance himself, resorting to fasting, because he considered himself responsible for the misdemeanor. It also opened the eyes of the students because they experienced his love for them.

He taught them hymns and read out passages from books on religion and morality. However, the cultivation of the spirit takes place not so much by reading books on ethics, or listening to lectures on morality, or by recitation of prayers and singing of hymns but primarily through the spiritual caliber of the teacher. Gandhi was convinced that the best book for the students was the living example of the teacher, both in the class and outside. Moreover, his students, in turn, became his teachers: he took upon himself to be more self-controlled so that he could be a good example to his students.

Hence, the formation imparted at Tolstoy Farm was not limited to the three Rs. Physical fitness was built through manual work, the mind was refined through mental exercise, and the spirit was transformed through spiritual exercise (Gandhi, 1958–1984, 1988, vol. 39, pp. 264–274).

Satyagraha Ashram at Sabarmati

After Gandhi returned to India from South Africa, he decided to start an institution similar to the Tolstoy Farm. He named the institution Satyagraha Ashram. '*Satyagraha*' means 'holding to truth'. For Gandhi it meant bringing about transformation through truth and nonviolence. '*Ashram*' is a community hermitage where people strive for spiritual and all-round development of oneself and society. He began the ashram in a rented house at Kochrab, but in a short while, he moved it to the banks of the river Sabarmati. He lived in this ashram for many years, inspiring and guiding fellow Indians in different spheres of life.

In the ashram he emphasized certain important values and practices: truth; prayer; nonviolence or love (see Sheth, 2006, pp. 33–49); simple living; 'bread labor' or manual work to earn one's keep; '*swadeshi*' or the sense of belonging to one's own country, that is, using locally made goods without having to import merchandise so that the local interests may not be adversely affected; getting rid of the caste system that included considering outcastes as 'untouchable' (without any discrimination against them, outcastes were welcomed to live with the others in the ashram); elementary agriculture; running a dairy to provide milk for the inmates; and education and the practice of chastity, including celibacy (Gandhi, 1958–1984, 1988, vol. 50, pp. 193–236). He did make exceptions, however, in reference to celibacy, including arranging simple weddings in the ashram; he also brought in competent teachers, some of whom were married (Gandhi, 1958–1984, 1988, vol. 50, pp. 212–213, 232). The daily routine in the ashram included personal and community prayer, manual work of various kinds, recreation and classes for the children and for adults who needed them, and so on (Gandhi, 1958–1984, 1988, vol. 36, p. 410).

With regard to the children, first general knowledge was taught, then reading, then drawing, and after that, writing. The medium of instruction was the mother tongue. In addition, the teachers introduced the children to Hindi and Urdu as national languages and taught English as an international language. Hindus were taught Sanskrit, and Muslims had Arabic. From the ages between nine and 16, instruction in world history, geography, botany, astronomy, arithmetic, geometry, and algebra was given. Students between 16 and 25 were free to choose their subjects. No coercion was to be used; in fact, it was made so interesting as to appear as a game for the children. However, religious education was essential, and the children learned it primarily from the teacher's life.

Manual education was more important than literary training, and the reasons for doing things as prescribed were given. The work assigned was in accordance with the abilities of the students, but all were taught to cook and to sew. Boys, not girls, were instructed in the hereditary crafts of their parents. As the children grew in age, they were expected to increasingly finance their own education.

All teachers were virtuous, had the spirit of service, and were paid a living wage. The school buildings were simple and inexpensive.

He wanted to have night schools for adult education. However, he thought they would be introduced to reading, writing, and arithmetic only if they desired these. It was more important that general knowledge be imparted to them. In the ashram, they were inspired to acquire the thirst for knowledge. Women were aided in acquiring freedom from fear and from antiquated customs like wearing a veil, child marriage, and the prohibition of widow remarriage. They were equal to men and had the same kind of ashram activities as the men; for example, both men as well as women cooked in the ashram.

Thus, education in the ashram was all-round. He was more interested in inculcating the value of studies so that both children and adults could educate themselves by reading books themselves, without having a teacher for every little thing. He felt that creating a proper environment for education was more necessary than resorting to spoon-feeding. While he regretted that the ashram did not have sufficient provision for literary education, which has its rightful place, he felt literary education, per se, was not that important. Many subjects could be studied with the aid of books, but numerous crafts required hands-on experience under the guidance of a qualified teacher (Gandhi, 1958–1984, 1988, vol. 50, pp. 233–236).

Not only all the studies, but also all the activities in the ashram, lead to the knowledge of our true self, truth and God; they build moral character and motivate the inmates to share their knowledge and expertise with one another. In order that the activities achieve this goal, they ought to be done with the conscious aim of achieving this end, an understanding of their significance and their scientific method (whether it be cooking, cleaning, or spinning, etc., every work has a science behind it), and with a sense of duty and the spirit of service. In this way, all the activities of the ashram, and not just study, are all educative. 'The ashram is a great school in which the inmates receive education not for a few hours only but all the time' (Gandhi, 1958–1984, 1988, vol. 50, pp. 182–183).

The Champaran schools

In Champaran, in Bihar, near the Himalayas, Gandhi started primary schools for the poor and ignorant children whose parents were exploited for years, first by other Indians and then by European planters of indigo. He made plans for the children to be taught the rudiments of arithmetic, history, geography, and science, together with training in crafts: the literary education would help them improve their traditional agricultural techniques and lifestyle, while the crafts would be useful to them as a supplementary source of income. The building of moral character was of prime importance. For this, he wanted the children to be in contact with teachers who were cultured and of impeccable moral fiber. These teachers were also required to work among the villagers, training them in building roads and digging wells, and so on, and bringing about the emancipation of women. The teachers were also trained in distributing basic medications. In this way, he ensured that these village schools had a holistic formation, and at the same time, the teachers reached out to the adult population, giving them the type of education they needed (Gandhi, 1958–1984, 1988, vol. 14, pp. 93–94).

National schools, colleges, and universities

Under the inspiration of Gandhi and as a protest against British government-recognized educational institutions, several national schools, colleges, and universities were established in India. Gandhi himself founded the Gujarat Vidyapith (University) in Ahmedabad. Several colleges and schools were affiliated to or recognized by it. The number of students in such institutions was 30,000 in 1923 (Gandhi, 1958–1984, 1988, vol. 18, p. 463, n. 1). These institutions were run according to the principles of holistic education that Gandhi had evolved.

The Wardha scheme of basic education

Gandhi founded another ashram, the Sevagram Ashram, near Wardha in 1932, where he lived until he passed away. This ashram was run on similar lines to the ashram at Sabarmati. It was at the Sevagram Ashram that he announced his national plan for the reorganization of education in India. Accepting a suggestion made to him to hold a conference on education at which he would propose his plan for education for the nation, he made a proposal (Gandhi, 1958–1984, 1988, vol. 66, pp. 193–195) that was later discussed at a national conference he had convened on October 22, 1937 at Wardha. His proposal was focused on primary (and secondary) education but also made a reference to college education, which he felt, would be resolved after the question of primary (and secondary) education, especially for rural children, would be settled. Essentially, for Gandhi, all education, that is, literary education, history, geography, mathematics, science, and so on would be imparted through crafts. For example, the craft of spinning also involves acquaintance with different kinds of cotton grown in a variety of soils in diverse parts of India, a history of how this craft declined, and the political reasons for this deterioration, which would involve the history of the British rule in India, the knowledge of arithmetic, and so on. In this way, it would also be possible for the students to pay for their education and be self-supportive (Gandhi, 1958–1984, 1988, vol. 66, pp. 263–266).

At the conference, in addition to discussions, a committee was formed to work out a detailed plan that, after the approval of Gandhi, was implemented in a great number of national schools in India. Of course, such education had its teething problems, such as a certain amount of neglect of some subjects, but what was satisfactory about it was that it responded to the existential circumstances of India, even if finances were not enough to ensure the adequate teaching of these disciplines.[2]

Later, in 1945, Gandhi supplemented the basic (primary) education scheme with plans for a follow-up scheme for children between the ages of 14 and 18, in which the students aimed at also paying for their food and clothing in addition to their education. University education was designed to meet national and social needs. A program for adults was also devised; it concentrated on community development. By 1947–1948, just around the time when Gandhi was assassinated (on January 30, 1948), there were 524 schools based on Gandhian principles. The number rose to 2,816 in 1954–1955 and 4,227 in 1961–1962. Unfortunately, however, the great tide of alternative education put into motion by Gandhi eventually ebbed away (Cenkner, 1976, pp. 122–124). This phenomenon occurs especially when the charismatic personality who inspired and impelled the movement expires and the impetus comes to a halt.

Ahangamage Tudor Ariyaratne

Ariyaratne's holistic formation in Sri Lanka

For Dr. Ariyaratne (born in 1931), the prime focus of education is the full development of human beings (*purusodaya* – the uplift or welfare of human beings), primarily spiritually and morally. Only such persons can help others to overcome spiritual and moral failures as well as socioeconomic evils. Such education is not focused on jobs and the acquisition of wealth, divorced from spiritual and ethical considerations. The one-sided concentration of European capitalist industrialization on mere economic production that made human beings mere cogs in the wheels of industry and neglected the spiritual and ethical dimensions also made inroads in the East. Ariyaratne attempts to build a bridge between modern, exclusively economic development and the wealth of traditional spirituality (Ariyaratne, 1999, vol. 1, p. 45). For him, education is not passive acquisition of information or competence by individuals and society but that which brings about creative transformation in individuals and society (Ariyaratne, 1999, vol. 1, p. 52).

A large part of Asia's population still lives in villages, but it is controlled by the urban population, which has lost its traditional spiritual moorings and is heavily influenced by Western consumerism. In the past, Asia was tutored by saintly sages and had a healthy balance between spiritual values and material progress, but now it is educated by a so-called elite whose attitudes and approaches are a continuation of the former colonizers: they promote impersonal technological progress, degrade human beings, and neglect spiritual and moral values, such as truthfulness, nonviolence, selflessness, and altruism (Ariyaratne, 1999, vol. 1, pp. 81–86). We need to avoid the characteristic Buddhist evils of greed, hatred, and delusion and cultivate loving friendship, compassion, sharing, ethics, meditation, and sagacity (Ariyaratne, 1999, vol. 5, p. 117).

Ariyaratne explains that there are three types of literacy:

1. Conventional Literacy. Here one gets the basics of the three Rs: reading, writing, and arithmetic. By this yardstick around 90 percent of the people in Sri Lanka are literate. But there is a two-level system: (i) the upper layer consists of those who can speak English, who constitute only 7 percent of the inhabitants, while economically speaking, just 10 percent of the populace receives 50 percent of the national income; (ii) in the lower layer, the lowest 40 percent receives merely 7 percent of the income. This sad state of affairs is due to the decision-making being vested only in the upper layer. Many in the lower layer feel that this sort of literacy does not do them any good and does not lead to development. Conventional literacy is necessary, but it is just an ordinary, manually operated instrument, compared to the two other superior forms of literacy.
2. Functional Literacy: In this type of literacy, people are helped to realize the social, economic, and political structure in which they are, and to improve their condition within the parameters of this structure, but without bringing about any structural change. Besides the three Rs, they are instructed in health, agriculture, and handicrafts and are initiated into basic mechanical and organizational skills. This kind of literacy is like a tool driven by electricity and hence more powerful than the previous type of literacy. But it does not equip the people to respond to and challenge the repressive structures of a society that is fiercely competitive and exploitative.
3. Enlightenment Literacy: In this form of literacy, the first two kinds of literacy are integrated by people into a 'process of total ideological, technological, methodological and structural change to bring about a total transformation of themselves and the society as a whole' (pp. 72–73). With this literacy, people have a vision of life and have the freedom to choose their place in it. The poor, in particular, are helped to recapture the traditional values, such as sharing, collaboration, and nonviolence, in place of selfish individualism, rivalry, and aggression, which characterize modern society, which pursues mere material progress. Moreover, various meditational practices help people become intuitive, humane, and just, something that is sorely neglected in modern literacy programs. The poor and the marginalized are initiated into 'bottom-up, communitarian and

participatory decision-making' (p. 74) to replace the top-bottom decisions made by the urban and privileged elite few. The oppressed people are led to discover the structural causes of their poverty and the ways to overcome and change the oppressive structures. This form of literacy brings about the awakening of persons, families, society, the nation, and the world without leaving out anyone, including women and children. In this kind of literacy not all may have the knowledge of the three Rs, but they would neither be 'uneducated nor unskilled'; there would be 'no category of people called the educated unemployed' (p. 75). This type of literacy is far superior to the power-driven tool of the second kind of literacy; it is like a sophisticated machine or the latest computer (Ariyaratne, 1999, vol. 5, pp. 71–75, 222–223).

University education too should bring about inner transformation and the transformation of society and nature. It should inspire us to let our hearts reach out in love to humans and to animals and plants and to extend our love even beyond all living beings. Information or knowledge is not enough. We must not only broaden our minds but should also enlarge our hearts. We need wisdom, which comes from linking knowledge to virtues. If university education had wisdom, human beings would not have invented weapons of mass destruction; the atom bomb would not have been dropped on Hiroshima.

Higher education is not just to produce outstanding intellectuals but to also generate truly great people who render altruistic service. University education is not a product to be marketed, nor is it meant to get jobs or to amass wealth. It is unethical to increase one's wealth and thus deprive others of their rightful share. This would generate social problems like poverty and crime and in the end boomerang on us.

University education should also include, in addition to psychology, sociology, and anthropology, the study of comparative religion and the ethics of different religions. This will lead to mutual understanding and tolerance (Ariyaratne, 1999, vol. 6, pp. 78–79).

Higher education is not a product to be marketed. In addition to wisdom and love, university education should help us to become more simple, more humble and patient, and more compassionate and tolerant. It should inspire us to reach out to the poor and the rural people, making them self-reliant and making village self-government accessible to them. Such transformative and overall development is the great wonder of true education (Ariyaratne, 1999, vol. 7, pp. 151–157).

Asia was the birthplace and cradle of many religions of the world. *Gurus*, or people with deep religious experience, taught by word and example. In the postcolonial period, Asia needs to rediscover its heritage, its understanding of life. and our relationship to nature, society, and the universe. What is needed in the world today is community education for the total transformation of human beings, society, and nature. We need to recapture the great values of the great civilizations like Egypt, India, China, and Greece. Rationalism and scientific developments in modern times have brought in excessive individualism and neglect of the cosmos. Modern society, both in the West as well as in Asia, has

> institutionalised the very values that in religion are known as deadly sins, namely, greed, pride, selfishness and hate. Such is the world we live in where crimes against humanity, whether in the battlefields of Sri Lanka, the ravaged cities of Kuwait or the starving land of Ethiopia, are accepted as an unavoidable part of life. This is the reality of today's world that community education guided by Asian [and world] heritage must seek to change.
> (Ariyaratne, 1999, vol. 5, pp. 217–221)

Alternative forms of education

Ariyaratne established his grassroots educational system, which he called the Sarvodaya Shramadana Movement. '*Sarvodaya*' means the 'uplift or welfare of all', and '*Shramadana*' is 'donation of labor' in village work camps. Volunteers share not only their labor but also their energy, time, motivation, knowledge, culture, expertise, and influence and their spiritual, educational, psychological, social and physical resources (Ariyaratne, 1999, vol. 3, p. 44; vol. 6, p. 51).

When Ariyaratne was teaching in Nalanda College, Colombo, he inspired the teachers and students to start and engage in the Sarvodaya Shramadana Movement. The college was predominantly Buddhist, but from the second camp onward they were able to persuade teachers and students from Hindu, Christian, and Muslim educational institutions to join hands with them in common Shramadana village camps (Ariyaratne, 1999, vol. 5, p. 143). Gradually they started community education in nutrition, health, sanitation, and cooking; child care, preschool programs, day-care centers for children and working parents; a children's library; leadership courses and youth guidance; training in agriculture and various crafts, such as carpentry, masonry, and different cottage industries and cooperatives, and so on (Ariyaratne, 1999, vol. 1, pp. 30–40, 76–77).

The Sarvodaya Educational System for the villages has five stages. The first stage consists in psychological infrastructure, which includes discussing their needs, organizing self-help activities, and voluntary sharing of the village resources. The second stage develops social infrastructure, wherein groups of mothers, children, youth, elders, farmers, and so on are formed. Village childcare centers and community kitchens are often started at this stage. Many formal educational programs are introduced, such as preschool teacher training, community leadership, community health, legal aid, organizational courses, savings and credit schemes, increase of water supply, and better sanitation. In the third stage the Sarvodaya Shramadana Society (SSS) is formed and legally registered. The village fulfils its fundamental needs by opening bank accounts, getting loans, and engaging in economic activities. In the fourth stage the villages become self-financing. In the fifth stage, they help neighboring villages and engage in mutually benefitting collaborative projects with these villages (Ariyaratne, 1999, vol. 5, pp. 76–77; vol. 6, pp. 58–60). Thus Sarvodaya leads the villagers into enlightenment literacy.

Auxiliary programs

To help the villages advance through the five stages, several auxiliary programs are organized: (i) The Poverty Eradication and Empowerment of the Poor Programme (PEEP); (ii) The Early Childhood Development Programme (ECDP); (iii) The Sarvodaya Rural Technical Services (SRTS); (iv) The Rural Enterprises Programme (REP); (v) The Management Training Institute (MTI), and (vi) The Rural Enterprise Development Services (REDS). In addition, there are several independent national Sarvodaya organizations for social welfare, women's development, prevention of drug abuse and rehabilitation, legal aid, assistance at festivals, cultural programs, calamities, and international relations. To run these vast and varied programmes, Sarvodaya has around 4,000 permanent employees, 5,000 volunteers, and more than 50,000 associated people (Ariyaratne, 1999, vol. 6, pp. 61–64).

Sulak Sivaraksa

The holistic formation of Sulak Sivaraksa in Siam[3]

Sulak Sivaraksa (born in 1933) traces the problems of modern, Western education to the dawn of the Enlightenment, when the mind and individualism were overemphasized. As a result, true wisdom was not nurtured, and warmth and collaboration were downplayed (Sivaraksa, 2009a, p. 41). The Enlightenment gave rise to scientism, which is quite different from science. Scientism pays exclusive attention to rationality, to quantity rather than quality, and the religious dimension is considered as irrational. Such scientism has made inroads into psychology, economics, and politics too and has vitiated human relationships. Sivaraksa quotes Thomas Berry, who writes that today's universities are 'the most dangerous institutions in the world': they churn out thousands of rationalists who do harm to society as well as the environment while propagating a self-styled, value-neutral science and economics devoid of ethics and religion. Sulak emphasizes that in modern universities, such value-neutral science neglects ethics and spirituality. Focusing on rationality and on the quantitative and the measureable, the qualitative and the spiritual are left out (Sivaraksa, 2009a, p. 42, 2009b, pp. 285–286). In today's universities, rationality has no place for 'intuition, transcendence and mystery' (Sivaraksa, 2009a, pp. 48–49). Rene Descartes proclaimed, 'I think, therefore I am'. Hence Western education deals with the head and not with the heart. And worse still, the 'I' in 'I think' has developed into egotism and individualism (Sivaraksa, 2009b, p. 302). In fact, in modern times, we have gone further by saying, 'I buy, therefore I am': our whole being revolves around consumerism:

we lose our very being when we cannot buy! Educational institutions are meant to get us jobs so that we can make money and acquire more goods. In this context, we could say that Buddhism would rather propose, 'I breathe; therefore, I am.' This breathing is a measured, controlled breathing of which we are deliberately aware. It brings about mindfulness – awareness of ourselves, of society and of nature, and a holistic and loving concern for all. With its focus on thoughts, Western education has scorned controlled breathing and, as a result, has been breathing in (and out) rage, animosity, revenge, anxiety, avarice, and delusion (Sivaraksa, 2005a, pp. 18–20). 'It is time for us to question the fundamentals of the Enlightenment in order to be truly enlightened' (Sivaraksa, 2009a, p. 45).

The achievement of modern education is measured only in terms of quantity but not quality: a rise in the number of educational institutions, the number of students, and the enlargement of the syllabus, but no attention is paid to finding out whether the education truly benefits the students: education does not contribute to the students' social, political, cultural, or religious well-being (Sivaraksa, 1994, pp. 56, 87). Contemporary education caters almost totally to the head but neglects the heart. Smart students are praised even if they are not bighearted or concerned about removing social inequalities. From the Buddhist perspective, this is truly ignorance (*avjijja*) or delusion (*moha*) (Sivaraksa, 1999, p. 63).

Students are taught to think in a compartmentalized manner and not holistically. They learn by rote a whole lot of useless facts, only for the examinations. Frequently they are trained merely to become underlings of multinationals and other corporations that abuse society and the environment. Such improper education results in ignorance, which especially for Buddhism, is the cause of suffering. Giving mere lip service to the humanities, universities have become big businesses or at least focused on business alone (Sivaraksa, 2009b, pp. 285–286). Modern intellectuals or technocrats attempt to respond to social problems only with their heads and not their hearts, and so their solutions are devoid of deep insight (Sivaraksa, 1999, p. 93).

Sneering at traditional and nonformal formation, modern education concentrates on degrees and jobs, on selfishness and attachment to material things, on competition and the acquisition of wealth, focusing merely on economic development and that, too, only for the privileged few (Sivaraksa, 1987, pp. 32–35). Particularly in Asia, even though more urban youth go to schools, the rural youth are sorely neglected: the children of farmers hardly ever go beyond primary education (Sivaraksa, 1994, p. 83).

Without ethical values, science and technology lead to covetousness and insensitivity. Even when it brings electricity, modern means of transport, and advances in medicine, it also produces weapons of mass destruction. Moreover, it destroys the environment and diverse species, modifies the genetic structure of plants and animals, and claims patent rights over them. The modern school of economics teaches free-market capitalism and does away with alternative forms of development (Sivaraksa, 2009a, pp. 42–43, 2009b, pp. 286–287). We may be experts in technology but should not be controlled by it. We should not value technology more than religion, but on the other hand, we should not be religiously conservative and reject science (Sivaraksa, 1994, pp. 140–141).

It should be remarked that while Sivaraksa severely criticizes Western universities, he also points an accusing finger at universities in Siam. For him, many of the Thai universities are just glorified producers of civil service clerks (Sivaraksa, 1994, p. 8). Quoting a British educationist who pleads for eminent professors who are dedicated, thought-provoking, creative, inspiring, and noble minded, Sivaraksa laments that professors in Siamese universities are worse than second rate and are not leaders in morality and academics. They have hardly made any substantial international academic impact. He exhorts the professors of Thammasat University in Siam to emulate the Fabians of England, who strived to put academic brilliance at the service of the destitute and, initiating a socialist movement, founded the London School of Economics and Political Sciences to foster ethical awareness (Sivaraksa, 1985, pp. 290, 292, 296).

Sivaraksa bemoans the fact that although Siam was never colonized politically, it was mentally colonized. The foreign educational system replaced the Buddhist triad of morality, wisdom, and meditation with a lopsided emphasis on the head alone, neglecting the heart. Western education lays stress on selfishness that makes one strive to be above others socially, economically, and politically at the cost of exploiting other human beings, animals, and the environment. The Thai administration introduced sudden and large-scale Westernization of education and culture. Western education was considered superior, and traditional Buddhist values and holistic education were looked down upon as inferior. Pali and Buddhist studies were pursued only from the academic point of view, eschewing the spiritual and transformative aspects. University education in Siam began generating skilled civil servants but not dependable and kindhearted citizens. Most Thais who went to the West to study lost their cultural moorings and blindly revered the West. Western ways of thinking and behavior, developmental policies, and legal and communications systems distorted the psyche of Siam. Traditional habits, like chewing betel nut in public and wearing the customary *panung* (trousers), were banned, Thai music and medicine were debunked as obsolete, and time-honored virtues like self-dependence, sharing, and meekness were thrown to the winds. Transnationals swooped in. Western-style supermarkets supplanted temples as the center of Thai life: people became so brainwashed by consumerism that they ceased to be human 'beings'; they became human 'havings'! Various forms of traditional contemplation, like Insight Meditation, were looked down upon as immunizing the mind to societal problems and especially toward the onward march of modernization (Sivaraksa, 2005b, pp. 81, 91, 97–98, 112–113, 118–119).

Unfortunately, many third-world countries ape the West and produce substandard reproductions of Western education that fabricates thoughtless and selfish education that leads to consumerism, techno-capitalism, and globalization. We need to recapture the integral riches of our local cultures and heritages through holistic education founded on spirituality and environmental concern (Sivaraksa, 2009a, pp. 50–51).

While Sivaraksa lambasts the West for its lopsided view of education, he also expresses appreciation for individual Westerners who speak of alternative forms of integral education, for example, F. E. Schumacher, Ivan Illich, Paolo Freire, and Catholic Liberation Theologians in Latin America. In fact, there are devoted people in different parts of the world working for holistic liberation of all. This kind of education blends contemplation and action, spirituality, politics, and even humor and gravity (Sivaraksa, 2009a, pp. 48–49).

A holistic formation imparts different types of knowledge for different situations: one kind of knowledge helps us reach the moon, another sort of knowledge generates ecological sustainability, and still another fosters peace (Sivaraksa, 2009a, p. 45).

What we need is a reformation of education. We need to bring back ethics and human values such as compassion and dialogue, awareness of socioeconomic diversity, and alternative forms of development. We also need to look inward through meditation that helps us to live life holistically. Villagers can teach us to live in communion with nature, in touch with the sacred. Scientific knowledge and education has to be complemented with the wisdom of indigenous culture. In short, we require holistic education that helps us to blend the different aspects of our lives (Sivaraksa, 2009a, pp. 42–44).

Authentic wisdom, and not merely academic knowledge, combines the head and the heart. It makes us humble as well as kind and compassionate; it makes us aware of ourselves and understand others and motivates us to share in the suffering of others and eradicate its roots (Sivaraksa, 1999, p. 60). Real education leads to true, all-round human development: it brings inner freedom and recognition of the freedom of others, replaces rivalry with teamwork, and motivates us to use our creative abilities for the uplift of all, reducing the economic, social, and political disparities among people (Sivaraksa, 1987, p. 32).

Buddhist formation is intrinsically linked with life. Buddhist training includes wisdom, compassion, humility, and selflessness. It emphasizes detachment from oneself, nonviolence toward oneself and others, and the fostering of inner peace. It promotes holism and good relationships with other humans as well as with nature (Sivaraksa, 2005b, p. 91). The purpose of Buddhist education is freedom from (spiritual) ignorance. The Buddha taught the threefold training (*tisikka*): wisdom (*panna*), ethics (*sila*), and meditation (*samadhi*). Buddhist formation cultivates the mind and emotions together. It helps us know things as they are, without bias, attachments, or selfishness. This knowledge of reality is combined with empathy and concern for others, bringing peace in the world through sympathy, meekness, benevolence, awareness, and sagacity. Buddhist pedagogy is meant to bring happiness through diligence, friendship, equipoise, and faith (Sivaraksa, 2009a, pp. 44–46).

Alternative forms of education

Spirit in Education Movement (SEM)

In collaboration with grassroots nongovernmental organizations (NGOs), Sivaraksa has started the Spirit in Education Movement (SEM). Inspired by the four noble truths of Buddhism, it blends spirituality and knowledge, goes beyond the limited and compartmentalized contemporary education, and tries to bring about a judicious balance between tradition and modernity (Sivaraksa, 1999, pp. 69–70, 148).

It fosters ideals shared by all religions and spiritualities, encourages participatory civil society, protects native and ethnic wisdom, inspires an ecological worldview, teaches management skills, works toward an integral sustainable development, and strengthens grassroots communities. It holds courses on alternative development, deep ecology, conflict resolution, nonviolent action, alternative politics, and meditation for social action. It organizes courses for people from Asian countries, arranging grassroots experiences for them, enabling them to integrate their different spiritualities with participatory development projects, and imparting training in starting credit unions, community income-producing activities, sustainable farming, and proper management courses to help find solutions to food shortages, lack of training, subsistence living, and debt. It is also planning a host of programs and initiatives for the future (Sivaraksa, 2009a, pp. 51–53).

The SEM is also associated with alternative education in the Naropa Institute in the United States and the Schumacher College and Sharpham College in the UK. Students are helped to use controlled breathing to discover themselves. They are motivated to respect not only human beings but also animals, plants, and the Earth, the whole of nature. People from different countries also come to participate in courses organized by the SEM in Siam. They are exposed to suffering, to meditation in the forests, and to learning from the educated as well as from illiterate farmers (Sivaraksa, 1999, p. 149).

SEM, therefore, questions the harmful tendencies of Western education and tries to inspire personal and group reliance on traditional Buddhist values of holistic education that will make people less selfish and more content and compassionate. Although it is founded on Buddhist principles, it is also receptive to and cooperates with other spiritualities (Sivaraksa, 2009b, p. 291).

The Centre for Sustainable Development

Sivaraksa has also begun the Centre for Sustainable Development. With a network of committed people, it is developing curricula for use in villages to give rise to grassroots leadership. The aim is to equip leaders with the ability to mobilize local resources to alleviate poverty and build an immune system to protect the villagers from the destructive effects of globalization. Founded on deep spirituality, the center will cooperate with people of different religions. The participants' link with their own spirituality will be broadened and deepened through forest walks, yoga and other meditational practices. A host of other initiatives, such as slope agriculture, sustainable forestry, sanitation, and water treatment schemes are also being envisaged (Sivaraksa, 2009a, pp. 53–55).

Midnight University

An educational institution, called Midnight University, brings together native and Buddhist insight and ethos, sustainability, conflict resolution, resource management and networking. It motivates people to cultivate confidence, and diminish manipulation and domination, to live a happy and successful life (Sivaraksa, 2009a, pp. 47–48).

Conclusion

All these three giant reformers of Asia have very similar views with regard to education, or rather formation, in Asia. Their understanding of formation arose in the context of colonialism, postcolonialism, social injustice, and poverty. They do not want education to be the privilege of a small elite; it is the birthright of every one. Although all three are concerned with university education, their prime interest is in the formation of the poor and the downtrodden masses. They want to keep a happy balance between the perennial values of tradition and the benefits of modernization. Education has to bring about transformation in oneself, in society, and in nature.

All three put their theories into practice by setting up innovative and alternative forms of spiritually based integral education in dialogue with other faiths. They emphasized sustainable development, conflict resolution, grassroots initiatives, nonviolent action, and social change.

All three, while rightly pointing out the lacunae in lopsided Western or modern or globalized education and while also blaming their own countries not only for aping the West but also for neglecting the perennial values in their own traditions, have perhaps been overcritical of the West, without realizing that their own countries, instigated by some undesirable facets of their own cultures, have also embraced capitalism without always being influenced by the West.[4]

It will be noticed that Ariyaratne, in particular, but Sivaraksa too, were both influenced by Gandhi's ideas, not just on education but also in other areas. However, it is important to point out that as we have seen, both of them draw inspiration and support from their own Buddhist tradition and not from the Hindu tradition of Gandhi. The Hindu Gandhi wants people to attain their true self through all-round education, while the Buddhist Ariyaratne and Sivaraksa look at holistic education as a manifestation of one's non-self (Kantowski, 1980, pp. 74–75). Hence, although there are many similarities in all three with regard to what they propose and practise, the underlying worldview of Gandhi's Hinduism differs a good deal from the worldview of Buddhism.

Their views might in some respects appear to be idealistic and utopian. Gandhi, in particular, while emphasizing productive work, does not give sufficient value to creative work, although he had a great appreciation for poets like Tagore. On the other hand, their concept of integral education is a clarion call to remedy the lopsided, value-less, and commercialized thrust of modern education in Asia and in the world.

Notes

1 On their Hindu and Buddhist philosophical background, see Noel Sheth, S. J., 'Alternative Development Models in Response to Globalized Development', uploaded on the website of COMIUCAP: www.comiucap.net.
2 See, in this context, the approach to the earlier problems in national education (Gandhi, 1958–1984, 1988, vol. 26, pp. 274–276).
3 Siam is the ancient name of Thailand. Sivaraksa prefers the earlier name to the partially anglicized Thailand, which for him, epitomizes the erosion of traditional Buddhist values in Siam and the dehumanization of his country. A note to this effect is found at the beginning of several of his books and occasionally also inside a book (See, e.g., Sivaraksa, 2005b, p. 92).
4 See Grant A. Olson, 'Editor's Introduction' (Sivaraksa, 1987, p. iii).

References

Ariyaratne, A. T. (1999). *Collected Works* (2nd edn.). Eds. Nandasena Ratnapala (vols. 1–3, 6–7), B. A. Tennyson Perera (vol. 4) and Jehan Perera (vol. 5). 7 vols. Ratmalana, Sri Lanka: Sarvodaya Vishva Lekha.
Cenkner, William. (1976). *The Hindu Personality in Education: Tagore, Gandhi, Aurobindo*. New Delhi: Manohar.
Gandhi, M. K. (1958–1984/1988). *The Collected Works of Mahatma Gandhi*. 90 vols. (1958–1984); plus, Index (1988). New Delhi: Publications Division, Government of India.
Gomez, Rosa Aparicio and Cubillo, Andres Tornos. (2014). *Youth Cultures in Catholic Universities: A Worldwide Study*. Paris: Centre for Coordination of Research, International Federation of Catholic Universities.
Kantowski, Detlef. (1980). *Sarvodaya: The Other Development*. New Delhi: Vikas Publishing House Pvt. Ltd.
Sheth, Noel S. J. (2006). The Nonviolence of Mahatma Gandhi. In Karikottuchira K. Kuriakose (Ed.). *Religion, Terrorism and Globalization: Nonviolence: A New Agenda* (33–49). New York: Nova Science Publishers.
Sivaraksa, S. (1985). *Siamese Resurgence: A Thai Buddhist Voice on Asia and a World of Change*. Bangkok: Asian Cultural Forum on Development.
Sivaraksa, S. (1987). *Religion and Development* (3rd edn.). Tr. Francis Seeley. Ed. Grant Olson. Bangkok: Thai Inter-Religious Commission for Development.
Sivaraksa, S. (1994). *A Buddhist Vision for Renewing Society* (3rd printing with addenda). Bangkok: Thai Inter-Religious Commission for Development.
Sivaraksa, S. (1999). *Global Healing: Essays and Interviews on Structural Violence, Social Development and Spiritual Transformation*. With a Foreword by Ravindra Varma. Bangkok: Thai Inter-Religious Commission for Development, Sathirakoses-Nagapradipa Foundation.

Sivaraksa, S. (2005a). *Sixty Years of Achieving Peace in Siam*. Bangkok: Santi Pracha Dhamma Institute, Sathirakoses-Nagapradipa Foundation.

Sivaraksa, S. (2005b). *Conflict, Culture, Change: Engaged Buddhism in a Globalizing World*. With a Foreword by Donald Swearer. Boston, MA: Wisdom Publications.

Sivaraksa, S. (2009a). *The Wisdom of Sustainability: Buddhist Economics for the 21st Century*. Kihei, HI: Koa Books.

Sivaraksa, S. (2009b). *Rediscovering Spiritual Value: Alternative to Consumerism from a Siamese Buddhist Perspective*. Bangkok: Sathirakoses-Nagapradipa Foundation.

6 MacIntyre, rationality and universities

Steven Stolz

Introduction

The most obvious starting point to understanding MacIntyre's (2009) views on the university can be found in *God, Philosophy, Universities*. Representing his most recent thoughts on the Catholic philosophical tradition and how this has played out in universities, MacIntyre provides a compelling argument why theology and philosophy should be a necessary part of the contemporary university curriculum, particularly within the Catholic university. MacIntyre argues that the rise of secularism in Western culture has resulted in both secular and religiously affiliated universities either eliminating God from the curriculum altogether or restricting it to certain departments of theology. Indeed, MacIntyre laments the place of theology and philosophy within the contemporary research university because each have become highly specialised areas of study that tend to be taught in relative isolation from other discipline areas and essentially treated as subjects amongst many with no serious claims to truth, rational justification and meaning. Unfortunately, this has contributed to the perception that theology and philosophy have nothing useful to add to the academy, particularly compared to the natural sciences. In saying this, MacIntyre is laying the preliminary groundwork for his main thesis that the absence of theology and philosophy from the contemporary Catholic university has ultimately led to the disintegration of the curriculum, fragmented enquiry, and "multiversities" which have no shared understanding of the universe, and no overall understanding of the whole which the various disciplines are all parts of, but instead a multifarious set of assorted subject matters with a range of plural views and positions. It is important to note that MacIntyre is at odds with the academic culture of the contemporary university of the late 20th-century because it tolerates a diverse array of competing ideological and philosophical positions that are often incommensurable to each other.[1] He argues that the reason why theology and philosophy cannot find their proper place within the curriculum of the contemporary university is due to the dominant educational ideals of Western culture presupposing a morally heterogeneous and divided society that must choose amongst a variety of different and rival goods. MacIntyre, however, makes his position quite clear that a good education, particularly a good university education involves students being confronted with alternative – sometimes rather hostile – rival traditions, so they both come to see rival points of view and understand that each tradition, including their own, does not come from a neutral or value-neutral standpoint (MacIntyre, 1964, 1977, 1981, 1988, 1990a, 1998, 1999a, 1999b, 1981/2007, 2009; MacIntyre and Dunne, 2002). Not only is such a view contrary to the hegemonic culture which seems to take for granted that there is no such thing as *the human good*, but more importantly it highlights how the conception of the good is not something that can be *chosen*.[2] This is further reinforced by the moral reasoning of agents within contemporary Western culture which seem to be guided by a range of incoherent rules or principles that are both constantly changing and have no rational way of securing moral agreement (MacIntyre, 1981/2007). In fact, MacIntyre's (1988, 1990a, 1981/2007) well-known trilogy of *After Virtue, Whose Justice? Which Rationality?* and *Three Rival Versions of Moral Enquiry* all seem to be preoccupied with providing an account of rationality, overcoming rival and incommensurable traditions of moral enquiry and helping those agents who have yet to give their allegiance to some coherent tradition of enquiry. A central theme of this work highlights how the conception of good cannot be presupposed because it is contingent upon the agent possessing certain skills and characteristics, such as the virtues, habits of practice, a shared understanding of the good and an ability to exercise independent practical reason and exercise good judgement about what is good or bad, particularly the reasons for acting in the former way (MacIntyre, 1990c, 1999a, 1999b). So an education in which there emerge virtuous and independent practical reasoners will be one already informed from the outset by a conception of the good. Consequently, for the purposes of this chapter, I will be concerned with critical discussion of three issues: firstly, I provide a brief critique of MacIntyre's work that outlines the reasons why theology and philosophy should play a central and crucial role, particularly within the Catholic university; secondly, I turn my attention to MacIntyre's theory of rational vindication, which is concerned with the conditions of dialectical encounters between traditions as a crucial starting point in rational enquiry that is grounded in conceptions of first principles and standards of justification; and lastly, I revitalise and extend MacIntyre's argument that a university is set up for constructive engagement in conflict that also highlights the importance of reason or wisdom and its development because it enables us to see the interconnectedness and interrelationships among different forms of knowledge that can lead us to truth and the good.

MacIntyre's critique on the primacy of theology and philosophy in the Catholic university

Taking his cue from Aquinas, MacIntyre redefines the relationship of theology to philosophy in the sense that each provides an account of human nature, human activity and human goods and in part address the same subject matter (MacIntyre, 1998). Indeed, there is much about theological enquiry where philosophy cannot contribute (and vice versa); however, theological enquiry cannot be carried out adequately without recognising the important role philosophy has to play in making things such as the Catholic natural law tradition intelligible in terms of providing a corresponding account of human rationality, agency and the relationship of human beings to their good.[3] Although, such an account highlights how philosophy complements theological enquiry, however, to MacIntyre (2009), an understanding of how each contributes to an overall understanding and nature of things is crucial, particularly a university education that claims to be professedly Catholic. MacIntyre goes on to bemoan that with the advent of the contemporary research university, it makes little difference whether a university professes to be Catholic or secular because the place of theology and philosophy has become almost exclusively specialised and segregated from other disciplines to the point where they have either been expelled or marginalised altogether. To overcome this disintegration and marginalisation, MacIntyre (2009, p. 135) argues that the main task of the Catholic view of the world requires the study of the different aspects of "nonhuman nature and human society that provides each of the secular disciplines with their subject matter" and contributes to the "knowledge of the whole", which is the role of theological enquiry, whereas the role of philosophy in the Catholic view of the world is to "exhibit the relationship between a theological understanding of the world and the kinds of understanding provided by the various secular disciplines" (MacIntyre, 2009, p. 135). MacIntyre (2009) acknowledges that he has been influenced by John Henry Newman's (1852/2009) account of a university found in *The Idea of a University*, and so it is no surprise that he argues that if a university is functioning how it should, then "philosophical truths, arguments, and insights" should be taught in every discipline, particularly their relationship to other discipline areas in order to understand the universe as a whole (see Chapter 16 titled "Newman: God, Philosophy, Universities").[4]

Central to MacIntyre's account of a Catholic university is the role theology and philosophy should play in a university curriculum. In a sense, MacIntyre makes a strong point that although philosophy has become a highly specialised form of activity for those who have already been initiated, it has become marginalised within the university because it is claimed to be irrelevant. MacIntyre (2009, p. 176) challenges this claim and argues that "human beings *need* philosophy" more so than any other period because it still has some relevancy in that it can teach (or maybe train) agents to both think rationally and moves toward "answering questions the asking of which is crucial for human flourishing." In another sense, MacIntyre sees philosophy's role as making sense of both the Catholic theological tradition and the secular disciplines and how they contribute to a unique way of understanding the world. As a result, there is a real risk that if God is removed from the curriculum of the Catholic university, we will of course have no knowledge of God from a Catholic point of view but, more importantly a fragmented view of the universe and an assortment of different kinds of discipline-related knowledge with no way of relating them to each other.

Although faith is important in terms of turning us toward God, it certainly does not mean we follow the teachings of the Church or the claimed truths of Christianity blindly without rigorous scrutiny because truth (or falsity) is often tradition dependent in the sense that if we are an agent fully committed to a tradition, then we generally come to know what is the common good and how to achieve it through inculcation. Although the accepted standards of rationality may be shared by those agents who are members and committed to the tradition, MacIntyre argues that irrespective of whether we are committed members of a tradition or not, the point and purpose of a university education is to test every point of view in a systematic fashion to see if it withstands rigorous scrutiny from different and rival points of view using first principles and at the same time learn to understand that certain social concepts are essentially contestable, such as justice, love, human nature and so on.[5] Here we start to see an internal tension between theological and philosophical positions and how we cannot study each in isolation from each other, or privilege one at the expense of the other in the teaching and learning of the curriculum, because we would be led seriously astray as both provide an understanding of each other and an overall understanding of the whole, particularly how the Catholic philosophical tradition plays an "integrative" role in connecting Catholic views of the world and a whole range of secular disciplines. This is further reinforced by MacIntyre (2009, p. 179) when he states:

> Because of the integrative function of philosophy in the Catholic tradition, because of the way in which philosophy has to open up and illuminate relationships between theology and a whole range of secular disciplines, philosophical enquiry cannot be pursued in isolation from enquiry in those other disciplines. For both reasons its projects require the setting of a university.

As such, a Catholic university is very different from a secular university, and not just because it advocates for the primacy of theology and philosophy in the curriculum, but due to the fact that it does not ignore contemporary moral conflicts and competing conceptions of the good found in our social life. According to MacIntyre (1998), we need to confront rival and often hostile and alien points of view from the outset to test our own conclusions as comprehensively and rigorously as possible by viewing an education, particularly a Catholic university – as in Aquinas' own time – as a site of mutually constrained disagreement and conflict.

In this section I have provided a brief critique of MacIntyre's work that outlines the reasons why theology and philosophy should play a central and crucial role, particularly within the Catholic university. Consequently, in the next section, I turn my attention to MacIntyre's theory of rational vindication as it reminds us that a central feature of successful philosophical enquiry aims at both truth and rational justification.

108 Steven Stolz

MacIntyre's theory of rational vindication

The intellectual history of MacIntyre's oeuvre is crucial to understanding his theory of rational vindication. For instance, in *After Virtue*, MacIntyre's intellectual-*cum*-historical account of traditions of moral enquiry identifies how contemporary Western culture are inheritors of rival and incommensurable systems of ethical belief with no rational means for deciding which tradition of moral enquiry we should give our allegiance. Later, in *Whose Justice? Which Rationality?* MacIntyre sets out to answer his own self-imposed question of "whose" justice and "which" rationality now that there are a multiplicity of choices available. MacIntyre's position in this work is quite clear in terms of how contemporary moral agents should think about and approach disputed moral questions. He states that when

> a person is confronted by the claims of each of the traditions which we have considered as well as by those of other traditions. How is it rational to respond to them? The initial answer is: that will depend upon who you are and how you understand yourself. This is not the kind of answer which we have been educated to expect in philosophy, but that is because our education in and about philosophy has by and large presupposed what is in fact not true, that there are standards of rationality, adequate for the evaluation of rival answers to such questions, equally available, at least in principle, to all persons, whatever tradition they may happen to find themselves in and whether or not they inhibit any tradition.
> (MacIntyre, 1988, p. 393)

Here we start to see MacIntyre's account of rationality that is a hybrid of historicism and epistemological and metaphysical realism. The main thing to take away from this passage at this juncture is that rationality according to MacIntyre requires an agent to be aware of their own history of belief and realise that traditions that seek their rational allegiance are contingent until they have been dialectically established through a rigorous process of systematic testing for falsifiability through first principles and rational standards of justification.

So what role do first principles play in MacIntyre's theory of rational vindication? In MacIntyre's Aquinas lecture titled *First Principles, Final Ends, and Contemporary Philosophical Issues* delivered at Marquette University in 1990 and the chapter titled "Moral Relativism, Rationality and Justification" – originally published in 1994 in an edited book and now republished in his selected works – are two primary sources which outline his conception of first principles, rational justification and truth. It is important to note that the former was written around the same time *Three Rival Versions of Moral Enquiry* was published and so is quite useful in outlining his interpretation and subsequent reformulation of Aristotelian and Thomistic conceptual accounts of truth and rational justification that are central to his account of rational enquiry. It is made clear from the outset that his Aristotelian and Thomistic account is not like Descartes's epistemological first principle of which the Cartesian cogito is viewed as being self-justifying. He then goes on to contrast Cartesianism with Aristotelian and Thomistic views of knowing as a means to highlight that all knowledge that has been gained from enquiry in a sense is unstable with respect to the achievement of knowledge and hence problematic when it comes to claims to truth. Although this is presupposed as an embodied feature in Aristotelian and Thomistic conceptions of enquiry, unfortunately this has largely gone unacknowledged according to MacIntyre. In addition, it is the analytic antifoundationalist rejection of epistemological first principles that served as the catalyst for a very different contemporary philosophical system in the form of deconstructive denials in the possibility of metaphysical first principles. It is at this point that MacIntyre notes that Aristotelian and Thomistic conceptions of enquiry emerge unscathed from both the analytic antifoundationalist rejection and deconstructive critiques of first principles in part due to the philosophical distance between each being so great that it is impossible that an alternative conception of enquiry could be envisaged. Likewise, the Aristotelian and Thomistic conceptions of enquiry are directed toward the *telos* of truth through a systematic and rigorous process of dialectical exploration that share similarities with both historicism and the rationalism of the scientific method. In this case the latter is of interest to this section, and so in MacIntyre's own words (MacIntyre, 1990b, p. 38), the transition from dialectical to apodictic and necessary theses is established through a

> series of stages in the progress towards the *telos* of a perfected science. There will be dialectical conclusions of both initially in the first characterizations of the *archê/principium* of that particular science, which provides the earliest formulations of the *telos/finis* of its enquiries, and later on in the arguments which relate empirical phenomena to apodictic theses. There will be provisional formulations of such theses, which in light of further evidence and argument, are displaced by more adequate formulations.

It is at this point we start to see the role first principles play in MacIntyre's account of rational vindication that is predicated on truth and rational justification. The genesis of MacIntyre's thinking about the relationship between the ideas of dialectical encounters, intellegiability, rationality, truth and scientific enquiry can be found in "Epistemological Crisis, Dramatic Narrative and the Philosophy of Science" (MacIntyre, 1977). This earlier work is useful to understanding what MacIntyre means by his more mature conceptual account of first principles and its relationship with scientific enquiry. In particular, his critique of Karl Popper and Thomas Kuhn's scientific method and his subsequent criticism and revision of Kuhn's work represents a turning point in MacIntyre's thinking as it formalises his ideas about rationality which are developed further in *Whose Justice? Which Rationality?*, *Three Rival Versions of Moral Enquiry* and other later works. It is also where we encounter his notion of the "conversion experience" in which a theory or tradition transcends a rival theory or tradition in the progress towards truth in the same subject matter. Here we start to see MacIntyre's tradition-transcendent account taking form that characterises the transition from the dialectical enquiry stage of deciding between the claims of rival theories or traditions to the formulations of apodictic and necessary theses that conform to the essential features of truth. Such a mode of enquiry is essentially non-linear in the same way that scientific progress is not straightforward due to the doctrine of falsifiability possibly providing evidence or rational argument that contributes to its vulnerability and hence leads the theory to be either rejected, reformulated, revised, amended and so on in light of the new evidence or argument.[6] It is this rigorous process of dialectical enquiry found in scientific method that MacIntyre has in mind when he deploys the term "dialectical construction" as a means to demonstrate that the logical form of first principles must satisfy the conditions of truth and rational justification. For something to be called true for MacIntyre (1990b, pp. 44–45) means that it essentially expresses

> the truth of the intellect in relation to the objects, since insofar as they afford such expression they present to us actually how things are and cannot but be. Each type of predication of truth and each type of activity of rational justification stand in a relationship to others specifiable only in terms of their place within the overall teleological ordering of the intellect's activities of enquiry.

As such, the relationship between truth and rational justification is an essential feature of MacIntyre's theory of rational vindication. Not only does it presuppose a certain kind of intentionality in an overall scheme of teleological ordering of ascriptions of both truth and rational justification, but more importantly it provides a mode of enquiry which can transcend the limitations of particular and partial standpoints in a movement directed towards truth (or its limitations) and, where possible, provide rational justifications for why a particular standpoint should be rejected, revised, accepted and so on (MacIntyre, 2006). Thus, the role of first principles in MacIntyre's account of rational vindication is threefold: (i) members of a tradition need to be continually willing to engage in rigorous dialectical exploration by intentionally exposing the claims to truth and rational justification found in their tradition with rival and competing traditions to test for fallibility, falsifiability and rationality; (ii) if the test proves to be false, an openness to both considers the inadequacies of the preceding tradition or the superiority of the alien point of view in the dialectical construction of a new tradition which can claim truth; and (iii) if the test demonstrates superiority, then this demonstrates progress because certain incommensurabilities and limitations have been transcended and overcome in the rational vindication, that is, until such a refutation is forthcoming.[7] Consequently, in the next section I revitalise and extend MacIntyre's argument that a university is set up for constrained disagreement and conflict that also highlights the importance of reason or wisdom and its development because it enables us to see the interconnectedness and interrelationships among different forms of knowledge that can lead us to truth and the good.

Revitalising the university as a place for cultivating independent rationality and wisdom[8]

MacIntyre (1987) in his paper titled "The Idea of an Educated Public" provides an account of what he considers to be the demise of an educated public that shared a belief in the unity of rational enquiry through the following conditions: (i) shared forums of intellectual and political debate; (ii) shared standards used to judge an argument for victory, defeat and progress in enquiry; and (iii) shared canonical texts. Later in *Three Rival Versions of Moral Enquiry*, MacIntyre (1990a) outlines the reasons underlying this transformation. He argues that by the ninth edition of the *Encyclopaedia Britannica*, encyclopaedias served the function of both unifying a secular vision of the world and also providing a place of knowledge and enquiry within it; however, by the eleventh edition it no longer embodied the advancement of reason and became instead a pragmatically ordered collection of facts. Furthermore, during the period from the ninth to the eleventh editions (published in 1910) – a period of approximately 30 years – the nature and form of academic enquiry fundamentally changed due to the professionalisation and subsequent specialisation of each discipline area into narrowly focused disciplines for a select few. Not only did this result in the fragmentation and marginalisation of academic enquiry, but it highlighted how the educated public had been replaced by a heterogeneous set of specialised publics that no longer believed in the unity of knowledge, and essentially expelled the conditions by which the educated public flourished. This subsequent impoverishment has led to what MacIntyre refers to as the "post-Encyclopaedic university" that claims to be producing rational consensus on a range of matters but instead conceals and domesticates these conflicts because the nature of rational debate is unpredictable and hence would seriously undermine the perception trying to be portrayed that there is no dissensus on various matters of enquiry, particularly between rival traditions.

MacIntyre's views since *After Virtue* and beyond have been rather consistent concerning the lack of widespread consensus on a range of matters of substance, particularly issues crucial to the life of society. To MacIntyre, the liberal university spawned in the late 19th and early 20th centuries have not delivered on its promise of producing constrained rational debate and conflict that cultivate independent rational thinkers. Instead, MacIntyre (1990a, p. 222) responds to his own self-imposed questions of "What are universities for?" and "What peculiar goods do universities serve?" by arguing that:

> universities are places where conceptions of and standards of rational justification are elaborated, put to work in the detailed practices of enquiry, and themselves rationally evaluated, so that only from the university can the

> wider society learn how to conduct its own debates, practical or theoretical, in a rationally defensible way.

MacIntyre's (1990a, p. 231) central thesis is that today's contemporary university should be aware of its post-Encyclopaedic status and become places of "constrained disagreement, of imposed participation in conflict . . . [and as a result the] . . . central responsibility of higher education" is to initiate students into both enquiry and controversy. To bring this about MacIntyre goes on to argue that members of an academic institution will have to "play a double role" of both acknowledging that they belong to a particular tradition of enquiry and at the same time intentionally enter into controversy with rival traditions. The latter of the two tasks is of interest here in this section because to enter into controversy with rival traditions of enquiry serves *both* the task of exhibiting what is mistaken in the rival point of view compared to one's own tradition *and* tests the central theses advanced in one's own tradition with rational examination from one's opponent. MacIntyre acknowledges that his re-creation of the university as a place of constrained disagreement is a 20th-century version of the 13th-century University of Paris, where Augustinians and Aristotelians developed their own traditions of enquiry and engaged in systematic debate for mutual rational benefit. Although MacIntyre clearly advances his proposal as something which adherents of any tradition of enquiry would be attracted to, he is not unaware of the charge of "utopianism" ascribed to it. Later towards the end of the same chapter in *Three Rival Versions of Moral Enquiry*, where this proposal is made, MacIntyre responds to this accusation by arguing that those who are prone to "accuse others of utopianism" are deluded by a form of "pragmatic realism" which proscribes immediate and concrete results that are measureable and predictable. In his words (MacIntyre, 1990a, p. 234),

> They are enemies of the incalculable, the skeptics about all expectations which outrun what *they* take to be hard evidence, the deliberately shortsighted who congratulate themselves upon the limits of their vision. Who were their predecessors?

In response, MacIntyre calls for the re-creation of the university into what he refers to as a "postliberal university" which is set up to serve, more or less exclusively, the rational justification of one tradition of enquiry. What he has in mind here is the University of Paris in 1272, which fostered a form of Thomism and the University of Vincennes in 1968, which nurtured Nietzschean genealogists. Likewise, at the same time to ensure the progress and flourishing of rational enquiry in institutions, he calls for a "set of institutionalized forums" in which academic debate between rival traditions of enquiry can find expression, presumably through journals, societies, institutes and so on. Unfortunately, MacIntyre's proposals are underdeveloped toward the end of *Three Rival Versions of Moral Enquiry*, particularly the role of the "Great Books" approach to addressing the moral malaise of contemporary Western culture. In saying this, enough can be gleaned from this and other pieces of work to understand that to MacIntyre, debates within texts put students in "touch with the best that has been said, written, done, and made in the past", and as a result we are the inheritors of a "number of rival and incompatible traditions" with no way of evaluating what should be read or taught from an alleged neutral point of view (MacIntyre, 1990a, p. 228). Indeed, MacIntyre has been rather consistent about what he considers should be the aims of education from "Against Utilitarianism" in which he argues that the key role of education is to develop students with the ability to move from dependent to independent reasoners in the cultivation of rationality (or intellectual virtues). This is reinforced when he (MacIntyre, 1964, p. 21) states:

> the values of rational critical inquiry seem to me to stand in sharpest contrast to the prevailing social values. The task of education is to strengthen the one and weaken the other. Above all the task of education is to teach the value of activity done for its own sake. And this will only be partially done if it is restricted to rational inquiry in the narrow sense; for rational inquiry in the narrow sense will not remain rational. Unless the feelings too are sifted and criticized, the feelings are simply handed over to unreason. We have to allow those whom we teach to remake themselves through their activity. And if we do this, we shall be educating those who may in the end help remake society itself.

It is worth dwelling on this quoted passage about both the value of rational critical enquiry and the cultivation of rationality momentarily as this is a consistent theme in MacIntyre's corpus. For instance, his latest iteration of this theme can be found in *God, Philosophy, Universities*, where he (MacIntyre, 2009, p. 147) argues that the:

> aim of a university education is not to fit students for this or that particular profession or career, to equip them with theory that will later on find useful applications to this or that form of practice. It is to transform their minds, so that the student becomes a different kind of individual, one able to engage fruitfully in conversation and debate, one who has a capacity for exercising judgement, for bringing insights and arguments from a variety of disciplines to bear on particular complex issues.

Without a doubt this is no easy undertaking as it requires students of enquiry to find their way through a multiplicity of rival traditions of enquiry, disagreements, of disputed questions in the direction of finality of understanding. This disequilibrium, albeit existentially unsettling, according to MacIntyre is crucial in the cultivation of rationality.

MacIntyre's (1977) earlier thoughts on the cultivation of rationality can be found in the work titled "Epistemological Crises, Dramatic Narrative and the Philosophy of Science". It is probably one of his most powerful pieces he has authored because it utilises a narrative to highlight what an "epistemological crises" means, which he develops further in *Whose Justice? Which Rationality?*. In the former piece of work, the paradigm example he uses is the predicament of Hamlet arriving back from Wittenberg and the radical interpretative doubts of events at Elsinore and what schema to apply. As MacIntyre poignantly notes, Hamlet does not know what to regard as evidence, and so without knowing what to treat as evidence, he cannot decide which interpretative schema to adopt. In this case, the agent (Hamlet) is now faced with task of reconstructing a "new" narrative in which the criteria of truth, intelligibility and rationality have been undermined by what was formerly intelligible but now seems false in light of contravening evidence. To overcome this epistemological crises, a new intelligible narrative needs to be reconstructed that synthesises past schemes of beliefs with new forms of understanding and truth. It is not too difficult to tease out MacIntyre's account of rationality and its cultivation from these related remarks and other works. Clearly, MacIntyre is committed to truth and to acknowledging how things really are as opposed to how they may be from some limited point of view. In a sense, this regulative veridical ideal founded in first order principles of enquiry relegates an agent's original beliefs as provisional because "all understanding and all knowledge is acquired as dependent upon its own past intellectual background and is to that degree historical" (MacIntyre, 1964, p. 20). This tradition of rational enquiry is reinforced by MacIntyre (1994, p. 295) in his response to his critics, when he states:

> within every major cultural and social tradition we find some distinctive view of human nature and some distinctive conception of the human good presented as – *true*. And although these claims to truth are supported with different traditions by appeal to rival and often de facto incommensurable standards of rational justification, no such tradition is or can be relativistic either about the truth of its own assertions or about truth . . . and so . . . how can this ant-relativistic commitment to truth coexist with(out) an awareness of those facts about different and rival standards of rational justification.

As such, rationality coexists with truth as a regulative veridical ideal because it requires an agent to be open to the transformative possibility of reason radically undermining their original schemata of beliefs and at the same time recognises as possible that the future requires the forming of new schematas of belief. As MacIntyre sees it, the point and purpose of cultivating rationality as an agent can both establish truths and/or tests for truth with methods that either highlights error or vindicate truth, irrespective of the tradition they may belong to. Actually, MacIntyre's (1988) theory of rational vindication is a central feature of *Whose Justice? Which Rationality?* (see, e.g., Chapter X).

According to MacIntyre (1988), to overcome rival and incommensurable traditions of enquiry requires both a rare gift of empathy and an ability to understand alien points of view which have the potential to lead to an "epistemological crises". Extending on my earlier critique of this occurrence, the solution to genuine epistemological crises requires the development of new concepts and frameworks which meet three conditions: (i) a solution needs to be found to the intractable problem; (ii) the solution needs to provide an explanation of what rendered the tradition as inadequate or misleading (or both); and (iii) the defeated tradition is compelled to give up its allegiance to the tradition in crisis in the development of new concepts and frameworks (see Chapter XVIII titled "The Rationality of Traditions" from MacIntyre, 1988). Quite rightly, MacIntyre cautions that not all epistemological crises are resolved successfully and hence why some traditions either dissolve into two warring parties or become extinct. In saying this, it is important to note that when traditions are vital, they will experience from time to time conflict, and only when devotees of these same traditions recognise a crisis is progress possible between rival traditions.

It is at this point that I want to extend upon MacIntyre's conception of the university by drawing on the work of Jānis Ozoliņš (2012, 2013a, 2013b, 2015) who argues that the main aim of an education, particularly the learning that takes place within universities, should be concerned with the gaining of wisdom because it enables us to see the interconnectedness and interrelationships among different forms of knowledge that can lead us to truth and the good. It is important to note from the outset that Ozoliņš's work shares many similarities with MacIntyre's work as both are informed by and utilise the works of Catholic scholars, such as Aquinas, John Henry Newman, A. D. Sertillanges and Bonaventure to name a few. For instance, each agrees that a university education is more than the preparation of students for a profession or career. Rather, it should transform minds so that the student becomes a different kind of person. It could be argued that each aim to argue for the same end but come at it from different perspectives according to the literature engaged with. In this case, Ozoliņš (2013b) conceptual account of the intellectual life and its relationship with the development of wisdom is most relevant to this section. His conceptual account of the intellectual life as vocation requires some unpacking, and as a result due to space restrictions, I will limit my critique to the latter part of the article, which is concerned with bringing various specialisations into contact with many disciplines because knowledge of the truth and the good will not be found in just one specialisation. According to Ozoliņš (2013b, p. 72), to lead an "authentic intellectual life", we need to both "read around" our area of study so that we have "sufficient breadth" and "depth" in those areas which are closest to our area of study. He goes on to argue that a special place is reserved for philosophy "because without it, the sciences lose their direction and human knowledge lacks unity", and without theology, philosophy is not grounded. This does not mean that the intellectual life should consist solely of studying philosophy and theology in a narrowly specialised way, rather the point that Ozoliņš is arguing for concerns the essential unity of all knowledge and its interconnectedness and interrelationships with other bodies of knowledge found in other discipline areas, which the former (philosophy) can provide. Likewise, the idea that someone can work in an intellectual field without seriously considering what constitutes knowledge and hence how to determine truth in it seems nonsensical because once anyone starts enquiring into such matters, they are doing so from a distinctly philosophical point of view. In some respects, such views are a precursor to Ozoliņš's (2015) four interconnected and interrelated elements of knowledge that apply to an understanding of wisdom: (i) technical know-how and the art of applying skills and knowledge; (ii) education of our senses to be able to see things; (iii) being able to look deeply into questions and see them from a philosophical point of view and see the interconnectedness of values and ideas; and (iv) concern with our relationships with each other, our community and with the world in which we have our being (Ozoliņš, 2015, pp. 7–9). Ozoliņš makes the strong point that the first and second forms of wisdom are mostly catered for by university educations because they can be measured, quantified and reported on easily; however, the third and fourth forms of wisdom present a number of problems for the contemporary university. The main concern being is that the development of the third and fourth forms of wisdom are not contingent upon acquisition of more knowledge per se but dependent upon the formation of character and the inculcation of the intellectual virtues of disciplined study, an ongoing commitment to truth and the good. To a large extent, such an account has strong connections with older conceptions of education which are concerned with the formation of the human person. Not only is such an account contrary to contemporary assumptions of education but intentionally challenges the status quo of the university which views and distorts knowledge as a type of commodity that can be bundled and packaged as something that can be sold to clients (namely students) in their studies, so they can emerge at the end with skills X, Y and Z. Such a distorted view completely misses the point that universities were initially set up for the gaining of wisdom – this being that wisdom is not a skill or technical knowledge but more so an understanding of the interconnectedness and interrelationships of what is known and an appreciation that knowledge leads to truth and the good (Ozoliņš, 2013b). In a sense, Ozoliņš's (2015) third and fourth forms of wisdom share similarities with MacIntyre's (1977) conceptual account of epistemological crises because the reformulation of a new narrative leads agents to become aware of their original beliefs and why they may have been deceived but more importantly becomes committed to a rational – as opposed to ideological or distorted view of truth – in the reformulation of new beliefs. Without a doubt, this is no easy undertaking, nor is this something that most university students at a university seek out or are ready for as it is existentially unsettling. Understandably, this is a natural human response when our deep-rooted schematas have been put into question; however, I would argue that this is a crucial part of making these invisible schematas visible and come to understanding of alternative and rival traditions of enquiry. Likewise, I agree with MacIntyre that the place of the university within society has an important role to play as a site of constrained disagreement that cultivates rationality or wisdom. As a result, the cultivation of rationality and wisdom is concerned with human formation and the development of the intellectual virtues that is concerned with the interconnectedness and interrelationship of what is known and an appreciation that knowledge leads to truth and the good or what Ozoliņš refers to as the gaining of "wisdom" (Ozoliņš, 2012, 2013a, 2013b, 2015).

Conclusion

In the first section of this chapter I have argued that the place of theology and philosophy within both secular and religiously affiliated universities have either eliminated God from the curriculum altogether or restricted it to certain departments of theology. To make sense of the demise of theology and philosophy, particularly within the Catholic university, I drew on MacIntyre's critique of the contemporary university to outline the reasons why theology and philosophy should play a central and crucial role within a university education that claims to be professedly Catholic. Understandably, a Catholic university is very different from a secular university, not just because it advocates for the primacy of theology and philosophy within the curriculum that provides a Catholic view of the world, but more importantly it does not ignore contemporary moral conflicts and competing concepts of the good. As a result, part and parcel of a good education, particularly at a Catholic university (and I might add a secular university) is to test every point of view in a systematic fashion – as in Aquinas's own time – to see if it withstands rigorous scrutiny from rival points of view using first principles.

Then in the second section of this chapter, I turned my attention to MacIntyre's theory of rational vindication, which is concerned with the conditions of dialectical encounters between traditions as a crucial starting point in rational enquiry that is grounded in conceptions of first principles and standards of justification. To bring this about, MacIntyre argues that the role of first principles and their relationship with truth and rational justification is a sine qua non of rational vindication. What MacIntyre has in mind here is a systematic and rigorous process which transitions from dialectical to apodictic and necessary theses to establish truth with methods that share similarities with the scientific method to either highlight error or vindicate truth. I made the point that rational enquiry is an activity that is non-linear and dynamic in the same way that scientific theory is not straightforward due to the testing for fallibility and falsifiability in truth claims. In a sense, it is irrelevant whether an agent is faithful to, ambivalent towards or consciously rejects a tradition and claims to be outside it because those who are committed to truth will be governed by common standards of truth and hence why MacIntyre claims that truth is tradition transcendent.

118 Steven Stolz

In the final section of this chapter I revitalised and extended MacIntyre's argument that universities should be sites of constrained disagreement, participation in conflict and the initiation of students into both enquiry and controversy. Central to MacIntyre's account of university education is rationality and its cultivation. To bring this about, MacIntyre argues that contemporary universities should be more aware of the dissensus surrounding rival traditions of enquiry and as a result initiate students into both enquiry and conflict, particularly incommensurable forms of enquiry that lead to epistemological crises – the reason being that when epistemological crises are resolved, they bring about the reformulation of a new narrative that leads agents to become aware of their original beliefs and why they may have been deceived but more importantly become committed to a rational – as opposed to an ideological or distorted view of truth – in the reformulation of new beliefs. To MacIntyre, this is one of the aims of an education, particularly a university education. To further highlight how rationality can be cultivated, I called on the work of Ozoliņš, whose conceptual account of wisdom is useful to understanding how its development enables us to see the interconnectedness and interrelationships among four different forms of knowledge or wisdom – (i) practical knowledge, (ii) perceptual knowledge, (iii) philosophical engagement traditions enquiry and (iv) relational or community-orientated ways of seeing ourselves in the world – that can lead us to truth and the good. Ozoliņš makes the strong point that the first and second forms of wisdom are usually found in most university educations, but the third and fourth forms of wisdom and their development clearly present a number of significant problems that may be insurmountable in the fragmented and corporatised university that is concerned with the commodification of knowledge into products for sale to clients (students). It was argued that such a view completely misunderstands the point and purpose of a university as sites of gaining wisdom, particularly how such an understanding can lead to truth and the good. I made the point that this was not an easy undertaking, nor is this something that most students at a university necessarily seek out or are ready for as it is existentially unsettling, but if we are serious about the place of universities in society as sites of constrained disagreement, then we need to initiate students into enquiry and controversy that cultivates rationality or wisdom. I concluded that the cultivation of rationality is fundamentally concerned with human formation and the development of the intellectual virtues or what Ozoliņš refers to as "wisdom".

Notes

1 This list is indefinitely long, and so I will only list a few to highlight the diversity of ideological and philosophical positions which present us with no way of dealing with conflicts or how to successfully overcome rational impasses between competing traditions. Some worth noting are as follows: utilitarian justifications, contractual justifications, universal justifications and intuitionist justifications.
2 The analogy of the "smorgasbord" is apt in this instance to explain the moral reasoning of *choice*. The idea that agents can pick and choose according to how they feel nicely sums

up the approach often adopted by agents within contemporary culture when it comes to moral deliberations and associated actions.
3 According to Aquinas (1265–1274/1993), philosophers have much to learn from theology, particularly the incompleteness of their understanding and limitations of their mode of enquiry because they first need the gift of faith to understand God (see, e.g., the second part from the *Summa Theologica*). Of course, it goes without saying that philosophy can arrive at conclusions from its own mode of enquiry; however, when it comes to understanding the nature of God, "faith is the First Truth". I would also like to point out that this critique is not meant be about the differences between theology and philosophy as this would be contrary to the intention of this section and the role each play, particularly in the Catholic university.
4 Borrowing heavily from Newman's (1852/2009) account of a liberal university, MacIntyre's thinking about a Catholic university education is quite similar in the sense that it is concerned with the following: (i) pursuing knowledge for its own sake; (ii) broadly based student experiences (rather than narrowly specialised); and (iii) the development of independent rational agents. The latter of the three will be of interest in the second section of this chapter.
5 See MacIntyre's (1973) paper titled "The Essential Contestability of Some Social Concepts" for more detail about contested social concepts.
6 One of the criticisms leveled against MacIntyre's general project is the perennial charge of relativism. Just because theories and traditions may be provisional does not mean that truth is relative. In a sense, disputes between MacIntyre and his critics are not surprising and remind us that fundamental philosophical disagreements are essentially disputes about the why and the wherefore of first order principles and their relationship with truth and rational justification. Indeed, Haldane (1994, 1999, 2009) has consistently argued that due to an absence of any agreed set of norms or standards external to a tradition renders tradition-dependent accounts tradition relative due to the plurality of rationalities generated. The latter is one of his theses leveled against MacIntyre's general project. Unfortunately, further discussion of Haldane's criticisms would take us both too far afield and distract from the point and purpose of this chapter.
7 In *Three Rival Versions of Moral Enquiry*, MacIntyre (1990a) provides an example of his theory of rational vindication in the form of a demonstration of the rational superiority of Thomism against what he considers to be its two main rivals in the form of Nietzsche's genealogical subversions (post-Enlightenment irrationalism) and a form of Encyclopaedic rationality (Enlightenment rationality).
8 This section extends on some of the themes found in my paper titled "MacIntyre, Managerialism and Universities" (Stolz, 2016). Earlier versions of this paper were presented in Melbourne (Australia) at the following international conferences: Conférence Mondiale des Institutions Universitaires Catholiques de Philosophie (COMIUCAP) in July 2015 and the Philosophy of Education Society of Australasia (PESA) in December 2015. For other works on MacIntyre, see my paper (Stolz, 2015) titled "MacIntyre, Rival Traditions and Education".

References

Aquinas, T. (1265–1274/1993). *Summa Theologiae*. Tr. English Dominican Fathers. Ed. electronic. Charlottesville, VA: InteLex Corporation. (Original work published circa 1265–1274).
Haldane, J. (1994). MacIntyre's Thomist Revival: What Next? In J. Horton and S. Mendus (Eds.). *After MacIntyre*. (91–107). Cambridge, UK: Polity Press.
Haldane, J. (1999). Virtue, Truth and Relativism. In D. Carr and J. Steutel (Eds.). *Virtue Ethics and Moral Education*. (155–168). London and New York: Routledge.

Haldane, J. (2009). *Practical Philosophy: Ethics Society and Culture*. Exeter, UK: Imprint Academic.

MacIntyre, A. (1964). Against Utilitarianism. In T. H. B. Hollins (Ed.). *Aims in Education: The Philosophic Approach*. (1–23). Manchester, UK: Manchester University Press.

MacIntyre, A. (1973). The Essential Contestability of Some Social Concepts. *Ethics, 84* (1), 1–9.

MacIntyre, A. (1977). Epistemological Crises, Dramatic Narrative and the Philosophy of Science. *Monist, 60* (4), 453–472.

MacIntyre, A. (1981). A Crisis in Moral Philosophy: Why Is the Search for the Foundations of Ethics So Frustrating? In D. Callahan and H. T. Engelhardt (Eds.). *The Roots of Ethics: Science, Religion, and Values*. (3–20). London and New York: Plenum Press.

MacIntyre, A. (1981/2007). *After Virtue: A Study in Moral Theory* (3rd edn.). Notre Dame, IN: Notre Dame University Press.

MacIntyre, A. (1987). The Idea of an Educated Public. In G. Haydon (Ed.). *Education and the Values: The Richard Peters Lectures*. (15–36). London: University of London.

MacIntyre, A. (1988). *Whose Justice? Which Rationality?* London: Duckworth.

MacIntyre, A. (1990a). *Three Rival Versions of Moral Enquiry: Encyclopaedia, Genealogy, and Tradition*. Notre Dame, IN: Notre Dame University Press. (Gifford Lectures delivered at the University of Edinburgh in 1988).

MacIntyre, A. (1990b). *First Principles, Final Ends and Contemporary Philosophical Issues*. Milwaukee, WI: Marquette University Press.

MacIntyre, A. (1990c). The Form of the Good, Tradition and Enquiry. In R. Gaita (Ed.). *Value and Understanding*. (242–262). London and New York: Routledge.

MacIntyre, A. (1994). A Partial Response to My Critics. In J. Horton and S. Mendus (Eds.). *After MacIntyre*. (283–304). Cambridge, UK: Polity Press.

MacIntyre, A. (1998). Aquinas's Critique of Education: Against His Own Age, against Ours. In A. Rorty (Ed.). *Philosophers on Education: Historical Perspectives*. (95–108). London and New York: Routledge.

MacIntyre, A. (1999a). *Dependent Rational Animals: Why Human Beings Need the Virtues*. London: Duckworth.

MacIntyre, A. (1999b). How to Seem Virtuous without Actually Being So. In M. Halstead (Ed.). *Education in Morality*. (118–131). London: Routledge.

MacIntyre, A. (2006). Moral Relativism, Truth and Justification. In A. MacIntyre (Ed.). *The Tasks of Philosophy: Selected Essays*. Vol. 1. (52–73). Cambridge, UK: Cambridge University Press.

MacIntyre, A. (2009). *God, Philosophy, Universities: A Selective History of the Catholic Philosophical Tradition*. Maryland, MD: Rowman & Littlefield.

MacIntyre, A. and Dunne, J. (2002). Alasdair MacIntyre on Education: In Dialogue with Joseph Dunne. *Journal of the Philosophy of Education, 36* (1), 1–19.

Newman, J. H. (1852/2009). *The Idea of a University: Defined and Illustrated in Nine Discourses Delivered to the Catholics of Dublin in Occasional Lectures and Essays Addressed to the Members of the Catholic University* (2nd edn.). Ed. T. Iglesias. Dublin, Ireland: UCD International Centre of Newman Studies.

Ozoliņš, J. T. (2012). Newman and the Idea of a University. *Études Newmaniennes, 28*, 97–117.

Ozoliņš, J. T. (2013a). R. S. Peters and J. H. Newman on the Aims of Education. *Educational Philosophy and Theory, 45* (2), 153–170.

Ozoliņš, J. T. (2013b). A. D. Sertillanges on Wisdom and the Intellectual Life. *Res Disputandae, 19*, 60–77. (This journal was formerly known as *Ethics Education*).

Ozoliņš, J. T. (2015). Reclaiming Paedeia in an Age of Crises: Education and the Necessity of Wisdom. *Educational Philosophy and Theory, 47* (9), 870–882. Advance online publication. doi: 10.1080/00131857.2015.1035154.

Stolz, S. A. (2015). MacIntyre, Rival Traditions and Education. *Discourse: Studies in Cultural Politics of Education, 37* (3), 358–368.

Stolz, S. A. (2016). MacIntyre, Managerialism and Universities. *Educational Philosophy and Theory*, 1–9. Advance online publication. doi: 10.1080/00131857.2016.1168733.

7 Values as a basis for human education
Personalistic approach[1]

Wladyslaw Zuziak

The human being as a value (theoretical ethics)

Values that emerge in the contemporary world are often strange to us as Christians. They can even be repulsive or offend our feelings. Frequently we see that while man can discover himself as a result of values, he can also get lost because of values that are harmful to him. Thus, we begin to wonder if there are true values and apparent values, honest and dishonest values, or humane and inhumane values? In a world which is increasingly losing its humane traits, where, as in a Kafkaesque labyrinth, we feel increasingly lost and dehumanized, we still want to find something dear to us and to share those things which matter and the things we care about with others.

John Paul II was certainly correct when saying that it is necessary to continuously seek

> ever more consistent rational arguments in order to justify the requirements and to provide a foundation for the norms of the moral life. This kind of investigation is legitimate and necessary, since the moral order, as established by the natural law, is in principle accessible to human reason. Furthermore, such investigation is well-suited to meeting the demands of dialogue and cooperation with non-Catholics and non-believers, especially in pluralistic societies.
>
> (John Paul II, 1993)

However, as Christians, we need to consider what common ground we still have with "the rest" of the world. There certainly exist many global values recognized by most states and compatible with Christian teaching: freedom, equality, fraternity, solidarity, responsibility for the natural environment, pluralism, democracy, and tolerance.

Unfortunately, these values do not always contribute to the improvement of the world. Their meaning is changing, and what is even worse, they can sometimes be morphed into their opposites. As E. Pickert (2007, p. 182) points out, "[I]n the situation of the increasing aporia of values the only remaining possibility is to resort to the last taboo of a secularized society. Axiological and functional fusion of vital goods with dignity as the highest value becomes a necessity in such circumstances." Human dignity or, more precisely, the personal value of someone equipped with specific characteristics and dignity is commonly recognized in this world, so it may provide a starting point for discussing the world of values and everything that is important to a human being (cf. Spaemann, 2001, p. 10).

> Research indicates that the educational ideal has an essential dependence on values and human beings. Indeed, the educational ideal should stem directly from the analysis of the axiological character of human nature and those values that are indispensable for achieving a more perfect human existence and the optimal development of man in all important aspects and on all levels of his structure.
>
> (Cichoń, 1996, p. 93)

Of course, these issues are crucial for us as educators and for our students who we need to provide with the right "tools" for fruitful functioning and development in this world.

At the same time there is a broader perspective to see in the world of values in which we live and in which our pupils will live. Thinking about values always entails not only the question of our own value but also the value of the world in which people come to live. Not only do we begin to see how much we are still lacking the ideal, but we see more clearly how much the ideal in which we want to live is missing in the present world. So the process of improvement cannot be limited to the aspirations of an individual, but it must include the ability to determine his or her own existence in a broader, humanistic perspective as well as the ability to influence the reality to improve it as well. Similarly, the educational process cannot be limited to supporting the development of personal qualities, but by learning critical thinking it should help, or even encourage, active involvement in improving the world.

The most important value in Christian teaching is the human person. What does it mean that the human person is the highest value? It means that he is a goal in and of himself. His development is the most important factor. He cannot be treated as an instrument and the most important moral imperative is to respect the dignity of every human being. Therefore Christian understanding of humankind is in radical opposition to many of the proposals of the modern world that are trying to reduce man and rob him of his uniqueness. The question about the value of humans in those conceptions comes down to the question of the market price or value of the services which they can provide or their skills useful in the production of consumer goods. In this sense, people are treated instrumentally, as a tool, as one of many replaceable parts, which can be exploited as long as they are useful. It is difficult to accept this reduction of a person to a number of useful (for the market) functions.

What does it mean to be "a human being"? Every science focused on the human being, and especially "education . . . must from the outset provide an answer to the question: 'who is man?' "(Maritain, 1993, p. 135). Without an answer regarding "who" he is, what is his structure, what are his needs, or what his essence is, it is difficult for man to find his place and even more difficult to set educational goals.

What can we meaningfully say about the human being? Certainly that "he is more of a process, continuously becoming, and he is never a separate, self-reliant individual being" (Gogacz, 1993, p. 9), but rather he recognizes himself through life and experience. By experiencing, he becomes the subject and the object of cognition (Wojtyła, 1976, p. 7), and he discovers his own personal nature. Because of philosophical dialogue it becomes increasingly clear that

> the human being becomes a person only in relation to another human being as a person. An individual discovers his subjectivity and personhood in a dialogical relationship. As a result of this, he discovers not only himself but also the world of values on which he bases his whole axiological world and the quality of his life.
>
> (Pasierbek, 2002, p. 5)

It should be added that the dialogical situation is not restricted to a dialogue with another person, but it also applies to dialogue with past generations, one's own conscience, or with God. "The human being develops when he grows in the spirit, when his soul comes to know itself and the truths that God has implanted deep within, when he enters into dialogue with himself and his Creator" (Benedict XVI, 2009).

In these dialogues human beings discover, through the wisdom and beauty that is revealed to them, what they already suspected: the good that is in them and in the world, which encourages and demands perfection. This imperative is probably best expressed by the words: "So be perfect, just as your heavenly Father is perfect" (Mt. 5:48). Only someone who can live up to his full personal potential and direct his life is able to reach his full humanity.

Practical axiology

If we recognize the sanctity of the world and the sanctity of the life given to us, we must assume the human being to be of the highest value in the natural order and his relation with God to be the main source of his efforts to improve himself and the world.

Values show a human being the world of opportunities and motivate him to fulfill them. By following the good, revealed by these values, the human being becomes himself.

> The human being lives through various values, but in his deeds he makes good real. It is the goodness of his own being, the objective personal perfection. It is also the good of the world of which the human is a part. . . . And finally the good of God. . . . By sheer acting, man reveals the perfection of

the Creator. Christian ethics teach a man how he can and how he should attach the value of an objective good to his actions. The human being is aware of this good and directly experiences values. Man's whole moral life consists of experiencing values.

(Wojtyła, 1983, pp. 72–73)

Only with the belief that there are values that are embedded in the structure of the world can these values be sought in the world, found, experienced, and followed.

It must be added that the dynamic character of human nature and aspirations to become better reveal values that stimulate individual development. These values are real and authentic. However, there are also aspirations connected with false values. For example, young people, observing the difficult lives and sacrifices of their own parents, often aspire to have better lives. This is especially true of immigrant populations. When compared with their peers, many immigrant children often work harder academically and are more determined to strive to succeed. They are more systematic in their quest to achieve their full potential. They want to grow and improve themselves. In their quest to realize their goals, they display many inherently good values such as self-discipline, motivation, and hard work. However, if left without guidance and a spiritual direction, the quest for self-improvement can turn into a self-defeating struggle to be better than those around them, a struggle in which materialistic gains are of paramount importance and the "end justifies the means." In such instances good and true values such as motivation can be replaced by false values such as obsession, teamwork by cut-throat competition, and altruism by selfishness. Although seemingly successful on the surface, individuals who fall into this trap never really achieve pure happiness and self-realization. Only by following authentic values can a human being discover his own dignity, his own value, and, in consequence, integrate his pursuits and focus on what is of real importance in life

Many of peoples' aspirations are the result of promotion of excess in contemporary culture. They largely coincide with the ancient "hybris," crossing the measure, which in the belief ancient Greeks, everyone has and must find. The implementation of apparent values has long-term effects, causing stagnation, apathy, frustration, despair, and a sense of powerlessness and futility. It is worth considering whether current ideologies, leading to the modern diseases of civilization, are not too expensive for humanity and whether the discredited ideal of "success" is worth promoting. The negative effects of this ideal were thoroughly analyzed half a century ago by Thomas Merton (see Merton, 1982, p. 196), who pointed out that it was the source of conformism, achieving goals by illegal means, falling into routine, rebellious escape from the pattern, or falling into resentment, which manifests itself in an effort to redefine values and change their meaning (see Merton, 1982, pp. 203–204) or even deny the previous meaning.

Although this ideal does not promote the development of personality or even, what is increasingly evident, does not favor harmonious existence of community, it remains the last ideal of modernity, which still dynamically affects the imagination of members of democratic-liberal communities. The problem to solve is to find an ideal that could not only compete with the present one but also could effectively organize and utilize the potential inherent in people, the ones living nowadays and those who will come after us. This competitive ideal exists and has been trying to reach peoples' awareness since at least two millennia. Its last version was the conception of personalism,[2] formulated in the 20th century. In the broadest sense personalism is considered to be "any philosophy that defends the dignity of the human person in ontological, gnoseological, moral and social spheres" (Stefanini, 1969). Personalists want to express what is the most difficult to grasp by the scientific worldview and what is the most mysterious and unique in the human person. This broad intellectual movement, including not only Christian thinkers,[3] considers humans as the main value. All other values serve the development of the potential that is in all human existence.

In this concept the actualization of genuine values enables humans to discover their dignity, learn their own value, and in further consequence, achieve a state of spiritual maturity that allows them to integrate their own aspirations and focus on what is really important in life. Only someone who can live up to his full personal potential and direct his life is able to reach his full humanity. Each step toward authentic values leads to self-improvement, whereas implementation of false values degrades humankind.

It can be noted here that only someone who believes in the sanctity of the world and in the sanctity of the life offered him has he a solid basis for finding his own dignity and striving for perfection. Of course, this recognition of holiness does not necessarily have to be expressed in religious practices. There are many people, such as mystics, scientists-cosmologists, poets, climbers, sailors, and many, many others who recognize and feel the sanctity, for whom it is obvious, although it is not associated with participation in religious practices. On the other hand, there are many people who live in a world of interpretation, of cultural products, and in different virtual realities. Due to the weak or only mediated contact with the world, for them sanctity is far from being obvious. They also must face the problem of choosing the vision of the world and the definition of their role in it. To some extent this choice determines further choices. If individuals assume that humankind is a part of a mechanism or organism, it is difficult to find themselves in their uniqueness, their irreducible specificity, and they only find an excuse for their passivity.

If we notice the sanctity of the world and the sanctity of life given to us, we must accept that in the natural order, human beings are of the highest value, and their relation to God is the main source of the effort to improve themselves and the world. This highest value exists in the world and chooses different values. Through these choices and their consequences, humans recognize themselves, their own capabilities, and also they are able to recognize mistakes and eliminate them. We can risk the assertion that man does not know his nature as it is not fully given from the beginning of his life, but he knows or feels his desires in which this nature manifests itself. Undoubtedly, we must agree in this matter with existentialists L. Lavelle and J. P. Sartre, who say that "existence precedes essence." The question of who we are remains a mystery to us, which only life enables us to resolve. All previous attempts to determine the essence of personal being, although necessary, are only hypotheses that are verified by the choices we make in our lives and our self-identification caused by those choices. It is the world of values that allows such self-identification. Every thought and every decision, conscious or not, is a choice of values, and establishment of our own hierarchy of values that we choose and reject, which we are trying to accomplish right now or we decide to postpone. Those choices reveal our personal structure – our essence.

We recognize values gradually through desires, longings, experiences, and events that force us to make a choice.[4] Choices reveal the values we prefer and those we respond to. In accordance with these values, we make judgments, intuitive at first and then more and more conscious. We perceive ourselves, and the world, through the perspective of our values, and they allow us to comprehend it (cf. Ingarden, 1989, pp. 348–349). One cannot live without value judgments. Modern theories establishing reason as the supreme value, as a measure of every act of thinking or nonthinking, action, or inaction, make such judgments as well, according to their own understanding of normality. However, reason that lacks reference to the human being can often misguide us. One mistaken path is the attempt to eradicate some values from social life – stripping human beings from some sources that stimulate their desires and satisfy them. If the "higher" values are depreciated and repressed from public consciousness, they do not disappear, they still exist, but human unsatisfied desire to fulfill themselves through values causes a number of negative consequences. It seems that each of us has experienced such a tear between the pursuit of what we are expected to do by institutions, groups, and social patterns and the desire to pursue what we think is important, beautiful, good, and wise. The effects of such tears are a number of so-called diseases of civilization: frustration, depression, drug addiction, alcoholism, and others.

The diversity of values remains necessary for action and self-fulfillment as a subject. At the same time, it serves as a means of communication for a varying consciousness, leading to their unification or separation. The harmony of the world, the human world, is based on such diversity, which can trigger a full range of capabilities dormant in humanity. Their continuum, engaging and conditioning all values, allows some reference to other hierarchies of values. Perhaps it is not a precise communication, which is preferred by poor, formalized languages of science, but it is sufficient for making it possible to meet and have at least an intuitive feeling that there are some other goals just as important as our own. The lack of precision can even be an advantage because it allows the communication between people viewing reality from different perspectives, who indeed perceive the world differently but have common intuitions focusing on values. An example of such an intuitive "understanding" is a respect that is shown by their adversaries to people who consistently implement their desires. I believe it is justified to illustrate this thesis by the respect for Pope Francis among the representatives of other religions and non-believers.

Communication becomes impossible when the continuum of values is destroyed or when some of the values are depreciated and repressed from public consciousness. It is clear that this is happening nowadays. Contemporary attempts to reduce the world to lower values are the main causes of the disintegration of spiritual unity of the people participating in social communication. The limitation of this communication contributes to the lack of understanding by its participants – understanding of themselves and others.

One can easily notice that freedom provides the basis for finding one's place in the world of values. As T. Gadacz concisely put it, "[F]reedom always gives us reference to the world of values" (Gadacz, 1994, p. 138). Regardless of one's views, freedom remains one of the most important demands of people participating in social life.

Thanks to freedom, we discover the world of values, but also the world of values discovers our freedom for us. We see that we cannot avoid freedom, although today there are attempts to provide us with only a small range of actual possibilities under the guise of the freedom of choice or even to suggest false values. People are told: you are free, you can choose between many different kinds of cars, TV sets, and shoes. Each of them has some specific "value," like durability, low price, or the prestige offered to its buyer. In reality, however, the opportunities offered to us are small and are only intended to divert our attention from the real possibility of the freedom to pursue our own aspirations.

Therefore, to make use of freedom one also needs to understand it. It is impossible to grasp it in a speculative way as it manifests itself only through the action in which it is fulfilled in deeds and participation undertaken by man. However, it remains a gift from God, challenging us to become what we are. As the French philosopher L. Lavelle wrote, "[T]he relationship between our freedom and the freedom of God contains the mystery of creation" (Lavelle, 1995, p. 224). Due to this reference to God, authentic and full freedom enables one to learn the difference between things that are valuable and those that are convenient. It allows a distinction between created and genuine values found through creativity. This might be the source of an axiological intuition that allows us to recognize the very "height" of values (Ingarden, 1989, p. 341) and their importance to our existence. The ability to see their rise makes it possible to realize what is important to us and orders various values and their hierarchies. Here, of course, we are referring to internal freedom, the freedom "to" – the one that gives us the feeling of integration and gives meaning to our actions. Freedom "to" is the freedom of the person who wants to express himself through his actions, seeking its meaning. A person who continues to seek meaning is responsible not only for this meaning but also for others around him, trying to find this meaning together with him.

An internally free person, finding his "own" values and realizing himself through their implementation becomes authentic and finds his own value. At the same time, someone who has a feeling of self-worth feels responsible for his own development and those around him. He pursues an internal and external integration, compatibility of thoughts, words, and actions toward self-fulfillment. It must also be emphasized that only someone who has a sense of his own value can take an attitude of "openness" toward the world of other values and is able to find value in another human being. Such a person is ready to ask: how can you help me, and how can I help you? An example of this manifests itself each day at countless universities around the world. It is often the case that professors who themselves feel successful and self-fulfilled usually strive to promote and elevate their students through teaching, scholarship, and positive feedback and evaluations. On the other hand, professors who themselves are struggling with their own work are often the first ones to bring their students down, giving out poor marks and harsh criticism. They do not realize, however, that each poor mark given to a student is also an evaluation of their own work and ability as a teacher. Therefore, having a sense of self-worth is an important step toward what Karol Wojtyła called "integration of love *in a person* and *between persons*" (Wojtyła, 1976, p. 125). Only someone who has a sense of his own value, who has "reclaimed" his own dignity and has found the truth of his own existence, is ready to go "beyond himself," toward selfless love. What is more, as Benedict XVI emphasized,

> Truth, by enabling men and women to let go of their subjective opinions and impressions, allows them to move beyond cultural and historical limitations and to come together in the assessment of the value and substance of things. Truth opens and unites our minds in the *lógos* of love: this is the Christian proclamation and testimony of charity. In the present social and cultural context, where there is a widespread tendency to relativize truth, practising charity in truth helps people to understand that adhering to the values of Christianity is not merely useful but essential for building a good society and for true integral human development.
>
> (Benedict XVI, 2009)

Love, disinterested by definition, in the world of postulated and promoted self-interest is both desired and undervalued. On the one hand, everybody wants to love and be loved, but on the other hand, understanding of feelings, despite the centuries of philosophical reflection on this issue and 2,000 years of Church teachings, is alarmingly superficial and inadequate. The essence of Christian love and the lack of understanding of this essence were analyzed in the last century by, among others, Max Scheler and Erich Fromm. The current use of language reveals this lack of understanding. Love is sometimes conceived as a form of ownership: a girl wants "to have" a boyfriend, a woman – a husband, a man – a wife, that is, "to have" someone, not "to be" with someone. Such use of language suggests instrumental treatment of other human beings. In this kind of relationship, love does not grow out of compassion, mutual respect, or joy of the mutual exchange of gifts but from calculations and self-interest. It certainly is not the love described by John Paul II and Benedict XVI or called for by Pope Francis.

This love is also based on the concept of external freedom – freedom from responsibility for themselves and, above all, for other people. Freedom, giving importance to their own life, with responsibility for their own feelings and the feelings of others, for their own dignity and the dignity of others, has been replaced by the freedom of self-management and – if possible – the management of others. In this process of dehumanization of each other, we become treated as objects. Things, even those that are loved strongly, will never love us, whereas love is a largely mutual relationship.

The volume of this article does not allow me to go into detail on the cause of the escape from freedom, love, agency, and aspirations bigger than collecting and consuming. These issues have been repeatedly and thoroughly analyzed by many philosophers. It is worth it to remember what was written on the subject in the last century by Max Scheler, Erich Fromm, Martin Buber, and many others. The fact is that this escape remains an essential feature of modern culture.

Objectives and stereotypes shaped by the positivist utilitarianism and propagated in the last two centuries led to the flattening of the hierarchy of values and, consequently, to a significant reduction of human capacity of development, both in social and individual dimensions. This refers not only to the development but also to the perspective that would enable us to go beyond the more and more dehumanized social reality.

Here we recognize the first important goal of Christian education. It must focus on the liberation of the human being from the stereotypes of social behavior, stemming from the concept of external freedom. It must also give rise to dignity, showing the perspective of inner freedom, and teach how to use it. Values, such as dignity and freedom, are not gifts; they are tasks. They are to be discovered by both the teacher and the pupil. To call attention to dignity, to restore a sense of dignity, is the first step in finding personal being. That is why on this question John Paul II took a decisive, uncompromising attitude: "Because there can be no freedom apart from or in opposition to the truth, the categorical – unyielding and uncompromising – defence of the absolutely essential demands of man's personal dignity must be considered the way and the condition for the very existence of freedom" (John Paul II, 1993). Only free and dignified people are capable of "[a] love which thus causes each of them to be loved for himself, so that through him, and for him, other men will open their souls to the love of humanity" (Bergson, 1935, p. 81).

By finding their own freedom, dignity, and love, human beings are able to find communion with God, the world, and other people. We must remember here that everyone is different, and everyone realizes this based on various hierarchies of personal value. People can express themselves and find this communion through poetry, science, music, or helping others – the diversity of values is given so that all can choose their own path to self-fulfillment. There are many Christian values – not only love but also compassion, humility, and others that can prove useful on the way to self-fulfillment.

There are also many "worldly" values that can bring about self-realization. The previously mentioned global values such as liberty, equality, fraternity, solidarity, and environmental responsibility; local values such as motherland, the place with which we can identify, and friendship; and individual values such as justice, truthfulness, wisdom, diligence, honesty, and responsibility. All these values, as long as they are implemented with God and the universal values, center around the transcendental triad of truth, goodness, and beauty in perspective are Christian values, and what is more, they stem from the Christian tradition (Denek, 1996, p. 75).

Educational imperatives (applied axiology)

Christian pedagogy faces a great challenge: unless it is to repeat its own and others' mistakes, contributing to worsening the axiological crisis, it needs to develop its own educational methods, based on the Christian vision of humankind and Christian values.

T. Gadacz took up this important issue when he asked what Christian education should be like. Gadacz proposed a being-centred education that "is creative and dynamic, open, and always tends towards what is better, truer and more beautiful. Its purpose is the love of God, which is the source of all creativity" (Gadacz, 1991, p. 68). I fully agree with the author that the latter model is more suitable for not only Christian education but education in general. Especially, in my opinion, the purpose of education should be to awaken man to his dignity and to further his sense of self-worth. If we forget about dignity, then we forget about the purposefulness of human existence (cf. Wojtyła, 1994, p. 419). Who, or rather what, man becomes when he is deprived of this dignity can be seen in many spheres of social life – he becomes a function, a replaceable tool, anything but human.

Secular theorists also see the need of changing the educational model, as evidenced by their appeal:

> We want to teach how to adapt, how to operate in the world as it is, but also to warn against the dangers of conformity and to some degree encourage revolt. We want to nurture criticism and creative thinking, but also to shape the attitude of fidelity to reality or even 'the love of everything that exists.'
> (Radziwiłł, 1991, p. 12)

This appeal recalls the comparison, made by Z. Bauman, of the old education model and the one postulated by, among others, T. Gadacz. In the previous model, a human being was treated like a ballistic missile. The educators thought that it was enough to set goals and distance, determine the initial parameters, and fire the pupil into the world. However, nowadays we can see all too clearly that this model fits neither the modern world nor humankind.

The human being is more like a cruise missile that must change its course during flight, must learn all the time, update, and process data (cf. Bauman, 2007, pp. 219–220) but also must have a designated purpose. For Christians, this goal is of course an encounter with God, but we have to find the right path to this goal in our earthly existence. This is why we must educate for freedom and responsibility. The responsible approach is toward a life associated with freedom and creativity and open to values. Karol Wojtyła (1976, p. 213) emphasized this aspect, adding: "Man can be liable for his actions and experiences responsibility because he has the power to respond to values with his will." Freedom and responsibility are shaped alongside the pupil's character. This character cannot be forged by force but by showing positive examples and the opportunities that the beautiful, wise, and good world opens for us.

The contemporary world is affected by a crisis of will, as F. W. Foerster already recognized in the first half of the last century. "The desperate need for entertainment today, this passionate bustle, this feverish activity, are in fact nothing more than man's escape from himself and from a deeper knowledge of himself" (Foerster, 1938, p. 55). People make easier, more superficial choices, ones that bring quicker results, without sufficient care. They sell their souls for trinkets. They do not see much point in their own existence, and having lost respect for themselves, they do not see the possibility of enjoying their own inner life. This does not mean that they cannot get back this inner life and spontaneous joy or satisfaction with their own actions. It is necessary to show the person both his potential greatness and his vanity and to give him a choice. Young people quite often spontaneously choose striving for the better, and we need to support them in this. We need to "encourage" the hidden persons in them and help them develop self-awareness as well as assist them in identifying their own strengths, weaknesses, and goals; show positive examples of best practices; and strengthen their best traits of character.

Let us not ask our pupils to abandon the natural world — we cannot all be saints — but show them that with the divine perspective in mind, they can gain a sense of their own worth and can change the world with their power. This is not about some sentimentality but about supporting the strength of character — the kind that will resist false pretences in the modern world and will provide an example that one can be oneself.

This is another important "anti-system" purpose of Christian education. Contrary to widely accepted mechanisms of justifying all weaknesses, the point is that the pupil should not seek justifications for mistakes or look for an alibi for the belief that something is not possible, but he should responsibly learn from his mistakes and correct them, shaping his own character. Character is not a value of its own — it remains just a tool. It enables the agency of will, allows independence and perseverance in the pursuit of the undertaken objectives, and finally — together with a sense of freedom — it gives a sense of self-esteem.

It is beneficial to recall once again the pedagogical proposals of F. W. Foerster. Moral perfection is just a means for him, not the ultimate goal. The desire to learn the truth about oneself always returns the knowing subject to the source, to the truth of God, the image of what a human being is in his essential, personal structure (cf. Smołka, 2005, p. 40). It is important that man, who remains the greatest value in the natural world, does not lose sight of the highest good, which is God, because only with a perfect example in mind can he strive for perfection himself.

> God gives what in us is higher, the light of conscience, a clear sense of purpose and unwavering stability. He alone saves us from all the pettiness, from terrors and contradictions, typical of a being that only revolves around itself and tells us that our every action refers to something infinitely higher than what is human.
>
> (Foerster, 1926, p. 144)

God is the purpose present in every man, the hidden Good News that needs to be discovered.

Today's educational projects lack an ideal that would provide a point of reference for students and yet "[l]ife exists for a purpose, which makes it worthy of living" (Maritain, 1993, p. 140). Moving toward God by doing good is an ideal attractive to many. Foerster, as cited, assumed that by choosing a direction compatible with the God, a human being can act in accordance with free will. Then every step will be guided toward moral perfection. Foerster emphasized, however, that one of the "basic conditions for the formation of character is to know and to understand the values that constitute the educational ideal" (Cichoń, 1996, p. 103).

Here we come to another question, the question of competence. Our requirements toward pupils may be effective only when we deeply understand the values that constitute the educational ideal of Christianity. Only then will we be able to pass on this profoundly understood knowledge to others.

An educator is someone who helps the student discover the world of values while respecting his autonomy. Values must have an impact through their strength – but first they must be uncovered for the student, preferably through dialogue. One of the best teachers I have ever had, J. Tischner, emphasized this: "Education is work with a person – one who is in the state of maturation. Education creates a bond between the teacher and the pupil analogous to the relationship of paternity.[5] . . . Through the work of the educator truth is born in a human soul. Truth becomes human strength. The educator does not create this truth. . . . He only helps, joining the man's efforts with his own"(Tischner, 1981, p. 74). Referring to the thought of Levinas, Tischner tried to show that the relationship between a teacher and pupil has a special, dialogical nature and that through this relationship the pupil gains his identity.

It is also important for the educator to be the one who bears witness, presents, and represents values. Even the most knowledgeable teacher is not able to pass on his knowledge if he has no authority; it is not about the authority of the institution, his authority as a teacher or even a professor but personal authority, obtained as a result of the adequacy of the truth proclaimed by his own actions, which makes him credible. Such an exemplary educator, giving testimony of his own truth, experienced and understood, can reach everyone, even when talking to a great many people. John Paul II, J. Tischner, and Pope Francis, as well, were capable of this art. Jesus Christ was also such a teacher, uniting divine and human nature in one human person, the perfect model for us. Christ showed us the proper way of teaching. He did not denounce but gave the example of fidelity to his teaching through his own actions, through his courage and determination in the pursuit of being the Son, more and more worthy of God the Father. Of course, "Jesus Christ was not only a great model to follow as a person, but he was also an ethical lawmaker, preaching to the whole of humanity the will of God" (Wojtyła, 1991, p. 52). His teachings and the call to love have been the moral imperative for our culture and for every human being for more than two millennia. In a world that is turning away from His message, we see with increasing clarity that morality and natural law are not enough for us. We need love as well.

As emphasized by John Paul II: "You cannot understand who a person is nor what is his proper dignity, his vocation, or ultimate destiny. You cannot understand any of that without Christ" (John Paul II, 1984, p. 39). Therefore, our teaching must still refer to His wisdom, goodness, and love and to everything he has given us.

Christian call to wisdom, goodness, and love is valid not only for Christians themselves. These are universal values, without which our world will not survive. It is noticed by the representatives of Buddhism, Hinduism, or moderate versions of Islam. In the depths of the soul the lack of these values is felt by many agnostics, deists, and atheists – people who are often sensitive, seeking confidence and the sense of their existence. For them the divinity or sanctity of the world and humanity is an equally obvious starting point for their own pursuit of wisdom, goodness, and love, although it is expressed in different terminology.

Each of us believes in something – these beliefs are based on peoples' desire to live their lives as best they can. Some believe that to accomplish it that they need a world better than the one that surrounds us; others believe that they can improve the world. There would be no reason to want to improve something without a perfect model, which for religious people is God. Confronting with His perfection makes it is easier to see our own shortcomings and find incentives for development.

This better world needs to be built with joint effort. This can be done only by people who want to improve themselves, people having the character and the will that allow them to make wise decisions and good changes. Only those people who have self-esteem, people who are able to love and take responsibility for their own actions and for someone else's destiny, can become not only the creators of a better world but also role models for the masses who are confused in today's world. The goal of Christian education is not so much to shape but rather to free from traps, illusions, lies and the network of apparent values. Lost and overlooked opportunities of development should be restored. If it is noticed that human culture created not only materialistic determinism, but also many other models of the world with much greater potential for the development of humanity, then there is a chance that this development will occur.

In this project of education, every human being is important because each of us is a value. Everyone can become a role model for others; everyone can give an incentive and contribute to create the common good, forgotten in the utilitarian world, but still important for all of us.

Notes

1 This is an extended version of the paper first published as "Values as a Basis for Human's Education" in *Logos i ethos* 2/2014 (20), pp. 7–20.
2 The origins of personalism go back to the second half of the 19th century. G. Teichmüller (1889) described his conception of the defense of human person as "personalism."
3 Among different varieties of personalism, we can distinguish idealistic, panpsychic, dual, critical monadistic, phenomenological, pantheistic, relativistic, absolutist, and even atheistic personalism, represented by the English philosopher J. E. McTaggart (cf. Rogalski, 1950, pp. 559–591; Wojtyła, 1961, pp. 664–674).
4 The analysis of this process was performed by a French existentialist L. Lavelle (cf. W. Zuziak, 2012, chapter II.2).
5 Although J. Tischner mentions paternity as a metaphor that illustrates the relation between student and teacher; using maternity instead appears to be fruitful as well. It has a long tradition, started by Socrates, who famously compared education to the process of bearing a child. In a sense, the teacher, by developing the student, gives him a new life.

References

Bauman, Z. (2007). *Szanse etyki w zglobalizowanym świecie*. [*The Chances of Ethics in a Globalized World*]. Kraków: Znak.
Benedict XVI. (2009). *Caritas in Veritate*. Rome: Libreria Editrice Vaticana.
Bergson, H. (1935). *Dwa źródła moralności i religiii*. [*Two Sources of Morality and Religion*]. Polish transl. P. Kostyło and K. Skorupski. Kraków: Znak.
Cichoń, W. (1996). *Wartości, człowiek, wychowanie. Zarys problematyki aksjologiczno-wychowawczej*. [*Values, Man, Education: An Outline of the Axiological and Pedagogical Issues*]. Kraków: Wydawnictwo UJ.
Denek, K. (1996). Uniwersalne wartości edukacji szkolnej. [Universal Values of School Education]. *Dydaktyka Literatury*, 16, 69–90.
Foerster, F. W. (1926). *Chrystus a życie ludzkie*. [*Christ and Human Life*]. Polish transl. J. Mirski. Warszawa: Gebethner i Wolff.
Foerster, F. W. (1938). *Światło wiekuiste a ziemskie ciemności. Nasza współczesność z punktu widzenia wieczności*. [*Eternal Light and Earthly Darkness: Our Present Day from the Point of View of Eternity*]. Polish transl. Z. Starowiejska-Morstinowa. Katowice: Księgarnia i Drukarnia Katolicka S. A.
Gadacz, T. (1991). Wychowanie jako spotkanie osób. [Education as the Meeting of Persons]. *Znak*, 436, 67–68.
Gadacz, T. (1994). *Wychowanie do wolności*. [*Education for Freedom*]. In H. Kwiatkowska (Ed.). *Ewolucja tożsamości*. [*Evolution of Identity*] (38). Warszawa: Polskie Towarzystwo Pedagogiczne.
Gogacz, M. (1993). *Podstawy wychowania*. [*Fundamentals of Education*]. Niepokalanów: Wydawnictwo Ojców Franciszkanów.
Ingarden, R. (1989). *Wykłady z etyki*. [*Lectures on Ethics*]. Warszawa: PWN.

John Paul II (Pope). (1984). *Musicie od siebie wymagać.* [*You Must Demand from Yourselves*]. Poznań: W. Drodze.
John Paul II (Pope). (1993). *Veritatis Splendor.* Rome: Gregorian University.
Lavelle, L. (1995). *De l'Intimité Spirituelle.* [*Spiritual Intimacy*]. Paris: Aubier.
Maritain, J. (1993). Od filozofii człowieka do filozofii wychowania. [From the Philosophy of Man to the Philosophy of Education]. Tr. A. Ziernicki. In F. Adamski (Ed.). *Człowiek, wychowanie, kultura. Wybór tekstów.* [*Man, Education, Culture: Selection of Texts*] (61–79). Kraków: WAM.
Merton, R. (1982). *Teoria socjologiczna i struktury społeczne.* [*Sociological Theory and Social Structures*]. Polish transl. E. Morawska and J. Wertersein-Żuławski. Warszawa: PWN.
Pasierbek, W. (2002). Człowiek w dialogu ze światem. Wprowadzenie. [A Man in Dialogue with the World: Introduction]. *Horyzonty Wychowania, 1*, 5–7.
Pickert, E. (2007). *Godność człowieka a życie ludzkie. Rozbrat dwóch fundamentalnych wartości jako wyraz narastającej relatywizacji człowieka.* [*Human Dignity and Human Life: Division of the Two Fundamental Values as an Expression of the Growing Relativization of the Human Being*]. Polish transl. J. Merecki. Warszawa: Oficyna Naukowa.
Radziwiłł, A. (1991). O ethosie nauczyciela. [The Ethos of the Teacher]. *Znak, 436*, 10–15.
Rogalski, A. (1950). Personalizm katolicki. [Catholic Personalism]. *Życie i Myśl, 1*, 559–591.
Smołka, E. (2005). *Filozofia kształtowania charakteru. Fryderyka Wilhelma Foerstera teoria wychowania w świetle założeń personalizmu chrześcijańskiego.* [*The Philosophy of Character Development: Friedrich Wilhelm Foerster's Theory of Education in the Light of the Principles of Christian Personalism*]. Tychy: Maternus Media.
Spaemann, R. (2001). *Osoby. O różnicy między czymś a kimś.* [*Persons: The Difference between "Someone" and "Something"*]. Polish transl. J. Merecki. Warszawa: Terminus.
Stefanini, L. (1969). Personalismo. [Personalism]. *Enciclopedia filosofica.* [*Encyclopedia of Philosophy*]. Firenze, 4, 1511–1531.
Teichmüller, T. (1889). *Neue Grundlegung der Psychologie und Logik.* [*New Foundation of Psychology and Logic*]. Breslau: Wilhelm Koebner.
Tischner, J. (1981). Wychowanie. [Education]. In J. Tischner (Ed.). *Etyka solidarności i homo sovieticus.* [*The Ethics of Solidarity and Homo Sovieticus*] (77–81). Kraków: Znak.
Wojtyła, K. (1961). Personalizm tomistyczny. [Thomist Personalism]. *Znak, 13*, 664–674.
Wojtyła, K. (1976). Osoba: podmiot i wspólnota. [The Person: Subject and Community]. *Roczniki Filozoficzne, 24*, 5–39.
Wojtyła, K. (1977). *Znak, któremu sprzeciwiać się będą.* [*A Sign Which Will Be Contradicted*]. Poznań – Warszawa: Pallottinum.
Wojtyła, K. (1983). *Elementarz etyczny.* [*Ethical Primer*]. Lublin: Antyk.
Wojtyła, K. (1991). Ocena możliwości zbudowania etyki chrześcijańskiej przy założeniach systemu Maxa Schelera. [Evaluation of the Possibility of Building Christian Ethics on the Basis of Max Scheler's Approach]. In T. Styczeń, J. W. Gałkowski, A. Rodzinski, A. Szostek (Eds.). *Idem, Zagadnienie moralności* podmiotu [*The issue of the agent of morality*]. Lublin: KUL.
Wojtyła, K. (1994). *Osoba i czyn*, Lublin: KUL.
Zuziak, W. (2012). *Aksjologia Louisa Lavelle'a wobec ponowoczesnego kryzysu wartości.* [*Axiology of Louis Lavelle in the Face of the Postmodern Crisis of Values*]. Kraków: WAM.

8 The promise and risk of the university

Secular education in Paul Ricoeur

Jecko Bello

Refiguring the secular

Secularism is characterized by Ricoeur (1974a) as the 'the emancipation of most human activities from the influence of ecclesiastical institutions' (p. 182). If such is the case, in a way, it may exist only on the level of, or upon intervention of, (specific) institutional configurations. He characterizes this form of secularism as the secularism (only) proper to the state (as an institution) – it is defined in terms of abstention. Using the French Constitution as an example, Ricoeur further elaborates that in this form of secularism,

> the state neither recognizes nor supports any religion. This is religious freedom in negative, the price being that the state itself has no religion. This goes even further; this means that the state does not "think" in these terms, that it is neither religious nor atheist. We are in the presence of an institutional agnosticism.
>
> (Ricoeur, 1998, p. 128)

Thus, secularism is not universal. However, the non-universality of secularism is only true de facto. That is, insofar as it is only brought about by (political) institutional decision-making as exemplified in constitutions, it remains to be proper only for a specific community. This necessarily affirms that a state can be secular or non-secular. This exemplifies that there is an element of 'ambiguity,' 'contingency,' or 'irrationality' in the sphere of institutions. However, the universality of secularism can be justified as de jure – that is, insofar as secularism, in the level of institutions, is brought about by the unfolding of scientific progression of universal political rationality or humankind's accumulation of sociopolitical experience (technics). In other words, secularism, though not completely reduced, may now be thought of an effect of technical civilization.[1] In effect, this speaks of the depth of the phenomenon. It shows that secularism can be thought of as something that operates in the way we, consciously or not, willfully or not, understand society. To properly analyze the de jure universality of secularism, we survey how secularism operates.

Secularism constitutes what Ricoeur (1974a) calls as 'the elevation of man to the position of autonomous subject of history' (p. 183). That is, it is operating without due influence from some nonscientific rationality. This is 'characterized by the erasing of the distinction between the spheres of the sacred and the profane' (Ricoeur, 1974a, p. 183). This is made possible through, in an ironic manner, creating specific spaces where the sacred can only be expressed. This characterizes modernity as such. However, one must not easily fall into temptation in saying that secularism per se had caused the relegation of the sacred to a specific space in society. For it would be tantamount to say that institutional decision-making had full control over the totality of the unfolding of the universal political rationality. If it is true that politics (characterized as decision-making) is irreducible to the a-personal progression of the technical, it should be true likewise that what is technical is irreducible to what is political. It can easily be thought of as either the effect or the cause of the grand narrative of the progression of technics.[2] It is worth noting, further, that the progression of the scientific spirit and its tools paved the way to the dispersion of spaces in society; that is to say, since there are already developments in different disciplines, the same demands to be *emplaced* at the expense of the other, such as religion. The rise of technico-secular civilization did not merely relegate the place of religion but also limited its participation in human affairs. This is not only true between technics and religion; as we can see now, the diaspora of discipline from a mother discipline is symptomatic of the effect of the progress of technics. From this, the technico-secular age is an age of specialization – that secularism is indeed secularization.

In secularization, Ricoeur illustrates that external relations prevail over internal ones.[3] When one says external, it means that the manner in how people relate with one another is only at the level of the distinction of spaces. It is merely organizational and functional (Ricoeur, 1974a, p. 183).[4] The danger in this mode of existence is the reduction of what is ethnic, religious, or cultural to the grand operation of secularization. It assimilates traditions and beliefs to the general machinery of industry. A perfect example of this is the creation of 'human zoos,' wherein traditions of indigenous people are perfectly sedimented for industry. In allusion to Nietzsche's pronouncement through the madman, the 'churches have now turned to be the tombs and sepulchers of God.' In this, what is existential-ethical becomes fragmentary if not lost. Meaning, both as sense and direction, is absent, for it relies heavily on the constant unfolding of technics. In the age of secularism, the anonymity of relations due to the emphasis of what is external makes the human being anonymous likewise (cf. Ricoeur, 1974a, p. 183). This constitutes the subtle destruction not only of traditional values that constitute us but also what Ricoeur (1965) calls as the 'creative nucleus' of civilizations from which people interpret life itself (cf. p. 276).

Confronted with the tug-of-war between technico-secular assimilation and value preservation of cultures, we see now the crucial role of institutions. In this point, it is important to invoke that Ricoeur observes that the universal character of political technics or rationality is the movement of localized political regimes from a dictatorial to a more democratic form. It deserves our attention, for it would help us refigure secularism in institutions since institutional decision-making is based as well on the unfolding of universal history. In fact, in this juncture, one can argue that secularism proper to the state can only exist on the basis of the current democratic political rationality – that the de facto exists because of the de jure. Thus, Ricoeur illustrates a second form of secularism – the secularism of confrontation – one that is proper to 'civil society.' That, close to Habermas's notion of 'post-secular' society,

> there exists an active, dynamic, polemical secularism, tied to the spirit of public discussion. In a pluralistic society such as our own, opinions, convictions, professions of faith are freely expressed and published. Here, secularism seems . . . to be defined by the quality of public discussion, that is to say, by the mutual recognition of the right of expression, but even more so, by the acceptability of the arguments of others.
> (Ricoeur, 1998, p. 128)

Since plurality of convictions, cultures, and beliefs that every society encounters had penetrated political technics, abstention – institutionalized negative secularism – can now be interpreted as a means toward the configuration of a democratic plane for public discussion. As one can see, the negative paves the way for the positive – that is to say, secularism, in this level, should not be seen as an amputation of religion or any culture from public discussion but, quite remarkably, as a sort of legitimization of their participation. In this level of interpretation, one can see that democratic political organization is built upon 'mutual recognition.' It is on this point that one can properly place the notion of religious freedom and its necessary effect – that is, as Ricoeur (1974b) opines, that 'religion figures as cultural power, a recognized public force; and the freedom which one claims for *it is the more legitimate as religion is not its exclusive beneficiary*' (p. 402, emphasis is mine). Religion, in other words, becomes a resource. Appropriating Hegel, Ricoeur (1998) recognizes 'that the political is grafted on the socio-economic order (or what we call today "civil society"), which [is] designated by [Hegel] the name of "external state" ' (p. 97, brackets are mine). This is the 'anteriority' proper to the political per se (cf. Ricoeur, 1998, p. 102). This has been shown by different communities who found their forms of government to some founding act or principle, such as the 'Divine Right of the King' in monarchies. However, the multiplicity of cultural and religious resources for socio-political legitimacy already speaks of the 'ambiguous' side of institutions, especially when these convictions are institutionally recognized with equal weight. Despite this, Ricoeur (1965), speaking of theology, affirms that this is 'the very ground where theology (religion) may be propagated – the ground of ambiguity' (p. 92, parenthesis is mine).

Though the universal presence of this phenomenon remains to be ambiguous, it remains to be considered that in this re-figuration of secularism, cultures are now given space not to erase – to provincialize – their significance in the public sphere but to bring them back to the social. Ultimately, this dialectical relation of abstention and confrontation – even of the political technics and institutions – is close to Ricoeur's appropriation of Hannah Arendt's idea that what is presupposed in the vertical, institutional and administrative aspect of power is the primal horizontal element which speaks of people *wishing to live together, people wanting to coexist.*

The relationship between the secularism of abstention and secularism of confrontation does not undermine their distinctive characters. Such relationship remains to be a dream for Ricoeur. The realization of such a dream is what he calls as the dawning of the 'third secularism;' and he finds the intervention of institutions – specifically educational institutions – to be the promising, yet risky, ground for such actualization (cf. Ricoeur, 1998, pp. 134–135).

Why both a 'promise' and a 'risk'? Though institutions are informed by the unfolding of scientific rationality, the fundamental character of decision-making adds to the acceleration of technical civilization (especially to political technics). In the same manner, political decisions can affect the manner how cultures interact to what is technical. This is exemplified by the 'conquest' of the West and the liberation movements of 'colonies' that have cultural identity as their motivation. As one can see, the resistance (or consent) of colonies speak of a reaction to a political schema informed by political technics. That is to say, one can see that an approach of a culture to the technical has institutions for its medium. It is in this position that one can see that there is indeed a 'promise' and 'risk' in institutions in relation not only to cultures but also to the speed of progression in technics taken in the general sense. The progress that speaks of the *rational* nature of technics and the ethos that speaks of the *surrational* character of cultures are interwoven in the *irrational* ambiguity of politics (cf. Ricoeur, 1965, p. 94).

Thus, from the reasons aforementioned, my approach in analyzing education will be through its institutionalization.

The universe of the word: *institutionalizing* the university

'Ricoeur's reflection on the university has been ignored by most of his commentators despite the fact that there is much food for thought there' (Garcia, 1997, p. 103). Three reasons come to mind why understanding the university is relevant. First, it is an institution where its primal task is the pursuit for truth. Thus, it is an institution that engenders an integrative character with fewer constraints compared to other social institutions. Second, emanating from the first, it will allow us to reevaluate secular institutions – seeing the university as a microcosm of the society. Third, the university itself resides in an ambiguous position between civil and state responsibility – the university, as such, is a point of intersection.

For Ricoeur, contrary to the prevailing functionalist view of the university as totally serving capitalist cultural order, the legitimate task of the university is research – the pursuit of truth. Citing Jaspers: 'It is the right of humanity as humanity that the search for truth be pursued somewhere without constraint'

(Garcia, 1997, p. 104). This signifies the place of the school as an expression of the secular state's abstention from cultural and religious convictions to secure 'freedom of education' (Ricoeur, 1998, p. 129) – that is, a freedom *from* the dictates of religion and cultures. However, it is not only the state that is solely responsible for the education of its citizens, but the civil society is also charged to do the same. As Rawls would put it, education is one of the primary social goals which has to be distributed. From this, 'freedom of education' may mean how different cultures and religion have the freedom *to* choose the manner of educating their members. Truly, the school itself resides in ambiguous ground between the civil and political.

However, the search for truth demands to be elaborated further. From the context of secularism of confrontation, it has been affirmed that there can be other bearers of truth. This does not merely call for the sincere recognition of difference in the university. As observed in the progression of technics, the same spirit for research effects a form of diversification itself as exemplified further by the rise of specializations. However, to passively succumb to the functional segregation of sectors that characterizes the present progress of industrialization compromises the vision of coexistence in institutions, in this case, the university community. This is tantamount to loss of meaning or nihilism of a society as a society. It is in this juncture where one can bracket the nature of university.

'The university is the universe of the multiple powers of language in the moment of the communication of speaking' (Ricoeur, 1955, p. 193; as cited by Reagan, 1996, p. 22).[5] This preeminence opens up an aspect that the university is a place for confrontation. As such, diversification does not, and should not, necessarily imply atomization. The aforementioned diversification provides the presupposition for potent ground for the configuration of networks of confrontation (critique) that must be present in institutions. This implies further a refiguration of traditional pedagogical relation in education, for if what is preeminent in the university is communication, 'the university must imbue itself with the "egalitarian spirit by promoting the sharing of the right to the word' (Garcia, 1997, p. 104). Without effacing the distinctive roles of teacher and student, Ricoeur (1991) deems it necessary 'to incorporate the maximum of reciprocity in the non-symmetrical relation' of teaching' (p. 382). The student and the professor share the same responsibility in the search for truth.

From these considerations, I now propose the extent by which the university, as an institution, may realize its mission as a universe of the word through characterizing the manner confrontations may operate and their necessary effects. First, I will elaborate on the configuration of the field of confrontation itself. Second, I will present the manner of how such confrontation can engender a reinterpretation of cultures, and its effects, faced with the threat of assimilation of existing technico-secular civilization. Third, I will discuss the necessary effects of confrontation-reinterpretation of cultures with other cultures. The last point will be using translation as a paradigm. All of this is in view of the effort not to reduce education to professional training or to the tendency of elitism in humanities.

Critique in and of institutions

The institutional order is the sphere of confrontation – of difference. In emphasizing the recognition of difference, Ricoeur (1998) asserts that in education, 'we must [also] prepare children to be good participants in discussion; they have to be initiated into the pluralistic problematic of contemporary societies, perhaps by listening to opposing arguments presented by competent people' (p. 286). However, this training in discussion should not submit itself to 'an apology of difference for the sake of difference; [for] this will finally make all difference indifferent which will render all discussion useless' (Ricoeur, 1992, p. 288). Though Ricoeur (1998) admits his 'obsession for reconciliation,' wherein vestiges of Habermasian style of argumentation that assumes unlimited confrontation can be seen (cf. p. 61), he partially reproaches such a model of argumentation for its movement toward *purification* a la Kant since 'it makes impossible the contextual mediation without which the ethics of argumentation loses its hold on reality' (Ricoeur, 1998, p. 286). The movement toward purification divests the subject from its cultural background that constitutes it. This is tantamount to the elimination of the subject himself, and to eliminate the subject is ipso facto to eliminate the wish to live together, the idea of institution itself. Therefore, beliefs, cultures, or convictions, in their passage through institutions, rather than being eliminated in the progress of discussion, are carried to the level by what Ricoeur (1992) calls as 'considered convictions' (p. 288). Ricoeur further warns us that the resurgence or hospitality of/to cultures to the public sphere should not be thought as a form of 'tolerance' that merely puts up with what one cannot prevent. Ricoeur (1998) exhorts that tolerance should mean 'the genuine acceptance of diversity; the recognition . . . of the fact that there can be bearers of a share of the truth . . . [that] there is an idea that the public space is a the place of cohabitation of several religious traditions' (p. 64). By this, discussion, argumentation or confrontation now becomes the critical agency operating at the heart of convictions. As such, if education trains people for discussion, the university necessarily engenders a universal character that is *regulative* rather than *constitutive*. What is institutional clearly becomes mediatory.

Springing from such a notion of confrontation as critical agency, the university – to deserve the name institution – cannot be exempted in its own operation. Coming from the May 1968 revolution of students, Ricoeur affirms that oppositionists to the system – their dissidence – must be incorporated in the university framework. One must not be blinded by an either/or position between the university and protesters lest we allow ourselves to succumb likewise in choosing between rigid conservatism and radical nihilism. The university should be 'supple, flexible, and repairable . . . to allow it to exist anew, to [always] bring out the conditions of a contract' (Garcia, 1997, p. 106). In the 'egalitarian spirit' that moves the university, the students, professors and administrators are equally capable in questioning even the very end of its own ambiguous – thus fragile – role as an educational institution.

Technics and cultures: adaptation and dis-adaptation

This is where the institutional takes a crucial role in its arbitration of confrontation. It has been shown that the ascent of technics constitutes likewise the subtle destruction of what is cultural. Such being the case, it is easy for one to propose that the only way to preserve culture is to resist assimilation of technics – a form of 'dis-adaptation.' This proposal may only beget cultural provincialism – even elitism – which engenders further a complete detachment from whatever is real. However, it bears emphasis that against this nostalgia for traditions, adaptation is also necessary, for it is only through playing with the development of technics that cultures can survive and be relevant. In this tension, we find the important role of education. As Ricoeur (1965) opines: 'Education, in the strong sense of the word, is perhaps only the just but difficult equilibrium between the exigency for objectification [globalization in technics]–that is, adaptation – and the exigency for reflection and un-adaptation (pp. 213–214).

The task of education is to exercise a permanent arbitration between technical universalism and the personality constituted on the level of ethico-political plane (cf. Ricoeur, 1974a, p. 291). 'The University should be *par excellence* the seat of this pulsation' (Ricoeur, 1965, p. 218). The tension, mediated by institutions, allows us to broaden the concept of progression that is, up to this point, only proper to the unfolding of universal rationality. In here, progress becomes inclusive not through assimilation but in such a way that while institutions recognize the development of industrialization, they open up likewise spaces for the strengthening of certain values by reinterpretation *through* the current technico-secular rationality. The movement is not only a preservation of the cultural. Elsewhere, Ricoeur emphasizes the 'ethico-mythical nucleus' that moves great civilizations and defines how people value existing technical developments that characterize secularism. Evidently, technical civilization affects the cultural. However, if cultures define how people value what is technical, then it is logical to suppose that values likewise may affect the direction of the progression of technics. This does not deride the unfolding of universal progression, though valuation of technics (and its particular direction) depends on a particular community. This merely contributes to the mounting of universal civilization in its de facto aspect. In this way, one can see, in a sense, the unified humanity that subsists in the plurality of cultures.

Interpretation of cultures: 'the paradigm of translation'

The critical function opens up to a formative (*poetic*) one. To enrich further the critical function of institutions, and thus reinterpretation of cultures, one may look at how certain cultures – despite their singularity – confront other cultures. In this point, Ricoeur wagers that despite the fact that languages (as symbolic expressions of cultures) are multifarious, they can at least communicate – a wager, therefore, on translation (cf. Ricoeur, 1974a, p. 282).[6] A guiding thought on translation, to be faithful on Ricoeur's critique of constitutive universalization, would be that there can never be a perfect translation as to identification – humanity is always *after Babel*. Ricoeur (2006) affirms that 'a good translation can aim only at a supposed *equivalence* that is not founded on a demonstrable *identity* of meaning. An equivalence without identity. This equivalence can only be sought, worked at, supposed' (p. 22).[7] Without going to the complexity by which Ricoeur had explored translation as a problem of linguistics, for the purposes of this paper, I will present the ethico-poetic implications of translation. This is just to show the necessary effects of interpretation-translation of cultures. Thus, translation, for the purposes of this article, remains to be a paradigm.

Facing the problems inherent in translation, Ricoeur liberally employed as guiding points Freud's vocabulary of the 'work of mourning' and 'work of recollection' in view of Antoine Berman's *The Test of the Foreign*, the *desire* to translate. To put it in broad strokes, the work of mourning speaks of the renouncing the very ideal of perfect translation, while the work of recollection affirms that despite this, something can still be translated. Submitting to the impassable gap between the peculiar and the foreign, 'translation is [still] inscribed in a long litany of "despite everything"' (Ricoeur, 2006, p. 18). Why the incessant *desire* to translate? The work of mourning in renouncing the ideal of perfect translation gives the translator a vague hope of unification and, in hope, a form of responsibility. Translation, as such, becomes a task. Picking from Walter Benjamin, Ricoeur (2006) proposes that ' "perfect language", the "pure language" . . . appears as the *messianic horizon* of the act of translating, secretly ensuring the convergence of the idioms as they are taken to the pinnacle of poetic creativity' (p. 16, emphasis is mine). This grounds the *passion* to translate – poetic creativity. As Ricoeur (2006) observes in the great translators, that it is

> the *broadening* of the horizon of their own language – together with what they have all called formation, *Bildung*, that is to say, both configuration and education, and as a bonus . . . the discovery of their own language and of its resources which have been left to lie fallow.
>
> (p. 21)

This allows us to appreciate the foreign in relation to one's culture. It shows the limits of our own culture. Truly, through translation, the foreign remains to be a test of limits. However, the foreign is not only *extralinguistic* in relation to our own; as Ricoeur proposes, there is always an element of otherness in sameness – a translation *intra-linguistic*. This can be seen in the manner how one can say *in other words* what one has just said in the same language (cf. Ricoeur, 2006, p. 25). The test of the extralingual foreign in translation allows us to have a proper grasp of what is foreign in us. '[T]he task of *outer* translation finds its correspondence in the work of *inner* translation' (Kearney, 2007, p. 153). In this way, 'to understand is to translate' not only the other but also the other in oneself. This is precisely why the paradigm of translation gives us a *formative* promise and task through what Ricoeur (2006) calls as *linguistic hospitality* – that 'where the pleasure of dwelling in the other's language is balanced by the pleasure of receiving the foreign word at home, in one's own welcoming house' (p. 10), where the house that a guest has entered changes. If translation engenders understanding tested by the foreign, it is clearly poetic.[8] This is similar to Ricoeur's hermeneutic arc, where in understanding translating, a dialectical relation of sedimentation (inventory) and innovation (invention) takes place.[9]

Education and the humanity of man: a recapitulation

As we can see, it is in understanding, interpreting and translating cultures where the 'revolutionary' par excellence can be found – where it draws humankind ahead by projecting not only what is to come in technics – that characterizes secularism but, more importantly, since it is in cultures where the 'creative nucleus,' which moves humanity that his meaning resides, his meaning (cf. Ricoeur, 1974a, pp. 79–80). But how?

To recapitulate, one can see the pervasive nature of the university seen as an institution whose function is to be a critical agency in the heart of convictions – why it can properly be called as an educational institution that truly makes man understand the totality of his being and his humanity. In broadening the lines where confrontation may happen, we have broadened likewise reinterpretation. In effect, we have widened the lines of efficacy of the university. Other than reinterpreting cultural values or convictions through the current technico-secular condition, we have furthered such through showing the effect of reinterpretation-translation in the arena of values themselves. Thus, if cultures, convictions, religions, and the like arbitrate the value of technics, their reinterpretation will necessarily affect the speed – or even direction – of the progression of technics. Through the *mediation of institutions, to emphasize this, the rule remains to be critique*. This is precisely why education plays an important role in society. Educational institutions are loci where man is situated, and thus integrated, in his totality – technical, political, and cultural. It is in this way that it can be of service to the society. Thus,

> [t]he university does a disservice to itself when it simply and passively succumbs to the demands of industrialization. It also does a disservice to society when it fails to realize its being linked in the crisis of society, when it fails to show its solidarity with society by paradoxically putting into question the legitimacy of the present socio-cultural order.
>
> (Garcia, 1997, p. 105)

And how is it possible? Not only through educating a professional but also a person of culture. Cultures are sources of legitimization of sociopolitical orders through the mediation of what is institutional. In this way, the university is clearly an institution.

Elsewhere, Ricoeur (1974a) presents that humanism – the study of culture to be precise and due recognition thereto – 'is the *preliminary* conviction that through material determinations of a civilization. . . . [M]an chooses himself, and that *choice can be clarified and reflected on* and thus improved by the activity of a man of culture' (p. 75, emphasis is mine). We have seen the contours how the clarification, and reflection of convictions are brought about through forms of reinterpretation. However, as affirmed in translation, it remains to be a wager. This is precisely why the conviction starts always as *preliminary*. Ricoeur exhorts that this does not mean that such work on culture is bereft of rationality, which can predict development.

> It can only be presupposed with conviction as a *rational belief* in the possibility of existing historically as a man of culture. [A postulate] that the existential possibility of your activity is tied to a certain structure of history just as your existence has *power* over history.
> (Ricoeur, 1974a, p. 76)

It has been affirmed that cultures – the person of culture to be precise – stand as the critics of other cultures and of secularism. The orientation of culture as a limit-critic of world operations and other cultures is its own efficaciousness (cf. Ricoeur, 1974a, p. 79). The person of culture does this through rooting itself to his or her own traditions – knowing its values, symbols and expressions – in the hope of clarifying his or her own. This does not take away the relevant position of the man of culture in directly participating in what is political and technical. In fact, since he struggles in understanding the 'ethico-mythical kernel' or 'creative-nucleus' that orients the movement of civilization – the very resource, though dispersed, of the political – he or she opens up the horizon of possibilities where humanity may be realized. Again, it is only a horizon, it is limited, and it can only be hoped for. However, it is in this humble acceptance that the humanity of man is dignified and begins to be elevated. When one recognizes that '[m]an is man when he knows that he is *only* man' (Ricoeur, 1974a, p. 86).

Postscript: between theology and philosophy

It is erroneous to think that the reconstruction of secular society and education had placed religion in a privileged position. In its welcoming as a *cultural force*, it is likewise tasked to live up to actualizing this force. One can already see the contours that religious education may embody. Ricoeur (1965), in refiguring the Christian meaning of history, exhorts that 'it is the hope that secular history is also a part of that meaning which sacred history sets forth, that in the end there is only *one* history, that all history is ultimately sacred' (p. 94). If it indeed engenders unification, it must not only ambition to be in singularity with other cultures but permeate as well what unifies humankind – technical civilization.

In *Lectures on Ideology and Utopia*, Ricoeur showed how the utopian function of religion is effective in understanding-critiquing existing societal orders. Moving beyond Habermas, he pointed out that we can no longer think of religion as something that involves itself in the production of an ideology for the current configuration of secular society; the fetishism of functions and commodities, as affirmed earlier, can already work on its own. However, religion is not totally bereft of an ideological role; it is just that such function of the religious has been superseded by the ideological role of the market, science, and technology that characterizes the secular as such. In the present course of things, one can observe that whatever religion, taken on its own, can no longer justify existing systems of society. It is humbled. Despite this, religion's function as utopia should not easily be dismissed. Because of the mythico-ethical force that moves its history – projecting an eschatological hope for meaning – religion 'functions as utopia to the extent that it is a motivation nourishing the critique (of ideologies)' (Ricoeur, 1986, p. 231, supplement is mine). In other words, the emigration of ideologies from the religious did not merely humble the latter but, more importantly, did impose a task on it that must be endeavored. There will always be dangers in positing a utopia. We have to shatter the pretension of the utopian vision for absolute meaning to draw out fully the essence of eschatology – that eschatology adds meaning to history by adding the final meaning.

Unification can only be hoped for, but it is this hope that a certain 'responsibility' is imposed on the religious. The responsibility can be characterized through Ricoeur's three leitmotifs, wherein one can refigure a theology of the secular city, namely: '*disenchantment of nature, desacralization of politics, deconsecration of values*' (Ricoeur, 1974a, p. 185). These suggest readily the *corporealization* of theology – that for it to really be value laden, it must be *with* the world. In fact, Ricoeur had affirmed in his observation of American universities that the attitude of theology to integrate in its discipline the technical, political, and perhaps, diversified values had accelerated secularism in America. This allows us to see that religions are not always readily reduced to 'fundamentalism' (Ricoeur, 1998, p. 58) given the proper effort for integration that instead of thinking secularism as a threat, it should be confronted as a challenge for innovation. As such, the political rationality of mutual recognition does not only allow the religious to participate in the public sphere; much more, it imposes a task on the religious to be open in understanding-critiquing whatever is mundane and empirical and, ultimately, itself. As such, the religious pertains to a *disposition*.

How is this disposition characterized? Following Geertz, this dispositional function of religion makes it go beyond the opposition between the traditional and the Modern . . . that it provides a form of *stability* for the religious (cf. Ricoeur, 1986, pp. 260–261). Thus, to truly be innovative, religion, confronted by the technico-secular, agnostic, and even atheistic society, must be reinterpreted into a religion beyond morality, beyond the idea of accusation and consolation, of indoctrination to be precise. In giving up the hold that a supernatural moral order that accuses and consoles what is mundane, religion is brought back to the order of its founding principle – revelation of the Word. Following Heidegger, Ricoeur, in a highly theological tenor, asserts that language becomes something more practical than means of communication with others and of mastering things. This reduction of the Word to a tool is the same with what Heidegger reproaches as the forgetting of Being – that is, the distinction of Logos and Being, which encapsulated Western metaphysics. Rather than thinking that we speak a word, the Word speaks to us – we 'dwell' in the Word. 'Dwelling' in the Word does not make us fly from reality; in our dwelling or answer to the Word, we are called to be poetic. 'In its most inclusive sense, "poetry" is that which roots the act of dwelling between heaven and earth, under heavens and on earth, in the power of the Word, of discourse, of saying' (Ricoeur and MacIntyre, 1969, p. 97). This is the act of creation (*poiesis*) itself – of *gathering* together. This is religion's return to its fundamental impetus, *hearing* – faith.

Few words, if philosophy is the love to search for the ultimate meaning of reality – the truth – it can only thrive through dialogue with other disciplines, which in their own right, have something to say about reality. Philosophy is no longer the handmaid of theology; philosophy finds itself along the *in between*. It has no proper territory; it is within arts, sciences, literatures, and even theology. Philosophy is the *hospitable* effort to unify despite the originary situation of diaspora. For philosophy to be truly philosophical, it must strive to be the concatenation of dispersed disciplines, including theology.[10] In this way, the 'paradigm of translation' can properly be applied. As Richard Kearney (2007) characterizes Ricoeur's hermeneutic philosophy, it is 'both a philosophy *of* translation and philosophy *as* translation' (p. 147).

Notes

1 What I have in mind is *Foucault's (2010)* characterization that the French Revolution is an important event not only because of how it affected the course of French history but also of how it was seen by spectators from neighboring countries.

   Further, not to make the discussion longer than what is necessary, the propositions of this paper are based on Ricoeur's three-layered analytic reading of civilizations. It is through this analytic reading of Ricoeur of the levels of civilization where one can justify or, at least, see the universality (breadth) and depth of secularism. In broad strokes, Ricoeur analyzed civilization in three different yet overlapping levels, namely – 'industries/technics,' 'institutions,' and 'values.' Firstly, 'industries/technics' refers to the progression and geographical expansion of the scientific spirit – concretized in the creation of tools available to humankind (printing press, the Internet, trains, and the like); this is otherwise named as humankind's 'accumulation of experience.' Such characterization is very telling since it may include likewise the expansion of ideas from which we interpret or view reality – such as secularism itself. This characterizes the abstract universality of humankind. Secondly, 'institutions' refers to the 'historico-geographical complex which covers a certain domain and which although it may not be rigidly defined, has its own peculiar vital cores and zones of influence.' In contrast with the level of 'industries,' one can see that this level speaks already of an active element insofar as it shows an effort of a certain community to direct its own history. As such, humankind can be deemed to be plural. Thirdly, 'values' refers to the 'concrete valorization of such as could be apprehended in the attitudes of men in regard to other men – in work, property, power, temporal experience, etc.' (*Ricoeur, 1974a*, p. 279). 'Values' represent the sum total of all goals of certain community, which necessarily direct their attitude that decides upon the meaning of the tools themselves. In other words, it is 'the very substance of the life of the people' (*Ricoeur, 1974a*, p. 280). In this level, civilization is in the plural. These layers are distinct from each other, but the assertion of one necessarily affects the other, for example, erosion of cultural values (values) through the progression of globalization and secularism (industries).

2 In 'Christianity and the Meaning of History,' Ricoeur posits that the 'uninterrupted progress of mankind is the aftermath of secularization.' However, this is only true insofar as secularization had accelerated the progress of technics – that is, it does not necessarily follow that secularism per se is the reason for the uninterrupted progress of humankind. In 'Urbanization and Secularization,' Ricoeur points out that the city phenomenon accelerated the effects of secularism *despite* the fact that secularism itself is the cultural condition of the mobility and efficiency of the city.
3 According to Ricoeur, through the effacing of the distinction of what is sacred and profane, the city accelerates the secularization despite the fact that secularization is the condition that makes the phenomenon of the city emerge. This is similar to Ricoeur's distinction between the *socius* and the *neighbor*.
4 Cf. As Ricoeur further affirms, 'Organization is equally a secularization factor in that it requires social roles to be presented as essentially lay roles. As they become less and less "orders" with traditional and sacral foundation, i.e. institutions with mystical origins in the depth of the past, they become more and more functional relations, non-traditional, claiming no origin and no ultimate meaning. They are directed toward the future more than they are rooted in the past; they make no claim to give ultimate meaning to life; they are disjoint and not encompassing.'
5 While Ricoeur had used several terms to express his view of addressing conflicts, namely – discussion, argumentation, communication, and even critique – I will be using 'confrontation' as a term for it to be consistent with how Ricoeur had used it exploring the role of the schools in secular society. Much more, the term 'confrontation' readily suggests conflict.
6 'What we have said just said about language – signs – is also valid for values and the basic images and symbols which make up the cultural resources of a nation' (*Ricoeur, 1965*, p. 282).
7 The same essay of Ricoeur appears in *Reflections on the Just* (*Ricoeur, 2007*). Note that this is Ricoeur's effort to recognize and transcend the theoretical alternatives in translation, namely: 'either the diversity of languages is radical, and then translation is impossible by right, or else translation is a fact, and we must establish its rightful possibility through an inquiry into the origin or through a reconstruction of the *a priori* conditions of the noted fact' (*Ricoeur, 2006*, p. 14).
8 Ricoeur had used the paradigm of translation as a model for hermeneutics.
9 In Latin, *invenire* means both discovery and invention.
10 This is similar to Giorgio Agamben's characterization of philosophy: 'In a sense philosophy is scattered in every territory. It is always a diaspora, and must recollected and gathered up.' In Giorgio Agamben, 'What is a Paradigm?' lecture at European Graduate School, August 2002. Retrieved from: http://www.egs.edu/faculty/giorgio-agamben/articles/what-is-a-paradigm/v.

References

Agamben, Giorgio. (2002). *What Is a Paradigm?* Lecture at European Graduate School. Retrieved from: http://www.egs.edu/faculty/giorgio-agamben/articles/what-is-a-paradigm/

Berman, Antoine. (1992). *The Experience of the Foreign: Culture and Translation in Romantic Germany*. Tr. S. Heyvaert. New York: SUNY Press.

Foucault, Michel. (2010). *The Government of the Self and Others, Lectures at the Collège de France, 1982–1983*. Tr. G. Burchell. Ed. F. Gros. Gen Ed. F. Ewald and A. Fontana. English Series Ed. A. Davidson. London: Palgrave MacMillan.

Garcia, L. (1997). On Paul Ricoeur, the University, and the Philippine Culture. *Karunungan, 10, 14*, 102–114.

Kearney, R. (2007). Paul Ricoeur and the Hermeneutics of Translation. *Research in Phenomenology, 37*, 147–159.

Reagan, Charles. (1996). *Paul Ricoeur: His Life and His Work.* Chicago and London: University of Chicago Press.
Ricoeur, Paul. (1955). La parole est mon royaume. *Esprit. Nouvelle série, 223* (2), 192–205. Réforme de l'enseignement. February.
Ricoeur, Paul. (1965). *History and Truth.* Tr. Charles A. Kelbey. Evanston, IL: Northwestern University Press.
Ricoeur, Paul. (1974a). *Political and Social Essays.* Col. and Ed. David Stewart and Joseph Bien. Athens, OH: Ohio University Press.
Ricoeur, Paul. (1974b). *The Conflict of Interpretations: Essays in Hermeneutics.* Ed. and Intro. Don Ihde. Evanston, IL: Northwestern University Press.
Ricoeur, Paul. (1986). *Lectures on Ideology and Utopia.* Tr. George H. Taylor. New York: Columbia University Press.
Ricoeur, Paul. (1991). *Lectures 1. Autour du politique (La couleur des idées).* Paris: Seuil.
Ricoeur, Paul. (1992). *Oneself as Another.* Tr. Kathleen Blamey. Chicago: University of Chicago Press.
Ricoeur, Paul. (1998). *Critique and Conviction: Conversations with Francois Azouvi and Marc de Launay.* Tr. Kathleen Blamey. New York: Polity Press.
Ricoeur, Paul. (2006). *On Translation.* Tr. Eileen Brennan. With an introduction by Richard Kearney. London: Routledge.
Ricoeur, Paul. (2007). *Reflections on the Just.* Tr. David Pellauer. Chicago and London: University of Chicago Press.
Ricoeur, Paul and MacIntyre, A. (1969). *The Religious Significance of Atheism.* New York and London: Columbia University Press.

9 Teleological pragmatism
A MacIntyre-shaped university education

Philip Matthews

One of the central themes of this book is the role that philosophy plays for a renewed understanding of education in the formative process of individuals and of civil society. This theme has been pivotal to the thinking and writing, over several decades now, of one of Notre Dame's most influential philosophers, Alasdair MacIntyre. Like many contemporary philosophers, MacIntyre painted his view of what a moral education ought to look like using the original canvas that Aristotle provided two millennia ago. However, there is an important difference between Aristotle and MacIntyre over ethics and the limits of philosophy. MacIntyre remains frustrated that there is no consensus in moral philosophy over how moral enquiry ought to be conducted. Aristotle, on the other hand, thinks that one ought not to expect too much precision when it comes to deliberation about moral issues.

This essay will show why MacIntyre's pessimism about moral philosophy is overstated. First, by illustrating why a lack of epistemological consensus among philosophers is not in and of itself particularly problematic, and second, by showing how MacIntyre's triadic relationship among *narrative*, *practice*, and *tradition* can be utilized in a university setting. Many universities have schools of teaching, law, and medicine, and this is evidence in and of itself that a practical consensus already exists over the internal goods of education, justice, and health care. A MacIntyre-shaped approach to a university education can therefore build on this teleological agreement to show how a practice-based education might be implemented in a Catholic university setting.

Alasdair MacIntyre and incommensurability

MacIntyre's pessimism over the dire state of moral philosophy began early and continues today to be deep, unrelenting, and frustrating. In 1965, in an essay titled "Imperative, Reasons for Action and Morals," MacIntyre was already suspicious about the emotivist status of contemporary moral ought-type statements.

> Suppose a society in which there was a moral ethos of either the Aristotelian or the Judaeo-Christian kind or perhaps some synthesis of the two. . . . But

now suppose also that belief in the divine law declines and that the formerly shared conception of what human well-being consisted in is no longer shared. Nonetheless, people continue to use the word 'ought,' but in new contexts. Sometimes, indeed, they ask skeptically whether they ought to obey the divine law or whether one ought to preserve former conceptions of human well-being. The 'ought' of these inquiries clearly cannot be either of the 'oughts' previously current. When 'ought' is now used to reinforce an imperative injunction, it will add little but emotive force.

(MacIntyre, 1965, pp. 513–524)

In 1977 MacIntyre gives his frustration a name in an essay titled 'Epistemological Crises, Dramatic Narrative, and the Philosophy of Science.' Unlike Descartes, whose own epistemological crisis led him to advocate only ideas that were both clear and distinct, MacIntyre connects the concept of an epistemological crisis with both personal and communal relationships. A personal epistemological crisis occurs, for instance, when the *foundations* on which a loving relationship is *grounded* becomes untenable, perhaps when one partner betrays a trust. A communal epistemological crisis occurred among astronomers early in the seventeenth century when they were confronted by evidence from Galileo's telescope, evidence that *undermined* their geocentric worldview. Let me pause here to highlight the Cartesian foundationalism that remains embedded in epistemological language. In the previous few sentences I used terms that clearly belong to the Modern mind-set, *foundations*, *grounding*, and *undermining*; are all terms that presuppose that the Cartesian 'bottom-up' approach to knowledge is the only one available to us.

In 1979 MacIntyre published an essay with another provocative title 'Why Is the Search for the Foundations of Ethics So Frustrating?' Here he argues that ethics is frustrating because the types of debates we have are unsettlable at one level and interminable at another.

> Premises about moral law with a Thomistic and biblical background are matched against premises about individual rights that owe a good deal to Tom Paine, Mary Wollstonecraft, and John Locke; and both are in conflict with post-Benthamite notions of utility. I call such premises incommensurable with each other precisely because the metaphor of weighing claims that invoke rights against claims that invoke utility, or claims that invoke justice against claims that invoke freedom, in some sort of moral scale is empty of application. There are no moral scales . . . hence moral arguments terminate very quickly and in another way are interminable.
>
> (MacIntyre, 1979, pp. 16–22)

MacIntyre's conclusion is that moral arguments can never be settled conclusively because there is deep incommensurability over the premises from which moral conclusions are drawn. Furthermore, even when consensus is advocated in any particular tradition, it does not last because the tradition has to keep updating its epistemic grounding to avoid throwing the baby out with the bathwater when faced with an epistemological crisis.

In 1981 MacIntyre published *After Virtue*, the first of a trilogy of books that deal with incommensurability problems associated with rival moral traditions. The hypothesis that MacIntyre (1981/2007, p. 2) advances in *After Virtue* is that the language of morality is in a 'state of grave disorder.' In the chapter titled *The Nature of Moral Disagreement Today and the Claims of Emotivism* MacIntyre (1981/2007, pp. 6–7) explains that the disorder in moral enquiry can be seen in the adversarial mode of contemporary moral debate: militarism *or* pacifism, a right to bodily integrity *or* abortion is murder, justice as a form of socialism *or* justice as defined by the free market. MacIntyre argues that there are three characteristics of the disordered state of contemporary moral debate. First, using a concept adapted from the philosophy of science, MacIntyre suggests that rival moral arguments are conceptually incommensurable.

> Every one of the arguments is logically valid or can be easily expanded so as to be made so; the conclusions do indeed follow from the premises. But the rival premises are such that we possess no rational way of weighing the claims of one as against another. . . . From our rival conclusions we can argue back to our rival premises; but when we do arrive at our premises argument ceases and the invocation of one premise against another becomes a matter of pure assertion and counter-assertion.
>
> (MacIntyre, 1981/2007, p. 8)

The second characteristic of the disordered state of contemporary moral debate according to MacIntyre is that each of the moral discussants thinks that his or her respective propositions are based on impersonal rational argument:

> [T]he appeal is to a type of consideration which is independent of the relationship between speaker and hearer. Its use presupposes the existence of *impersonal* criteria – the existence independently, of the preference or attitudes of speaker and hearer, of standards of justice or generosity or duty.
>
> (MacIntyre, 1981/2007, p. 9)

MacIntyre's third characteristic is that the conceptually incommensurable premises of rival arguments all have diverse historical origins. MacIntyre says that some appeal to 'Aristotle's account of the virtues,' some to a Marxist 'concept of liberation,' some to a Lockean concept of rights, and some to a 'view of universalisability' following Kant or the 'moral law,' following Aquinas (MacIntyre, 2007, p. 10). Moral enquiry has evolved into discrete forms of emotivism, by which he means evaluative moral judgment based on expressions of personal preference, attitudes, or feelings. For MacIntyre (1981/2007, pp. 11–12), emotivism represents the current state of moral decay because it accurately describes what happens when philosophers advocate for impersonal and objective criteria for moral action. What flows from this advocacy is 'nothing but expressions of preference, expressions of attitude or feeling, insofar as they are moral or evaluative in character' (MacIntyre, 1981/2007, p. 12).

In 1988, MacIntyre encapsulated his distrust about the idea of moral progress in the title of the second book in trilogy, *Whose Justice? Which Rationality?*. Here again he argues (MacIntyre, 1988, p. 6) that the attempt to replace authority with reason should be rejected because the Modern appeal to principles that is 'undeniable by any rational person' and independent of 'social and cultural particularities,' is a mistake since neither the Enlightenment thinkers nor their successors could agree on what these undeniable principles are. MacIntyre contends that philosophy of the Modern period failed to see how connected moral arguments are to the historical tradition from which they emerge. The Modern concept of an impartial observer is fictional, according to MacIntyre, because a moral agent is already embedded in a social milieu in which the boundary conditions of rational argument have been defined in specific ways. He further claims (MacIntyre, 1998, p. 198) that the "Modern attempt to remove concepts such as truth and reality from their teleological framework deprives these terms of the only context in which they can be made 'fully intelligible and rationally defensible.'

> What the Enlightenment made us for the most part blind to and what we now need to recover is . . . a conception of rational enquiry as embodied in a tradition, a conception according to which the standards of rational justification themselves emerge from and are part of a history in which they are vindicated by the way in which they transcend the limitations of and provide remedies for the defects of their predecessors within the history of that same tradition.
>
> (MacIntyre, 1988, p. 7)

Because of this historical disconnect MacIntyre further contends that

> Modern academic philosophy turns out by and large to provide means for a more accurate and informed definition of disagreement rather than progress toward its resolution. Professors of philosophy who concern themselves with questions of justice and of practical rationality turn out to disagree with each other as sharply, as variously, and so it seems, as irremediably upon how such questions are to be answered as anyone else.
>
> (MacIntyre, 1988, p. 3)

In 1990 the third book, *Three Rival Versions of Moral Enquiry*, MacIntyre restates the problem in even starker terms. *Three Rival Versions* is based on his Gifford lecture series (MacIntyre, 1988), and MacIntyre uses the series as a launching pad for another attack on moral philosophy. He argues that in the hundred years since the death of Gifford, it is hardly controversial to claim that disciplines such as astronomy and chemistry have made significant and continuing progress. However, one cannot say this about natural theology, according to MacIntyre

(1990, pp. 9–10), particularly as far as the foundation of ethics is concerned because there is no agreement over what rational progress within the study of ethics ought to be. The level of disagreement exhibited by the Gifford contributors is symptomatic of a lack of consensus in academic philosophy in general over what constitutes moral argument.

> [D]ebate between fundamentally opposed standpoints does occur; but it is inevitably inconclusive. Each warring position characteristically appears irrefutable to its adherents; indeed in its own terms and by its own standards of argument it *is* in practice irrefutable. But each warring position equally seems to its opponents to be insufficiently warranted by rational argument.
> (MacIntyre, 1990, p. 7)

The conveners of a philosophy conference in 1991 were probably even more surprised, or perhaps a little perturbed, by MacIntyre's keynote address, 'What Has Not Happened in Moral Philosophy.' The conference theme concerned the demise of abstract principles and the renaissance of tradition, but MacIntyre's address contended that nothing of the sort has happened. In spite of numerous philosophers agreeing with the epistemological problems he presented in *After Virtue*, namely, that moral claims can only be intelligible from within the 'particularities and contingencies of historical movements,' MacIntyre (1992, pp. 193–199) contends that little has changed in the way practical rationality is currently portrayed.

The final nail in moral philosophy's coffin for this short review comes when MacIntyre was in his late 70s from the first chapter of the 2009 book *Intractable Disputes about the Natural Law*, a book advocated by Cardinal Josef Ratzinger to the president of Notre Dame, Father John Jenkins, CSC. MacIntyre restates the now familiar criticism.

> [I]f the precepts of the natural law are indeed established by reason, we should expect to find agreement in assenting to them among rational agents. But this is not what we find, at least if we judge the rationality of agents as it is usually judged. Many intelligent, perceptive, and insightful agents either reject what Catholics take to be particular precepts of the natural law or accept them only in some very different version, or, more radically still, reject the very conception of a natural law. And these disagreements seem to be intractable. How can this be? It seems that either the Catechism's account of the natural law must be mistaken or else it is possible for some theses to be rationally vindicated without thereby being able to secure the assent of all rational agents.
> (MacIntyre, 2009, pp. 1–2)

MacIntyre's diagnosis of the dire state of moral philosophy is sound because it is abundantly clear that the Cartesian search for a unified rational foundation for moral enquiry has not happened. Modern philosophers exaggerated the efficacy of their own approaches to moral enquiry but then had to patch up their respective theories when faced by the various epistemic crises to which MacIntyre refers. The various types of utilitarianism, for instance, evolved by patching up problems associated with Bentham's original version of the hedonic calculus. But even after this patch up was done, its advocates remain ideologically and uncritically committed to the cause. Australian preference utilitarian, Peter Singer (1981, p. 111), illustrates this overconfidence when he claims that utilitarianism's most recent formation, the impartial consideration of interests, is a 'uniquely rational basis for ethical decision making.' If this bold claim was true then philosophers, who are in the business of rational deliberation, it would have taken on board Singer's new understanding of ethics. This has not happened because Singer's *new understanding* of ethics is neither unique nor definitive.

From one perspective many philosophers share MacIntyre's pessimism over the incommensurability standoff between consequentialism and non-consequentialism, and they have voted with their feet by disengaging from moral philosophy as a discipline and thus from the public space that moral philosophy ought to inhabit. From another perspective, however, MacIntyre's analysis is overstated because he does not sufficiently appreciate that consensus among moral agents is possible even when they advocate incommensurable theories of ethics. The next two sections of this paper will unpack this consensus, first, by unpacking the thin (minimalist) consensus associated with universal propositions, and second, by unpacking the thick (maximalist) consensus associated with MacIntyre's concept of a practice.

Epistemological crisis versus thin moral minimalism

As indicated one of the central themes of this volume is the *Role of Philosophy for a Renewed Understanding of Education in the Formative Process of Individual Persons and of the Civil Society*. In the second part of this paper I will present a case that MacIntyre's pessimism is overstated because moral agents can and do agree on *thin* minimalists moral propositions that sustain a civil society even when they hold incommensurable views over *thick* issues in applied ethics. Stephen Toulmin, for instance, agrees with MacIntyre's diagnosis, but he rejects the pessimism because he thinks that the Modern quest for certainty was misguided. The Modern project, according to Toulmin (1990, p. 16), did not provide certainty for 'intellectual problems – let alone, practical ones,' and the claim that philosophical or scientific problems could be decontextualized was itself based on a historical motivation. After looking back on what he calls the 'received view' of Modernity, Toulmin says he is inclined to say, 'Don't believe a word of it' because 'that whole story was one-sided and over-optimistic.' The confidence that disengaged rationality would eventually transcend traditional religious or cultural moral claims has not happened. Further, Toulmin (1990, p. 11) rejects the Modern assumption that rationality was commonly available to anyone 'who sets superstition and mythology aside' in ways 'free of local prejudice and transient fashion.' Taking his cue from Wittgenstein, Toulmin suggests that the theory-centred focus of Modernity is over and done with because the 'destructive work of Dewey, Heidegger, Wittgenstein, and Rorty' has left philosophy with limited options. It can cling to a discredited research program that will eventually drive it out of business, it can look for new postmodern practical methods of decision-making, or it can return to premodern traditions 'that were side-tracked by Descartes, but can be usefully taken up for the future.'

Toulmin (1990, p. 21) has in mind here a way of doing philosophy that re-contextualizes the moral claims that Modern philosophers took pride in decon-textualizing. He claims (1990, p. 135) that throughout the Middle Ages and the Renaissance, clerics and educated laypeople understood that problems in social ethics were not resolved by appeal to any single universal tradition, so they appealed to multiple considerations and coexisting traditions that were weighed against one another. His suggestion (1990, p. 180) is that philosophy ought to 'reappropriate the reasonable and tolerant' legacy of humanism because humanity 'needs people with a sense of how theory touches practice at points, and in ways, that we feel on our pulses.' Jonsen and Toulmin (1988, p. 307) advocate a return to casuistry as a means to sidestep the incommensurability problems of philosophy. Toulmin and Jonsen contend that the benefit of casuistry is that it allows a moral agent to appeal to type cases or paradigm cases without becoming absolutist. A type case uses standard cases as referential markers so that an individual case can be compared and contrasted with the typical. Maxims such as 'don't use violence against innocent human beings,' 'don't lie,' and 'don't take unfair advantage of other people's misfortune' can serve as 'markers or boundary stones that delimit the territory of 'moral' considerations in practice.

Consider for instance the maxim: 'It is wrong to cause unnecessary suffering.' A *thin* universal maxim such as this has vast explanatory power because conse-quentialists and non-consequentialists interpret the maxim in roughly similar ways. Most moral agents will concur that the rational thing to do is to avoid causing unnecessary suffering whenever and wherever possible. The consensus over a thin universal maxim can and does break down in particular cases, but this makes only a marginal impact on the explanatory power of the maxim itself. If we ask, for instance, whether childhood circumcision causes unnecessary suffering, we might reach different conclusions about its prohibition depending on whether we are referring to males or females. It seems self-evident that because female circumcision provides zero benefit, it ought to be prohibited because it seems straightforwardly to be an activity that causes unnecessary suffering. The case against male circumcision is less clear because there is some evidence that there is a hygiene benefit and clearer evidence that it lowers transmission rates of sexually transmitted diseases, particularly in impoverished communities (WHO, July 2016). If this is true, then the suffering associated with male circumcision might be mitigated by these benefits, and therefore the activity might be considered to be neither unnecessary nor prohibitive.

This type of mitigation or contingency ought not to be a surprise to anyone because, as Bernard Williams has argued, moral life has to be perspectival, and therefore disagreement is exactly what one should expect from a complex discipline like ethics.

> Our ethical ideas consist of a very complex historical deposit. When we consider this fact, and the relations that this deposit has to our public discourse and our private lives, there seems no reason at all to expect it to take, in any considerable measure, the shape of a theory.
> (Williams, 1995, p. 189)

In MacIntyre's trilogy he does not sufficiently acknowledge that the study of ethics has limits and the epistemological consensus he longs for is a bridge too far. In the summary of MacIntyre's unrelenting pessimism, the final quotation from *Intractable Disputes about the Natural Law* does however reveal a significant shift in his thinking. Faced with a lack of consensus among moral philosophers over the precepts of natural law, MacIntyre suggests there are now only two options available. Either the 'Catechism's account of the natural law must be mistaken,' or it is possible 'for some theses to be rationally vindicated without thereby being able to secure the assent of all rational agents' (MacIntyre, 2009, p. 1). This shift is significant given, all that has come before because MacIntyre is conceding that consensus might not be as necessary as he has been claiming it ought to be. The concession he makes for the precepts of natural law can also be applied to other ethical theories as well.

Consider, for instance, what happens if we swap the subject of the either/or described here. The lack of consensus over Kant's deontic formulations leaves us with only two alternatives. Either we accept that the categorical imperative is mistaken, or it must be possible that some theses can be rationally vindicated without thereby being able to secure the assent of all rational agents. Similarly, the lack of consensus over what the hedonic calculus consists of leaves us with only two alternatives. Either we accept that the pain/pleasure calculus is mistaken, or it must be possible that some theses can be rationally vindicated without thereby being able to secure the assent of all rational agents. In some sense this leaves MacIntyre (1979, pp. 16–22) back where he started, 'Premises about moral law with a Thomistic and biblical background are matched against premises about individual rights . . . and both are in conflict with post-Benthamite notions of utility,' but there is no method for adjudicating which theory trumps the others.

A preferred option is to move on from the idea that philosophy can resolve complex moral issues because it simply does not have the tools to fulfil this vision. Aristotle is right; human flourishing (*eudaimonia*) begins with a rough sketch of the good life that is filled in with more detail depending on what activity or practice a rational agent engages in. For this reason, a rational agent ought not to look for more precision than the activity or practice allows (1098[a]). A rational agent acts 'for the right person, to the right extent, at the right time, with the right motive, and in the right way,' depending on what one is aiming to achieve (1109[a]). In this context a person can be an excellent surgeon (because he or she habituates the internal goods associated with surgical practice) but a failure as a human being (because he or she lacks appreciation for the Eudaimonic life).

Simplification in the sciences is a useful analytic process but Williams (1972, pp. 23–24) contends that we need to stop applying scientific analysis to moral enquiry because complexity and conflict are basic facts of moral deliberation. He prefers to see moral deliberation as a complex mix of local and universal concerns that includes the psychological and emotional concerns of the moral agent.

> There cannot be any very interesting, tidy or self-contained theory of what morality is, nor, despite the vigorous activities of some present practitioners, can there be an ethical theory, in the sense of a philosophical structure which, together with some degree of empirical fact, will yield a decision procedure for moral reasoning.
> (Williams, 1985, pp. ix–x)

In *Ethics and the Limits of Philosophy* Williams (1985, p. 17) ponders over why anyone would want ethics to be simple when he says, 'If there is such a thing as the truth about the subject matter of ethics . . . why is there any expectation that it should be simple? . . . Perhaps we need as many concepts to describe it as we find we need, and no fewer?' The fact that we appeal to a variety of ethical considerations is precisely what one would expect to find in the complex world we inhabit. Ethical considerations, according to Williams (1985, p. 16), are 'genuinely different from one another,' and this is precisely what moral agents should expect because all of us are 'heirs to different long and complex ethical traditions, with many different religious and other social strands.'

In the last part of this paper I will posit that MacIntyre's enduring legacy will not be his analysis of rival moral traditions but the method that he developed to undertake his research. Once having recognized that a thin moral consensus is not only possibly but common, we are in a position to fully appreciate how MacIntyre's analysis of a practice so neatly dovetails into the variety of habits of life that human beings engage in. The power of MacIntyre's process is that it allows university graduates to appreciate that actions associated with 'good practice' in their chosen disciplines have already been established because the establishment and maintenance associated with these goods has very little to do with them as individuals.

Epistemological crisis versus thick practices

MacIntyre's theory of rationality presupposes a method that is now referred to as tradition-guided or practice-guided inquiry. For MacIntyre (1981/2007, p. 187), the primary disposition toward the good life involves an appreciation for what he calls the '*telos* of the whole human life,' a fundamental contrast between 'man-as-he-happens-to-be' and 'man-as-he-could-be-if-he-realized-his-essential-nature.' This narrative quest is an individual's general search for the *telos* of human life via internal goods of particular practices. Beneath the teleological purpose that is integral to long-lived human societies, MacIntyre (1981/2007, p. 216) says a central thesis begins to emerge, namely, that humans are storytelling animals. So the key question for a moral agent is not, 'What am I to do?,' following Kant and Bentham, but to ask, 'Of what story or stories do I find myself a part?,' following Aristotle. MacIntyre (1981/2007, p. 218) contends that because stories are essential to understanding the unity of a person's life, questions about moral good are best understood in the context of how an individual can fulfil the teleological expectations in these stories. The unity of a human life *is* the unity of a narrative quest 'embodied in a single life.'

Practice-guided enquiry involves a primary disposition that accepts that human life is purposeful and a secondary disposition that accepts that a purpose-filled life is not lived out in a vacuum. Rather, a single human life involves an intricate connection to three conceptual themes, *narrative*, *practice*, and *tradition*. For MacIntyre (1981/2007, p. 222) *narrative* is the story-filled description of what good character means; *practice* is a cooperative human activity with established internal goods that are acknowledged and accepted by its practitioners; and *tradition* is an authoritative account of precepts and principles extended over time that have survived epistemic crises of the past. This primary top-down teleological disposition was obvious for philosophers from the classic to the medieval period, but Modern philosophers pushed it aside in favor of a bottom-up rational justification for ethics.

One aspect of Aristotle's genius was to acknowledge limits associated with rational deliberation over ethics and politics. He seems disinclined to offer advice on specific moral issues because he does not think that rational enquiry lends itself to this level of precision. When Aristotle argues that 'every art and every inquiry, and similarly every action and pursuit, is thought to aim at some good' (1094^a), he uses medicine to illustrate how this teleological imperative ought to be understood. He contends that there is general agreement about the *telos* of medicine because it is obvious to a rational agent that health is a necessary though not sufficient aspect of human flourishing (1101^b). Aristotle contends that a rational agent ought not to waste time deliberating about ends when he says, 'a doctor does not deliberate whether he should heal, nor an orator whether he shall persuade, nor a statesman whether he shall produce law and order' (1113^a). For Aristotle, a rational agent ought to be more concerned with practical intelligence or prudence, and thus the concentration of thought for doctors, orators, and statesmen is to 'assume the end' (health, persuasion, and law and order) and to spend time contemplating 'how and by what means' the end 'is to be attained' (1113^a). For Aristotle, practical ethics is forged in a shared teleological activity of a specific practice (medicine→health; law→justice; politics→civil society), and the virtues of these practices are shaped by hands-on engagement among the practitioners concerned.

Aristotle seems to have in mind here that prudence or practical wisdom involves habituation acquired over time. Young men, for instance, can become 'geometricians and mathematicians,' but Aristotle thinks that a 'young man of practical wisdom cannot be found' (1142^a). The reason for this is that intelligent young men can understand mathematics because mathematics requires knowledge but not skill. Practical wisdom, on the other hand, requires both knowledge and skill, and therefore young men have not had the time necessary to develop the skills associated with a complex social activity. All moral agents are involved in the *Eudaimonic* quest for fulfilment, but individuals live out this quest in pursuit of a secondary set of goods that are internal to long-lived practices such as playing chess, architecture, or the practice of medicine. MacIntyre (1981/2007, p. 219) says these internal goods are necessary both to 'sustain practices' and to form character because they supply a moral agent with both 'self-knowledge' and an 'increasing knowledge of the good.' These internal goods sustain both the form of life and the traditions in which an individual finds him- or herself engaged. The concept of a 'practice' in MacIntyre's work is sufficiently nuanced and useful to warrant it being quoted in full.

> By a 'practice' I am going to mean any coherent and complex form of socially established cooperative human activity through which goods internal to that form of activity are realized in the course of trying to achieve those standards of excellence which are appropriate to, and partially definitive of, that form of activity, with the result that human powers to achieve excellence, and human conceptions of the ends and goods involved, are systematically extended.
>
> (MacIntyre, 1981/2007, p. 187)

These secondary dispositions enable a moral agent to 'understand what more and what else the good life for man is' (MacIntyre, 1981/2007, p. 219) because it involves virtuous actions (internal goods) that sustain the practice in its teleological quest. For MacIntyre (1981/2007, p. 223), the virtues 'find their point and purpose' in the way they define the internal goods that sustain relationships within a practice. Practice-guided enquiry is therefore a type of analytic method that examines both the primary and secondary pursuits of a tradition by focusing on its own narrative account. A practice, moral or otherwise, is made intelligible, according to MacIntyre (1981/2007, p. 222), only from within a 'larger and longer history of the tradition through which the practice in its present form was conveyed to us;' thus, the history of a single life is therefore characteristically 'embedded' and 'made intelligible' in 'the larger and longer histories of a number of traditions.'

The teleological link between human beings and the practices that they engage themselves in is particularly important in a Catholic university. Medical schools everywhere ought to hold in common the internal goods of the practice of medicine, but only Catholic medical schools articulate these goods in the context of the purpose-filled narrative of the Catholic intellectual tradition. By definition this makes a difference to the types of training a Catholic medical school ought to provide because the internal goods of a practice cannot be divorced from the *telos* of the whole human life. Similarly, law schools everywhere ought to hold in common the internal goods of the practice of law, but only Catholic law schools articulate these goods via an understanding of what justice means in the context of the purpose-filled narrative of the Catholic intellectual tradition. Business schools everywhere ought to hold in common the internal goods of the practice of business, but only Catholic universities articulate these goods in the context of the purpose-filled narrative of the Catholic intellectual tradition. A MacIntyre-shaped approach to a university education provides a method for mapping disciplines to show how practice-based curricula might be implemented in a manner that articulates both moral excellence and practical excellence as necessary conditions for a proper university education.

References

Jonsen, Albert R. and Toulmin, Stephen. (1988). *The Abuse of Casuistry: A History of Moral Reasoning*. Berkeley, CA: University of California Press.

MacIntyre, Alasdair. (1965). Imperatives, Reasons for Action, and Morals. *The Journal of Philosophy*, 62 (19), 513–524.

MacIntyre, Alasdair. (1977). Epistemological Crisis, Dramatic Narrative and the Philosophy of Science. *The Monist*, 60, 453–472.

MacIntyre, Alasdair. (1979). Why Is the Search for the Foundations of Ethics so Frustrating? *Hastings Center Report*, 9 (4), 16–22.

MacIntyre, Alasdair. (1981/2007). *AfterVirtue: A Study in Moral Theory*. 3rd ed. Notre Dame, IN: University of Notre Dame Press.

MacIntyre, Alasdair. (1988). *Whose Justice? Which Rationality?* Notre Dame, IN: University of Notre Dame Press.

MacIntyre, Alasdair. (1990). *Three Rival Versions of Moral Enquiry: Encyclopaedia, Genealogy, and Tradition*. Notre Dame, IN: University of Notre Dame Press.

MacIntyre, Alasdair. (1992). What Has Not Happened in Moral Philosophy? *The Yale Journal of Criticism*, 5, 193–199.

MacIntyre, Alasdair. (1998). First Principles, Final Ends and Contemporary Philosophical Issues. In Kelvin Knight (Ed.). *The MacIntyre Reader* (171–201). Cambridge, UK: Polity Press.

MacIntyre, Alasdair. (2009). Intractable Moral Disagreements. In Lawrence S. Cunningham (Ed.). *Intractable Disputes about the Natural Law: Alasdair MacIntyre and His Critics* (1–52). Notre Dame, IN: University of Notre Dame Press.

Singer, Peter. (1981). *The Expanding Circle*. New York: Farrar, Straus and Giroux.

Toulmin, Stephen. (1990). *Cosmopolis: The Hidden Agenda of Modernity*. Chicago: University of Chicago Press.

Williams, Bernard. (1972). *Morality: An Introduction to Ethics*. Cambridge, UK: Cambridge University Press.

Williams, Bernard. (1985). *Ethics and the Limits of Philosophy*. London: Fontana.

Williams, Bernard. (1995). *Making Sense of Humanity and Other Philosophical Papers 1982–1993*. Cambridge, UK: Cambridge University Press.

10 Values education and Christological personhood

Philosophical and practical implications

Renee Kohler-Ryan and Sandy Lynch

A Catholic university engages with society through its graduating students as much as through its research. The more effectively we, as educators, prepare our students for working life, the more the Catholic university can exercise the influence on the world to which it aspires. In teaching ethics at the University of Notre Dame Australia (UNDA), we have been very much aware of the need to develop in our students both skills of reflection and capacities for well-formed relationships in a variety of personal and professional contexts. As is demonstrated in the Apostolic Constitution on Catholic Universities, *Ex Corde Ecclesiae* (*ECE*, John Paul II, 1990), promulgated by Pope John Paul II, such aptitudes are essential when set within the objectives of the Catholic university and the view of the human person expressed within those objectives; students must receive an "education offered in a faith-context that forms men and women capable of rational and critical judgment and conscious of the transcendent dignity of the human person" (1990, par. 49).

In this chapter, the first few lines of this constitution are analyzed to argue that the Catholic university emerges from the nature and purpose of the human person, understood through the self-giving activity of Christ. It then discusses the nature of "values" that are fundamental to the late John Paul II's philosophical analysis of what it means to act ethically and argues that these also form the basis of a curriculum developed by Mary C. Gentile: *Giving Voice to Values* (*GVV*, 2010), which we have found helpful for teaching ethics to those training for the professions at UNDA. Finally, the GVV curriculum is described to illustrate that the success of its approach within a Catholic institution may lie in the fact that its underlying presuppositions are in harmony with John Paul II's own vision of the human person. Examination of the latter's moral philosophy will take place mainly through developing his works under his given name, Karol Wojtyła.

Coming from the heart of the church: the Christological dimension

Given that the human person is central to the Catholic university, as John Paul II makes clear, study of human nature, of the various aspects of personhood and of our relationship to the world, is undertaken in the humanities and the sciences.

However this study is distinctive for its conviction that the community of knowledge is "born" from a particular person: Jesus Christ. This, effectively, is the argument made in the very first paragraph of ECE, when it states:

> Born from the heart of the Church, a Catholic University is located in that course of tradition which may be traced back to the very origin of the University as an institution. It has always been recognized as an incomparable centre of creativity and dissemination of knowledge for the good of humanity.
>
> (John Paul II, 1990, par. 1)

In these first few words, two points significant to our discussion are made. First, the university as an institution is rooted in a Catholic vision of the good for humanity. The initial universities in the West were Catholic, and so what a university is *for* can be traced back to the attitudes and values that gave rise to its beginning: such communities were focused on the goodness of knowledge for directing them toward God. That focus on what is good for humanity as a whole assumes that knowledge is discovered and disseminated with what is good for the individual human person constantly in mind. The work of the university can only support that good if it relies on the idea that there is a truth of the person, which according to John Paul II when writing as Karol Wojtyla, has both objective and subjective dimensions. Wojtyla argued that the human person holds a particular place within a metaphysically real world. Only with this in mind does John Paul II's insistence that knowledge must be constantly directed by and for the ethical, make sense since values are only intelligible when they pertain to knowledge and understanding of reality and when our feelings and intuitions reflect that knowledge. These claims are discussed in more detail as follows.

The second point that we can take from these opening sentences of ECE is more subtle, though just as important, and relies on an appreciation of what it means to be born from the *heart* of the church. One can glean this from the *Catechism of the Catholic Church*, which identifies the heart of Church as Christ, in his ultimate act of personal self-giving. It states:

> The Eucharist is the *heart* and the summit of the Church's life, for in it Christ associates his Church and all her members with his sacrifice of praise and thanksgiving offered once for all on the cross to his Father; by this sacrifice he pours out the graces of salvation on his Body which is the Church.
>
> (*Catechism of the Catholic Church*, 1997, par. 1407; author's italics)

Thus we may extrapolate to argue that the Catholic university is born out of Christ's Eucharistic act and that thereby the university is his community; formed by his self-giving; unified by and called to sacrifice, praise and thanksgiving. These are, of course, lofty thoughts, and they might seem fanciful and irrelevant to the actual day-to-day work of the university. The idea that the university is to be self-giving, or *agapeic*, to use a more philosophical term, seems particularly difficult to propose and almost impossible to live out in the current tertiary climate. Indeed, Haughey asserts that ECE has in this respect completely missed the point and that the contemporary Catholic university is the child not of the medieval university but instead of the research university instituted in Berlin in 1810.[1] Haughey seems to imply a complete division between research and teaching. He implies research is connected with the search for truth and leads us to conclude that the other crucial activity of the university (teaching) is not. However, John Paul II's essential claim is somewhat different: inasmuch as a Catholic university really is Catholic, it retains a Christological anthropology and thereby remains within the "tradition" to which the pope refers. While the institutional configurations of the Catholic university may have changed, and with that some deviations from original mission may well have occurred,[2] ECE's argument is at least implicitly for a return to its Christological foundations.

Considering the university as a center for research, this is perhaps nowhere more evident than in John Paul II's emphasis on the precedence that ethics should take in the realm of technological research and innovation (1990, pars. 7, 18, 45). However, our focus is somewhat different, in keeping with the challenges we have faced at the University of Notre Dame Australia, in preparing students to make and competently implement ethical decisions in the professional context and in their everyday lives. *Ex Corde* does not neglect this dimension of the contemporary university as a place for professional training. In fact, it directs that such training must assist students to realize their professional responsibilities (John Paul II, 1990, par. 23) and provide "formation in moral and religious principles and the social teachings of the Church", while at the same time providing "appropriate ethical formation in [their] profession" (1990, Article 4 [5]). But what constitutes "appropriate ethical formation", and how can this actually take place in the setting of the Catholic university? The answers to these questions can only really be ascertained after an analysis of the nature of the person who stands in need of such formation.

The theological framework necessary to finding what, or who, that person is, is specifically Christological: everything that the university does must have its source in Christ's self-giving love. The fruit of the work of the university, for its alumni, will be in the manner in which they bring the love of Christ to those they serve. However, the approach to teaching ethics and discussing vital notions of personhood here is philosophical in keeping with John Paul II's understanding that philosophy leads toward truth in ways that every human person can understand. Philosophy is, indeed, the mode of learning universal to all human knowers, as John Paul II argues in *Fides et Ratio*, and hence human persons naturally ask questions. When they do so well, using "right reason" (John Paul II, 1998), they inevitably discover and engage with reality. Thus,

> [a]lthough times change and knowledge increases, it is possible to discern a core of philosophical insight within the history of thought as a whole. Consider, for example, the principles of non-contradiction, finality and

> causality, as well as the concept of the person as a free and intelligent subject, with the capacity to know God, truth and goodness. Consider as well certain fundamental moral norms which are shared by all. These are among the indications that, beyond different schools of thought, there exists a body of knowledge which may be judged a kind of spiritual heritage of humanity. It is as if we had come upon an implicit philosophy, as a result of which all feel that they possess these principles, albeit in a general and unreflective way.
>
> (John Paul II, 1998, par. 4)

If it is the work of philosophy both to find these principles and to reflect upon them, then the university's role is to disseminate what such labor discovers. Notable in this passage is John Paul II's emphasis on personhood and morality. Human knowledge is first of all personal – even when it is directed at a nonhuman order, the mode and direction of knowledge still refers back to and influences the human person.

Some basic points can be derived now from *Fides et Ratio* and *Ex Corde Ecclesiae*,[3] which will directly concern the work of ethical formation for future professionals studying at the Catholic university. Bearing in mind that not every student will be Catholic, or even Christian, educators can turn with confidence to philosophy so that together educators and students can confront forms of human knowledge, which will always have ethical dimensions and implications. Working with that knowledge, the student is already being formed in the truth and can then reflect on that truth in ways that may in time open up a theological dimension of personal significance.

On practising values: an approach to teaching ethical decision-making

The challenge remains as to how students can come to the knowledge they uncover in ways that generate practical, rather than merely theoretical, engagement with the moral norms discussed and interrogated. Such guiding principles must be lived, practised and repeatedly reflected upon so that personal and integrated learning occurs. As educators we are responsible for ensuring that students are supported in coming to the immediate recognition of right action and in then living what is true. University students face a particular problem as they are about to embark upon, or have already begun, to work within a profession. They may not have had the opportunity, which is generally available through experience, to understand the possibilities for good or bad entailed in a particular workplace ethical conflict. The moments in which we most need ethical principles and guidelines are, after all, the messiest. Ethics itself is a messy business in which possibilities vie with each other to seem by turn fraught with good and bad consequences; where lack of information – perceived or real – makes us hold back; where feelings and reason might be in conflict; and where reasoned principles and belief may well conflict with commonly perceived morality.

The test for the educator of future professionals within a Catholic university is to ensure that ethical formation proceeds according to academic standards and involves the development of ethical awareness as well as an understanding of complex theoretical frameworks; at the same time that formation must enable students to make a difference in the world. Those of us who teach ethics in the tertiary context have discovered that an exploration of ethical decision-making at the theoretical level fails to engage a large proportion of our students in the ways that we had intended. When our university began to place a particular focus on teaching ethics within professional degrees, we became painfully aware of this discrepancy. A search of the literature uncovered the GVV curriculum noted, which has proven to be well suited to teaching ethics in a Catholic context to students training for professions.

Gentile developed the GVV curriculum at Harvard University in response to concerns about the ineffectiveness of business ethics education, given the part that MBA graduates played in the global financial crisis of 2008 and subsequent corporate collapses. The book on which the curriculum is based challenges traditional approaches to the teaching of ethics. It argues that developing ethical awareness and the skills of analysis and decision-making, requisite to understanding and resolving ethical conflict in the workplace, is insufficient preparation for good ethical practice in the same domain.

Gentile reinforces this critique by recounting the ethical decision-making strategy of one new graduate, who revealed that when deciding what to do in the face of an ethical conflict, he made a choice about right action and then supported that choice with whichever of the theories that he had studied at the university best justified his decision. Thus, his decision-making was reportedly based on "gut" feeling" or intuition and was essentially unreflective; his ethics education did not impact on the nature of the decision in any significant way, and hence the ethical dimensions of his life were unformed despite his ethics education (Gentile, 2010, p. xi). The cross-disciplinary GVV curriculum that Gentile has created is a response to the failure that anecdotes of this kind expose. Its thesis is not simply that a focus on awareness raising and ethical theorization can be ineffective but that this focus must be supplemented by an action-oriented pedagogical approach for developing the skills, confidence and competence required to implement morally defensible actions. The curriculum acknowledges the importance of developing ethical awareness and skills of analysis but diagnoses the difficulty as a failure to address ethical action.

Consequently, GVV does not focus on convincing students or practitioners to behave ethically; rather, it assumes that many individuals already want to act on the values to which they are committed and aims to empower them to become more proficient at doing so. While GVV is a secular curriculum, Gentile's focus on values is particularly fitting to the discussion undertaken in this paper, given that a substantial aspect of Wojtyla's discussion of ethical formation and action responds to a passive notion of value, replacing it with one that is active and practised. Our experience with this practical approach is that it works well within our Catholic context and that its underlying philosophical assumptions readily align with the approach recommended by John Paul II in *Ex Corde Ecclesiae* and *Fides et Ratio*. For example, it is premised on the assumption that humans share certain moral principles and values in common.

Gentile chooses to speak about values rather than ethics because she argues that, "in general usage, ethics suggests a system of rules or standards with which one is expected to comply.... [E]thics is often seen as rule-based and externally imposed, something that exists outside the individual" (2010, p. 25). Furthermore, theoretical education in ethics tends to focus on frameworks, like deontology, utilitarianism or virtue ethics, which can sometimes lead to scenarios in which different frameworks yield different results and make ethical decision-making even more puzzling (2010, p. 25). Gentile argues that speaking about "values" bypasses some of these problems. Akin to Wojtyla's vision, arguably they do something more, by bringing together the subjective and the objective dimensions of human action so that the person becomes intrinsically involved in what she does, by practising what she values. She makes real what she experiences as valuable through actions based on reflective understanding.

According to Gentile, values are "something that *we* own ourselves and hold dear – '*my* values' – and something we experience deeply and internally, which, although it possesses a cognitive aspect, is not exclusively about analysis" (2010, p. 27). That is, they are subjectively experienced. On the other hand, Gentile argues that "although differences do surface, what is important to remember . . . is that there is a great deal of commonality among the lists of moral or ethical values that most individuals identify as central, and . . . this shared list is rather short" (2010, p. 29). That is, there is an objective validity to what humans value – a shared human morality. Gentile gives two similar lists of core values. From Martin Seligman's research she derives "wisdom, courage, humanity, justice, temperance and transcendence"; while from Rushworth Kidder she takes a " 'more simply put' list: honesty, respect, responsibility, fairness, and compassion" (2010, p. 29). We might, Gentile says, "quibble around the edges" of such lists, but the fundamental point will remain: core values, which we hold in common, exist, and these form the basis for decision-making toward and with others, among the majority of reasonable and well-disposed persons. In other words, Gentile assumes a "common morality", which can offer both a defense of and agreement upon generally binding standards of action or rules of obligation; for example, respect for the lives of others allows us to infer obligations not to kill, not to cause pain or suffering to others, to rescue persons in danger and to nurture the young and dependent; a commitment to honesty obliges us to tell the truth and keep our promises.

Finding theoretical foundations of giving voice to values: approaching Wojtyla

Much work remains to be done here in terms of the theoretical underpinnings of such an approach, particularly within the Catholic context. Certainly, this exploration is an initial attempt at such a venture. Wojtyla's understanding of value, which is essential to his appreciation of what it means to act ethically, must be and will be examined, but it is worth indicating that other thinkers have carried out philosophical analysis that would support some of Gentile's claims. Thinkers such as Martha Nussbaum (1999), Sabina Alkire (2000), Beauchamp and Childress (2009)[4] and Gert (2005) have already examined notions of a common morality. Likewise, MacIntyre (1999) has already considered how law and morality interact, and Ralph McInerny has argued that "human language reposes on the assumption that there are common truths" (1999, p. 14). Philosophical work that bears upon much of what Gentile's curriculum proposes to achieve can also be found in analysis of the term "reflective equilibrium", which John Rawls in *A Theory of Justice*, and later Damian Grace and Stephen Cohen, argue is a way of thinking about how ethical decision-making often involves us in balancing a number of factors to come to a decision about which others might agree: "our feelings, judgements and intuitions about behaviour on the one hand and the principles to which we subscribe on the other – whatever the genesis of those principles" (2009, p. 9).

While all of these aspects will be essential in analyses of the role of Gentile's approach to professional training within the tertiary sector, Wojtyla is our focus in this section for three main reasons. First, he explicitly examines the subjective and objective dimensions of human values.[5] Second, ECE argues not only for ethical formation but also situates this within a discussion of the values most necessary to fostering Christian culture, as noted in the conclusion of this paper. Finally, Wojtyla is no stranger to the difficulties of conveying ethical concerns within a Catholic university, and he was very much aware of the need not only to theorize but more importantly to learn how to act well. Stefan Swiezawski thus observes:

> From the very beginning Wojtyla was keenly aware that the claims of ethical intellectualism were illusory and that by itself even the most perfect and penetrating knowledge of the inner structures and mechanisms of the human being does not guarantee proper human conduct and creativity. His own personal and pastoral experience taught him that even the best sermons and lectures do not automatically lead to real self-improvement. A person must also make a systematic effort to acquire the proper skills and virtues through the constant repetition of rightly performed acts.
>
> (Swiezawski, 1993, p. xiv)

This idea of constant repetition, coupled with reflection, is central to Gentile's curriculum. From Wojtyla's perspective, what is valuable calls for a response in action. When that action is willed, and at the same time is an answer to goodness, the human person is actively forming him- or herself ethically – and thus, in a profound sense, coming to understand what that means. The GVV curriculum prepares for such moments by helping students think through and practise voicing what they value in difficult situations.

Obviously, knowing better what a value is would enable such a process to happen more effectively. Wojtyla develops his notion of value both in relation to what it means to be a human person and in response to Max Scheler's "emotionalist" theory of values (Wojtyla, 1993).[6] Wojtyla is both a metaphysical realist and a personalist. That is, he thinks of the human person as a real thing in the world, and he maintains that a person holds the highest kind of value in reality as such. Each of these conceptual claims, furthermore, has an ethical dimension.

Let us first consider such results following from the position of metaphysical realism. One might say that, objectively, a human person is a thing like every other thing in the world (Wojtyla, 1993).[7] However, this is not entirely accurate because subjective experience, or consciousness – which is, of course, necessary for any kind of personal reflection – sets the person apart from all other things in the world. That experience always has an ethical component, which is inseparable from what the person is, as a real thing in the world. According to Wojtyla, the ethical dimension is readily apparent to the human person, who constantly experiences him- or herself as someone both existing and acting. Effectively, the person always experiences good and evil and can become more readily attuned to this. For Wojtyla, ethical subjective experience is always of something objective – only I have the experience of myself in an interior way. However, my experience of myself as an existing and acting object forms the basis for my appreciation of other human persons. At the same time, knowledge of myself actually relies on others and my experience of them. There is, for Wojtyla, no existing and acting person in isolation from others. This places ethical demands upon the human person toward others (1993, p. 221). So, my experience of good and evil always happens in community with world and others and not in isolation.

Considerations of what Wojtyla means by "personalism" offer another way in which to understand the importance of values within his philosophy. Personalism was the framework from within which Wojtyla and other members of the Catholic University of Lublin (so formative for Wojtyla's notions both of person and of Catholic university)[8] responded to reductionist claims about the nature of the human being. In keeping with his hesitancy to reduce ethics only to theory, as well as his insistence that the person always has ethical dimensions in operation, he cautions: "[p]ersonalism is not primarily a theory of the person or a theoretical science of the person. Its meaning is largely practical and ethical: it is concerned with the person as a subject and an object of activity" (Wojtyla, 1993, p. 166). Pawel Tarasiewicz describes that personalism as developed by Wojtyla and his university colleagues:

> [It] finds its essential justification in the metaphysical account of the transcendence of the human being . . . [which] emphasizes the two-fold transcendence of the person: (a) in relation to nature, through spiritual acts of intellectual cognition, love and freedom; and (b) in relation to community – through acts bound with the moments: subjectivity of rights, ontic completeness, religious dignity.
>
> (Tarasiewicz, 2014, p. 623)

Thus, personalism reacts against attempts to degrade the fundamental nature of the human person. It does so by insisting that every human person is embedded within a community. Personalism may have a theoretical dimension, but its starting point is intuition or experience. It is effectively a way of thinking about or, better put, reflecting upon what it means to experience and to act – with others.

Wojtyla's realism, mixed with personalism, constitutes a nexus in which one can find practical implications for ethical formation within the Catholic university; that is, his philosophical approach not only stimulates exploration of values, but it also emphasizes personal reflection and relations to self, world and others. Wojtyla's considerations of value began when he studied the philosophy of phenomenologist Max Scheler,[9] whom Kupczak argues based his ethical personalism on the idea that "the perfection of the person informs the goal of all human activity" (Kupczak, 2000, p. 14). Wojtyla wrote his Habilitationsschrift on Scheler, and eventually parted with him, specifically regarding the origin and ultimate significance of value. Eventually he claimed that Scheler's values, which are simply experienced and not reflected upon, cannot be considered morally significant. In précis, as mentioned, Wojtyla characterizes Scheler's ethics, which is grounded in an understanding of value as "emotionalistic". His arguments against Scheler's position are particularly helpful in thinking through the implications of only using gut feelings when making ethical decisions, and thus they assist us in elaborating upon the theoretical foundations of the GVV curriculum.

Wojtyla argues that for Scheler, a value is something felt – experienced – and a human being is "merely [a] conscious unity of experiences" (1993, p. 53). Thought and will are inconsequential to knowing what a person is and to describing his or her actions. Scheler's insistence on feelings constitutes his response to Kant, whom he thinks rules out the importance of feeling, or experience, by privileging the will and reason. While Wojtyla (1993) derives much from Scheler's concept of value, he criticizes it for going too far into passive experience.[10] Making values all-important and reducing these values to feelings, Scheler theorizes that human action is never the product of rational willing; it is only ever a response to something felt. Wojtyla characterizes this position as depriving human action of "the backbone of the will" (1993, p. 39). The Polish philosopher goes on to denounce Scheler's position even more decisively on phenomenological grounds: Wojtyla claims that we each "experience 'good' or 'evil' because we experience ourselves as the efficient cause of our own acts" (1993, p. 39). In other words, experience of what we value is always related to something real; as such, it is good or evil and forms the basis of any ethical decision and action. When we experience something as good per se, then we value that thing. Experience of the self in relation to others as good is fundamental to Wojtyla's enterprise; like other values it is to be acted upon and reflected upon. Values are not only felt but can and should be thought so that they can be found in their proper "teleological" order (Wojtyla, 2011, p. 36). Whereas for Scheler, values arrange themselves in priority according to gut feelings, for Wojtyla, those feelings do not have the last word in establishing what is more or less important in relation to human action. Wojtyla proposes to replace Scheler's detached, pure consciousness, disconnected with reality, with a person able to think about the objective values intuited in his experience and to act accordingly (Wojtyla, 1993).

That thought can only be mediated through an understanding of the role of the will in ethical action. Turning to Thomas Aquinas, whose metaphysical realism and particular brand of personalism are particularly helpful to the 20th-century Catholic phenomenologist, Wojtyla argues that the will works with reason (Wojtyla, 1993). Ethical action is, then, not about submission of the will to reason any more than it is an unreflective response to value. There may be an initial confused struggle, but truly good action, where an informed conscience reasons and chooses well, entails cooperation of reason, will and also passions.[11] The collaboration among these facets of the person depends upon a key term in Thomas's thought, which Wojtyla highlights: *bonum in communi*. *Bonum in communi* can be understood as "good in general"[12] and is the desirable aspect of the goodness of being as such. For Thomas, this good in general is the ultimate ethical context; so bountiful and intricate is its nature that no one ethical theory could encapsulate its demands since the good in general is goodness in its most universal sense. The fulfilment of human life is, then, the constantly concretized realization that we are made to live well, just as the whole of creation was ultimately made to fulfil God's proclamation that creation is indeed very good. Wojtyla observes that Thomas comes to the point of realizing what it means to "really want" – another term, one might argue, for "value" – via a metaphysical analysis, and he fleshes out the 13th-century saint's arguments through phenomenological analysis of ethical action. As Wojtyla explains:

> The lived experience 'I will' . . . is the simplest experiential fact in which the efficacy of the personal self is revealed. This simple experience, however, develops into a specific process thanks to the appearance of motives. The appearance of motives should lead to a decision. Frequently, however, in the course of the process of the will, a weighing or even a conflict of motives must take place. The result of such a weighing or conflict of motives is the victory of some one motive, followed by a choice made by the will.
> (Wojtyla, 1993, p. 12)

Far from being swayed by the experience of pure feeling, Thomas's acting subject is here instead enlivened by Wojtyla's phenomenologically explained experience and his personalistic norm,[13] which sees the fulfilment of the human person taking place only and always in relation to values willed and enacted. Primacy of place within the moral order is accorded to the person, known subjectively and objectively, and experienced as transcendent, irreplaceable and free. The central point at which all of this is realized is at the moment of ethical action, when the person knows fully the value of what he or she wants and invests the entire self into that moment. At such a point, willed action constitutes a moment in "self-determination." As Wojtyla puts it, "Through self-determination, the human being becomes increasingly more of a 'someone' in an ethical sense".[14] Willed, which is to say reasoned, action brings with it the experience both of self-possession and of self-governance – of making oneself. The personal act of the will, says Wojtyla, enables me to "become aware and also testify to others that I possess myself and govern myself. In this way, my acts give me a unique insight into myself as a person. By virtue of self-determination, I experience in the relatively most immediate way that I am a person" (Wojtyla, 1993, p. 193)

For Wojtyla, when I value something, I will it. If I really value it, then I will act upon it, and in that moment of action, I will experience even more the objective value in what I have done. (The reverse is, of course, also the case – in acting against values, I will also feel the consequences.) At that moment, having acted, I experience myself in a different way and have a further basis upon which to reflect about what is really good, in itself, but also in relation to all human persons. The notion of testifying is especially significant when considering how we might not only know but *voice* and act upon our values.

The practice of finding and voicing values

Before concluding with a brief reflection on the role of values in the Catholic university, we outline Gentile's method for ethical formation and draw attention to its synergies with Wojtyla's views. GVV asks: "What would I say and do if I were going to act on my values?" This approach recognizes that effective moral practice cannot be a matter of entirely impersonal and disengaged application to problems of general principles or values of the kind canvased by some modern deontological and cognitive moral developmental theories. Instead, it tries to emphasize that changing the world for the better is first and foremost a matter of changing ourselves by becoming aware of ourselves in respects that go beyond the internalization or application of abstract cognitive rules or principles.

Wojtyla has drawn our attention to the complexity of this process, which involves the thinking, willing, experiencing person at every turn. The onus of responsibility falls on the student in the end, who must make him- or herself more honest, courageous, self-controlled, just, caring and so on for other human virtues (Dunne and Hogan, 2004, p. 107). Jānis Ozoliņš makes the point that in effect, education should be in aid of making students wise so that they can "have understanding of themselves, of their relationships to others, to have an ability to make good moral and other judgements and to act on these" (Ozoliņš, 2015, p. 871). Ozoliņš argues that it will always be difficult to test whether or not a student knows what it means to value, and the only way that the educator can help students in this regard is to "encourage . . . [them] to be critically reflective, to question, but most of all to learn that the attainment of their own good requires commitment to, and responsibility for, the good of others" (2015, p. 879). Gentile's response to such a task is to create an accessible framework of seven pillars that assists students to reflect on and practise what they would do in the face of a difficult ethical situation. The first of those pillars reflects an initial assumption about a set of shared values, as we have seen. The second focuses on the fact of the choices we are free to make in regard to ethical action and recalls to mind Wojtyla's references to "the backbone of the will" (1993, p. 39) and his direction to us that what is valuable calls for a response in action. More specifically, Gentile encourages students to identify what is it that enables or conversely disables them in their choices to act in particular situations; the aim here is to help them recognize when they have acted on their values in the past and to encourage them to do so more often. Thus, what might appear to be an ethical impasse is recast as a choice. At the same time, and third, such conflicts are to be normalized. Helping students to appreciate that conflicts in which many factors are at play are a normal dimension of professional life, enables the future professional to "approach [conflicts] calmly and competently" (Gentile, 2010, Appendix). But equally, it resists tendencies to be overcome by negative feelings and can be taken to imply that we appreciate that we are engaged in a relation with all human persons, each of whom is equally valuable, despite disagreements.

Gentile's fourth pillar emphasizes the importance of reflecting on what we want from life, on our purposes – both personally and professionally – and the values implicit in them so that this is available to us when conflicts inevitably arise. The fifth and related pillar focuses on self-knowledge, self-image and alignment to recommend reflection on our own strengths and behavioral tendencies under pressure to play to our strengths; focusing on our particular style in dealing with conflict may help to form conscience. The focus of the sixth pillar is on the development of "voice". This refers to a style of communication with which the student is comfortable; it develops over time with practice and involves scripting what one *would* say or do in a moment of ethical conflict to habituate the response that testifies to one's values. The final pillar focuses on reasons and rationalizations that we often give to excuse us for not voicing our values. These could be as simple as wanting to avoid conflict or disapproval or as complex as being unable to appreciate the demands of an ethical code of conduct.

While this is a secular curriculum, it works well in a Catholic university context. Part of the reason is that it embeds itself within a particular conception of human knowledge – a personal experience of goodness or its lack. That GVV places such an emphasis on shared values is particularly fitting in that it coincides with John Paul II's idea that every human person can know goodness and truth and act accordingly. GVV encourages critical reflection, and one would hope that such reflection could be brought to bear on the values that John Paul II specifically identifies in ECE. The first of these is *"proclaiming the meaning of truth, that fundamental value without which freedom, justice and human dignity are extinguished"* (1990, par. 4). Others are the values of knowledge and research, of marriage and family, of religion, and of the human person (John Paul II, 1990, pars. 15, 33, 41, 45, 48–49). The university community is called upon to reflect on and evaluate the modern social values so that from the heart of the Church, academics and students can form adequate responses in action. Fundamental to that reflection and evaluation, we would suggest, is the recognition of what a value is and what it is not. Only when we own, testify to – voice – our values can the mission of the Catholic university be realized in the world. GVV is not the only possible response to the need for training in ethical reflection. However, its emphasis on what it feels like to act well, to experience the good, is well aligned with Wojtyla's understanding of the fulfilment and ethical formation of the human person.

Notes

1 It is telling that Haughey's 2009 book, *Where Is Knowing Going?*, is described as an "inquiry into the rationale for a Catholic university" (p. 140) but considers ECE only at the end. His discussion does not address and in fact appears to miss the Eucharistic point outlined in this paper. Rather, he asks whether the Catholic university of today does come from the heart of the Church, as the title of ECE asserts and answers: "Only in part. Historically, the Church was the patron of these educational institutions, but the university as a research institution – the target of the document – had its beginning not in the Church but at the University of Berlin in 1810, and later in that century at Johns Hopkins and the University of Chicago. From these beginnings, research universities have sprung up across the globe in various forms. Since the Church did not give birth to the form of these research institutions, they are not exactly *ex corde ecclesiae*, but *ex corde universitatis*" (pp. 139–140).
2 See Jānis Ozoliņš (2012) for an argument that the corporate structure of the current university actually impedes the work of the Catholic university from the perspective of its Catholic mission. The implications of such corporatization can also be seen in Wilson D. Miscamble (2009), while Neil Ormerod (2013) explores the difficulties the Catholic university faces in maintaining identity and mission while adhering to government requirements.
3 For a development of the relationship between ideas in *Ex Corde Ecclesiae* and *Fides et Ratio*, see David Ruel Foster (2002).
4 See Chapters 1 and 2 in the sixth edition, and also Chapters, 1, 3 and 9 in the forthcoming seventh edition.
5 For a broader framework of Wojtyla's understanding of personalist ethics, the following selected readings are helpful: Kupczak (2000), Wilk (2007) and Taylor (2009).
6 See pp. 35–38 in particular.
7 See pp. 221–228 in particular.
8 See Swiezawski (1993) and also McEvoy (2002) and Tarasiewicz (2014).
9 Besides the essays discussed by Wojtyla, see: Gorevan (2002) and McEvoy (2002).
10 See pp. 23–44.
11 "Passions", incidentally, seem a very appropriate rendering of what Scheler appears to mean by "value" and perhaps also what the MBA graduate in Gentile's analysis refers to in describing his mode of analyzing ethical decisions according to what he learned in the university.
12 See Wojtyla (1993, pp. 5, 14) and Kossell (2001, re Ia, IIae, pp. 90–97, 175).
13 The norm entails that a person can never be treated as a means toward an end. This is obviously consistent with Kant's view but on the basis of a personalist anthropology, rather than a strictly deontological framework. See Wojtyla (2011, pp. 74–77).
14 Wojtyla (1993, p. 192) in his chapter, "The Personal Structure of Self-Determination," immediately qualifies the claim that ontologically the person has always been a "someone" to note that now the experience of action is an engagement in self-making and at the same time a further realization that a someone is never a something.

References

Alkire, S. (2000). The Basic Dimensions of Human Flourishing: A Comparison of Accounts. In N. Biggar and R. Black (Eds.). *The Revival of Natural Law: Philosophical, Theological and Ethical Responses to the Finnis-Grisez School.* (73–110). Sydney: Ashgate.

Beauchamp, T. L. and Childress, J. (2009). *Principles of Biomedical Ethics* (6th edn.). New York: Oxford University Press.

Catholic Church. (1997). *Catechism of the Catholic Church.* (2nd edn.). Strathfield: St. Paul's Publications.

Dunne, J. and Hogan, P. (Eds.). (2004). *Education and Practice: Upholding the Integrity of Teaching and Learning.* Malden, MA: Blackwell Publishing, Ltd.

Foster, D. F. (2002). The Implications of *Fides et Ratio* for Catholic Universities. In J. McEvoy (Ed.). *The Challenge of Truth: Reflections on Fides & Ratio.* (109–128). Dublin: Veritas Publications.

Gentile, M. C. (2010). *Giving Voice to Values: How to Speak Your Mind When You Know What's Right.* New Haven, CT and London: Yale University Press. Retrieved from: http://www.babson.edu/Academics/teaching-research/gvv/Pages/home.aspx

Gert, B. (2005). *Morality: Its Nature and Justification* (2nd Rev. edn.). New York: Oxford University Press.

Gorevan, P. (2002). Karol Wojtyla in Philosophical Dialogue with Max Scheler. In J. McEvoy (Ed.). *The Challenge of Truth: Reflections on Fides & Ratio.* (134–153). Dublin, Ireland: Veritas Publications.

Grace, D. and Cohen, S. (2009). *Business Ethics.* Oxford: Oxford University Press.

Haughey, J. C. (2009). *Where Is Knowing Going? The Horizons of the Knowing.* Washington, DC: Georgetown University Press.

John Paul II (Pope). (1990). *Apostolic Constitution Ex Corde Ecclesiae of the Supreme Pontiff John Paul II On Catholic Universities.* Washington, DC: Office for Publication and Promotion Services, United States Catholic Conference.

John Paul II (Pope). (1998). *Encyclical Letter, Fides et Ratio, of the Supreme Pontiff John Paul II: To the Bishops of the Catholic Church on the Relationship between Faith and Reason.* Washington, DC: United States Catholic Conference.

Kossell, C. G. (2001). Natural Law and Human Law. In S. J. Pope (Ed.). *The Ethics of Aquinas* (169–193). Georgetown: Georgetown University Press.

Kupczak, J. (2000). *Destined for Liberty: The Human Person in the Philosophy of Karol Wojtyla/John Paul II.* Washington, DC: Catholic University of America Press.

MacIntyre, A. (1999). Theories of Natural Law in the Culture of Advanced Modernity. In E. B. McLean (Ed.). *Common Truths: New Perspectives on Natural Law* (91–118). Wilmington: ISI Books.

McEvoy, J. (2002). Singular Shape. In J. McEvoy (Ed.). *The Challenge of Truth: Reflections on Fides & Ratio.* (109–128). Dublin, Ireland: Veritas Publications.

McInerny, R. (1999). Are There Moral Truths That Everyone Knows? Natural Law and History. In E. B. McLean (Ed.). *Common Truths: New Perspectives on Natural Law* (1–18). Wilmington, DE: ISI Books.

Miscamble, W. D. (2009). *For Notre Dame: Battling for the Heart and Soul of a Catholic University.* South Bend, IN: St. Augustine's Press.

Nussbaum, M. (1999). *In Defense of Universal Values.* The Fifth Annual Hesburgh Lecture on Ethics and Public Policy: Women and Development. The Joan B. Kroc Institute for International Peace Studies: Occasional Papers. North Bend, IN: University of Notre Dame.

Ormerod, N. (2013). Mission Driven and Identity Shaped: *Ex Corde Ecclesiae* Revisited. *Irish Theological Quarterly, 78* (4), 325–337. doi: 10.1177/0021140013497441.

Ozoliņš, J. T. (2012). What Makes a Catholic University Catholic? *Ethics Education, 18* (1–2), 86–89. ISSN: 1444–8386.

Ozoliņš, J. T. (2015). Reclaiming Paedeia in an Age of Crises: Education and the Necessity of Wisdom. *Educational Philosophy and Theory, 47* (9), 870–882. doi: 10.1080/00131857.2015.1035154.

Swiezawski, S. (1993). Introduction: Karol Wojtyla at the Catholic University of Lublin. In K. Wojtyla (Ed.). *Person and Community: Selected Essays* (ix–xvi). Tr. T. Sandok, OSM. New York: Peter Lang.

Tarasiewicz, P. (2014). The Common Sense Personalism of Saint John Paul II (K. Wojtyla). *Studia Gilsoniana, 3* (Supplement), 619–634.

Taylor, J. (2009). Beyond Nature: Karol Wojtyla's Development of the Traditional Definition of Personhood. *The Review of Metaphysics, 63* (2), 415–454. Retrieved from: http://www.jstor.org/stable/40387698

Wilk, R. K. (2007). Human Person and Freedom According to Karol Wojtyla. *International Philosophical Quarterly, 47* (3), Issue 187, 265–278. doi: 10.5840/ipq200747321.

Wojtyla, K. (1993). *Person and Community: Selected Essays.* Tr. T. Sandok, OSM. New York: Peter Lang.

Wojtyla, K. (2011). *Man in the Field of Responsibility.* Tr. K. W. Kemp and Z. M. Kieron. South Bend, IN: St. Augustine's Press.

11 Adorno's critique of *Halbbildung*
Mapping an emancipatory educational program for critical consciousness

Ranier Carlo V. Abengaña

Introduction: why Adorno?

The mainstream scholarship on Theodor Adorno (1903–1969) often underscores his critique of society and culture in general, highlighting his reflections on the evils of modern capitalism, thereby making the *Culture Industry* as one of the most oft-cited theories in the wide range of subjects he has written on. But beyond this, Adorno also offered some thought-provoking insights regarding the education, formation, and development of an individual and society. Shedding light on this is a way of responding to the call for a "renewed understanding of the meaning of education".

Adorno's name is almost synonymous with the term "Culture Industry". His ruminations on the oppression and domination that happen beyond the workplace have indeed sparked a great number of discussions. However important, it would also be worthwhile to shift our attention from discussions about the "damaged life" to a way out of it. Certainly, the former substantiates our search for the latter. As such, the significance of shedding light on Adorno's educational theory lies precisely in accentuating education's emancipatory role. The way to freedom must begin in making man realize the negative conditions in which he is in.

The small percentage of engagement with Adorno's reflections on education, especially in English literature, may perhaps be due to the limited (in number, not in content) primary sources in which he directly dealt with the topic. Only three sources,[1] none of which are book length, come to mind: "*Erziehung nach Auschwitz*", "*Erziehung zur Mündigkeit*" (conversations with Hellmut Becker), and "*Theorie der Halbbildung*". This is understandable because Adorno is not so much a philosopher of education or a theorist in critical pedagogy with the same level of extensive focus on the topic that Paulo Freire or Henry Giroux, for instance, have.

But as our educational system is evidently exhibiting its characteristically socially mediated feature, it seems plausible that a renewed perspective on education might also be construed in the backdrop of critical theory. This chapter will thus be broadly divided into two main sections: first, I provide a justification regarding critical theory's role in educational theory; second, I focus on Adorno's perspectives regarding the meaning and value of education.

Between critical and educational theory: the desire for emancipation

There were a number of thinkers, prior to the formalization of critical pedagogy as a specific field of study (leading to Freire and Giroux's prominence), whose educational theories, as part of a larger system of thought, can be considered "critical" (see, i.e., Althusser, 2014; Gramsci, 1971). By "critical", I mean those who have been influenced by Marx's thoughts in understanding the crisis of modern education. That such "critical pedagogy" existed prior to Freire and Giroux is plausible as they themselves have been emphatic that "[c]ritical pedagogy is a movement and an ongoing struggle taking place in a number of different social formations and places" (Tristan and Giroux, 2013). They thus find it misleading to pinpoint a father, much less a beginning of critical pedagogy, for doing so devalues "those struggles and the collective efforts that have been made" prior to its supposed inception (Tristan and Giroux, 2013). Likewise, we cannot say that criticality in philosophy did not exist prior to Kant or the Frankfurt school, for after all, the foundation of the productive history of philosophy is none other than critique (Adorno, 1998a, p. 8).

Adorno was one of those thinkers who did critical pedagogy prior to Freire and Giroux. Giroux, aside from being influenced by Freire, would readily admit that the critical theory of Frankfurt School had significant contributions to the development of critical pedagogy (see Giroux, 1983a, 1983b). There are, thus, certain parallelisms. Giroux's notion of critical pedagogy is a "way of understanding education as well as a way of highlighting the performative nature of agency as an act of participating in shaping the world" (Tristan and Giroux, 2013). Education's task is beyond mere transference of knowledge, not merely emancipation from ignorance – which albeit important, is not the zenith of education. The emancipatory role of education carries with it a social, political, and moral import (see Tristan and Giroux, 2013).

The relationship between critical theory and pedagogy may, however, be questioned by discussing the presumptuous need for emancipation. Contemporary polemics on the politico-economic spectrum are often construed through left- and right-wing ideologies. While we may argue that modern educational system, culture, and society is indeed problematic, the opposite side would always disagree. Furthermore, even arguing from the standpoint of critical theory[2] is quite problematic, for it is difficult to define and encapsulate it into a fixed set of ideas and principles as those affiliated with the Frankfurt School alone shared different viewpoints and changed their minds over time (see Blake and

Masschelein, 2003, pp. 38–39). However, with a grasp on some of their normative claims (see Blake and Masschelein, 2003, pp. 38–39), it is possible to speak of critical theory as a school of thought.

What thus validates a critical theory of education? Primarily, I claim that we must address the problem of education vis-à-vis the problem of culture and society. As both are plagued with problems, philosophers' longing for a better world inhabited by a humane humankind has been a constant ideal. However, most proponents of critical theory agreed upon the dangers of promoting a positive ideal or utopia as attempts to realize it may be used to justify violence and injustice (see Blake and Masschelein, 2003, p. 39).

History has shown that progress was in truth regression (see Bronner, 2011, p. 5). Playing on Hegel's (1977) "the True is the whole" (§20), Adorno (2005) formulates that "the whole is the false" (§29). Given that our whole reality presents a false idea of progress, critical theory attempted to understand and reconstruct society not from some transcendent idea of a good life but from the existing negative conditions themselves – from the standpoint of the oppressed. This led to their gradually increasing pessimistic attitude – and Adorno's (see 1998c) thinking is typically characteristic of a resignation to a *cul-de-sac* – to the point that revolution has already become inconceivable. Culture Industry has rendered people pacified to an attitude of sheer conformity. In this case, we thus ought to take a step back – to treat the symptoms instead of the disease, that is, "to rescue the individual from a totalitarian world, totally bureaucratized, totally economized" (Blake and Masschelein, 2003, p. 40).

The task, therefore, was to map out an educational program that would restore the autonomy of individuals. Bronner (2011) says, "All members of the Frankfurt School agreed on the need for increased education to counteract authoritarian trends" (p. 5). However, it was unclear as to how such education might fare in a "totally administered society" (Bronner, 2011). Adorno would later on problematize this by asking how *Bildung* is at all possible in the age of *Halbbildung*.

Even educational institutions could become an avenue of "social and individual alienation" (Blake and Masschelein, 2003, p. 41). If this be the case, then the premier task of a critical theory of education would be a sort of intellectual revolution: making man aware of his vulnerable status in the plagued societal conditions he is in. Emancipation from ignorance – that is, ignorance on "the wrong state of things" (Adorno, 2007, p. 11) – precedes emancipation from those conditions.

Critical theory would thus argue that a proper education, that is, an education geared towards critical self-reflection, is the *conditio sine qua non* of autonomy. Critical pedagogy would later on similarly say that "pedagogy is a practice for freedom" (Giroux, 2010). If education were at all to become a transformative program, then we must first be able to comprehend its meaning and value. I shall thus proceed to briefly discuss the longstanding German tradition of *Bildung*.

Adorno's theory of *Bildung* and *Erziehung*

The notion of *Bildung* is central in Adorno's critical pedagogy. He builds this notion by supplementing it with his theories on *Erziehung* and *Halbbildung*. As such, for those restricted by the language barrier (myself included), I primarily find it important to try to unearth the meaning of *Bildung* – a term that bears such a "wealth of history" (see Gadamer, 2004, p. 9). With this, we could perhaps do more justice in comprehending Adorno's critique.

I opted to retain the German terms and titles of selected works from Adorno, not because the words are untranslatable, and we need not even be too idealistic for a "perfect translation". However, there is a great difficulty in trying to express a term that has been unique in one language to another. The translation does not often capture the very essence of the term. Non-English philosophical concepts translated to English produce a cacophony of disagreeing, yet complementary, voices. A number of words may correspond to the term being translated, and often these words may be distinguished from one another, but the term being translated encompasses all the possible translations and, yet, something more.

We experience a similar challenge in trying to unearth the meaning of the term *Bildung*. As Hegel (1961) so sublimely explains, the translated material's content

> can be approximately given [to] us by translations, but not their form, not their ethereal soul. Translations are like artificial roses which may resemble natural ones in shape, color, and perhaps even scent, but which cannot attain their loveliness, delicacy, and softness of life. Whatever daintiness and refinement the copy has belongs to the copy alone, and in the copy the contrast between the content and the form that has not grown up with the content makes itself felt unmistakably. The language is the musical element, the element of intimacy that fades away in the translation; it is the fine fragrance which makes possible the reader's sympathetic enjoyment of the [translated[3]] work and without which that work tastes like Rhine wine that has lost its flavor.
>
> (pp. 326–327)

Nevertheless, this restriction in language barrier could be temporarily remedied by getting to know the conceptual development of the term over the course of history. We thus owe a lot to the translators who made this highly alluring concept of *Bildung* accessible.

The German model of *Bildung*

Given that the "German notion of *Bildung* includes precisely an element of programmed incommunicability with regard to anyone who tries to approach the term from the outside" (Espagne, 2014, p. 111), it will surely take a great deal of philological, historical, and cultural scholarship – which I do not claim to have – to be able to grasp the essence of the term. With these limitations, I can only offer a glimpse into the profound richness of the word.

Coming from the word *Bild* (literally, "picture" or "image"), the term *Bildung* in its earliest sense may be taken to mean the "formation" of land, or mountain ranges, for instance. Later on, the word *Bild* developed a metaphorical connotation through its theological import made apparent by Meister Eckhart (see David, 2014, p. 107). *Bild* in this sense corresponded to the Latin *Imago*, while *Bildung* to *Formatio*. Much later on, and perhaps following Meister Eckhart, Humboldt (1988) would use a similar connotation of *Bildung* to distinguish it from *Kultur*, wherein the former is taken to mean a "higher and more inward" cultivation of one's "temperament and character" (see p. 34). This ancient mystical and theological import is both apparent in Meister Eckhart and Humboldt, who advocated that man's cultivation should be guided by the idea that "man carries in his soul the image of God, after whom he is fashioned" (Gadamer, 2004, p. 10).

Our concern, for this chapter, however, deals more closely with a "secular" notion of *Bildung*. The transition from the literal to the metaphorical (theological and secular) usage of the term suggested that "there is an especially complex set of words that are modeled on *Bild* and systematically related to it", one of which is "*Bildung* (education, culture)", and so "[t]he development of this system is representative of a large part of the history of German philosophy" (David, 2014, p. 107). Nevertheless, the intricacy remains. Schmidt remarked that *Bildung* is a complex term that can be translated as "culture", "development", "formation", or "education" (in Mendelsohn, 1996, p. 56). A combination of the senses of these words is how *Bildung* has been understood since the 18th century (see Gadamer, 2004, p. 8).

The notion of *Bildung* that we are precisely concerned with was determined by the definition given by Herder, which the 19th-century human sciences have preserved and appropriated. *Bildung*, according to Herder, is the "rising up to humanity through culture" (in Gadamer, 2004, p. 9). The word "culture" here must not be construed in its regular usage and basic dictionary definition (see Tylor, 1920, p. 1; Walton, 2012, p. 5), wherein it is understood as what we possess (e.g., the "culture" of bowing in some Asian countries). The difference between this and the German usage of the term precisely lies in the level at which we think culture is present.

While we typically regard culture as a "way of life", thereby regarding poor culture, or pop culture, or the culture of the hoi polloi still as culture, the Germans, however, take pride in their distinct "high culture". With their constant emphatic parallelism with Greek culture, culture is only culture insofar as it contributes to the development and formation of human beings toward an ideal. Espagne (2014) says, "By 'culture' we can mean . . . a certain amount of knowledge in the domains of history, literature, art, music, and language", which entitles a person to a certain level of distinction and recognition (p. 111). Being cultured is thus being erudite.

As such, *Bildung* is an "actualization of human perfectibility" (Espagne, 2014). However, I claim that it becomes complex as *Bildung* can be construed both as a process and an actualization. Espagne argues that as actualization, it cannot be reduced to any definite content, but on the contrary, as a process of development, *Bildung* is sure to have content. *Bildung* as a process contributes to the path of actualizing our human perfectibility via cultivation and constant formation.

Now, to what "projected ideal" is the process directed to? Mendelssohn (1996) conceptualizes the *"destiny of man"*, which is *"the measure and goal of all our striving efforts"* and must be "a point on which we must set our eyes, if we do not wish to lose our way" (p. 54). He uses the terms "enlightenment", "culture", and "education", all to refer to *Bildung*. As both a process and a goal, the three are the *requirements for our destiny* and, at the same time, *our destiny itself*. Therefore, *Bildung* has no goals outside itself. This playful notion connotes that we are dealing with a *moving target*. Gadamer (2004) drives a similar point by saying that *Bildung*, aside from the process of raising the mind to the universal (a Hegelian idea), "is at the same time the element within which the educated man (Gebildete) moves" (p. 13).

A society may benefit from the effects of having reached the status of *Bildung*. However, these should only come as secondary. Focusing on a "fixed goal" can lead to ideological formulations, wherein, instead of progress, we might turn to regression. This is a central theme in Adorno's appropriation of *Bildung*.

Culture industry and the emergence of **Halbbildung**

From three of the mentioned Adorno's works (*"Erziehung nach Auschwitz," "Erziehung zur Mündigkeit,"* and *"Theorie der Halbbildung"*) upon which I will primarily draw from, it is evident that only one involves the word *Bildung*. The other two works use the term *"Erziehung."* Note that there are several terms related to *Bildung*: we have *Aufklärung* (enlightenment), *Kultur* (culture), *Erziehung* (education, upbringing), *Ausbildung* (practical or vocational education, education that requires apprenticeship), and *Formierung* (formation), to mention some. All of the aforementioned terms have long vied with *Bildung*, but in fact, *Bildung* is distinguishable from the rest as it encompasses all of the these words and, yet, something more.

The concepts of culture and education are so closely intertwined in the German language that it thus becomes possible to understand Adorno's critique of education coming from and in relation to his critique of culture. What is then, the problem of culture according to Adorno? A plethora of noteworthy literature on this matter is readily available to the interested reader. Nonetheless, I shall provide a brief answer.

Adorno bemoans that modern sociopolitical phenomena, which people have so wrongly misconstrued for normality, have become avenues of oppression. Oppressive forces have already gone beyond the workplace and have made their way to the mass entertainment industry, whereby the culture it generated has led the people to become passive, thereby developing conformist attitudes. Modern capitalism has taken its toll in society. "Technical rationality today," says Adorno and Horkheimer (2002), "is the rationality of domination. It is the compulsive character of the society alienated from itself" (p. 95). Forms of mass entertainment – art, in its broadest sense – had become nothing but businesses. They used this as an "ideology to legitimize the trash they intentionally produce" (Adorno and Horkheimer, 2002). The pacified and subjugated masses in the culture of consumerism have inevitably led to society's decay. Adorno (1991) explains that the Culture Industry

> fuses the old and familiar into a new quality. In all its branches, products which are tailored for consumption by masses, and which to a great extent determine the nature of that consumption, are manufactured more or less according to plan. . . . The culture industry intentionally integrates its consumers from above. To the detriment of both it forces together the spheres of high and low art, separated for thousands of years. The seriousness of high art is destroyed in speculation about its efficacy; the seriousness of the lower perishes with the civilizational constraints imposed on the rebellious resistance inherent within it as long as social control was not yet total. Thus, although the culture industry undeniably speculates on the conscious and unconscious state of the millions towards which it is directed, the masses are not primary, but secondary, they are an object of calculation; an appendage of the machinery. The customer is not king, as the culture industry would have us believe, not its subject but its object. The very word mass-media, specially honed for the culture industry, already shifts the accent onto harmless terrain. . . . The culture industry misuses its concern for the masses in order to duplicate, reinforce and strengthen their mentality, which it presumes is given and unchangeable. How this mentality might be changed is excluded throughout. The masses are not the measure but the ideology of the culture industry, even though the culture industry itself could scarcely exist without adapting to the masses.
>
> (pp. 98–99)

Seducing us through the idea of progress in affluence, Culture Industry has rendered the people politically, materially, emotionally, and intellectually impoverished (see Walton, 2012, pp. 8–9). What was once highly regarded as *Bildung* is now reduced to *Halbbildung*. But how do we make people realize that the latter is simply masked as the former? If we answer "education", then how can proper education be possible in the age of Culture Industry, in the age of "pseudo-culture" (*Halbbildung*)?

Rescuing ourselves from *Halbbildung* means revamping the educational system, strengthening it, and protecting it from the further influences of pseudo-culture. Macroscale change will happen through microscale change. As Adorno (1993) narrates, "Culture was supposed to benefit the free individual – an individual grounded in his own consciousness but developing within society. . . . Culture is implicitly the prerequisite of an autonomous society – the more enlightened the individual, the more enlightened society as a whole" (p. 19). But if education is the way to enlightenment, how sure are we that it is immune from the effects of modern capitalism?

Thus, how is *Bildung* possible in the age of *Halbbildung*? Adorno does not give a very clear answer to this. He gives some insights about what education should be, despite not really saying whether we have the means to make education so. While pseudo-culture works its way to education, Adorno was emphatic that education must fight to resist it, for if it succeeds, education could become our salvation.

Adorno approaches the problem from this angle as he believes that *Bildung* "has a dual character: it refers to society and it mediates between society and pseudo-culture" (Adorno, 1993, p. 16). In other words, "*Bildung* is a socially-mediated phenomenon" (Stojanov, 2012, p. 126). A dialectical interplay exists between *Bildung* as education and as culture. As education, *Bildung* is not immune from the influences of culture. As culture, *Bildung* is affected by social phenomena that may either be beneficial or detrimental to it. But how do we solve this problem when it seems that we are surrounded by enemies from all sides?

Adorno's idea of *Bildung* as socially mediated may be interpreted as his critique of the traditional German model, particularly Hegel's, which Adorno thinks is detached from society. Hegel was stereotypically viewed as that classic elitist German professor who thought that the measure of one's education and being cultured is through one's knowledge of the Greco-Roman languages and classics. However, that Germany's *Bildung* during that time seemed to be detached from society and always grounded in classical literature and philosophical canon was because "they did not face the same needs of professionalization" (Blake, Smeyers, Smith, and Standish, 2003, p. 9) as did Germany during Marx's time and so on. Education's focus up to Hegel's time was the "transition [from] childhood to maturity, and the induction of the child into a cultural tradition, while it conceived this enculturated maturation as a form of emancipation" (Blake, Smeyers, Smith, and Standish, 2003, p. 9).

The transition to the capitalist age, however, paved the way for the overpowering of Germany's high culture. Adorno opposes the classical theory's rift between "culture" and "social practice" (Stojanov, 2012, p. 126), but not the rift per se, rather the reason for it. In Hegel's notion, culture as objective spirit ranks higher than society, "the latter simply a materialization of the former" (Stojanov, 2012, p. 127). But the gap must not be construed on the basis of some notion of pre-disposed hierarchy, but rather, "the conditions of modern capitalism" have made society "work against that spirit" (Stojanov, 2012, p. 127).

For Adorno (1993), this rift is not due to a lack of *Bildung*, but rather, high culture has been displaced by Culture Industry via the entertainment industry and consumerism, making society the "breeding grounds of pseudo-culture" (p. 20). Contra Hegel, if society is the materialization of objective spirit, then should it not work in accordance with the nature of the latter? However, given that pseudo-culture is socially-mediated, "its pathetic tendencies begin to infect the whole society" (Adorno, 1993, p. 36). I suppose this would lead to Adorno's main thesis: "the blithe dissemination of culture (*Bildung*) is the same as its destruction" (Adorno, 1993, p. 27). *Halbbildung* emerged from Culture Industry, producing a consumerist and conformist culture – a culture of pacified and subjugated individuals whose attempts to realize their ideals of progress led them to be assimilated into the capitalist machinery.

From the factory and beyond, "the measure of the bad new is merely the bad old" (Adorno, 1993, p. 23). This dehumanization further alienated people from authentic *Bildung* (see Adorno, 1993, p. 20). The only thing worse than this is perhaps being oblivious about it. Not having the mind-set for dissent, people think that there is no alternative to the status quo. If only we could be made aware, even in hypothetical terms, of this question of *eternal recurrence*.

> What, if some day or night a demon were to steal after you into your loneliest loneliness and say to you: "This life as you now live it and have lived it, you will have to live once more and innumerable times more; and there will be nothing new in it, but every pain and every joy and every thought and sigh and everything unutterably small or great in your life will have to return to you, all in the same succession and sequence. . . . The eternal hourglass of existence is turned upside down again and again, and you with it, speck of dust!"
>
> . . . If this thought gained possession of you, it would change you as you are or perhaps crush you. The question in each and every thing, "Do you desire this once more and innumerable times more?" would lie upon your actions as the greatest weight.
>
> (Nietzsche, 1974, §341)

To posit a better, alternative reality, even in the realm of fantasy, indeed bears the greatest weight. Lucky are those who can think of the possibility of such even just in hypothetical terms. However, Adorno was more skeptical. The masses are so deep in the machinery that they could no longer imagine any kind of reality apart from it.

One of the crucial effects of *Halbbildung* on cultural objects is making them easily assimilated, leading to the loss of subjectivity (see Stojanov, 2012, pp. 127–128). This loss of autonomy is what Adorno initially seems to problematize as authority and tutelage. Individuals deceived in capitalism's constant fiction of progress in affluence produce a mind-set akin to the Darwinian theory of the "survival of the fittest", thereby generating a "conformist society" (Adorno, 1993, p. 17). Formation degraded to conformation, and consequently, we lose ourselves. Once the capacity for autonomy has been curbed, people would tend to blindly acquiesce to the whims and fancies of those in authority, as history itself would not deny. Adorno (1998b) thus challenges us that an effective counterculture should envision that "[t]he premier demand upon all education is that Auschwitz not happen again" (p. 191).

Halbbildung generates a mind-set that people must conform "submissively to what is supposedly inevitable" (Adorno, 1993, p. 37). Man's desire for belongingness has overpowered his primal instinct to be disturbed. Practising a culture of dissent has thus been frowned upon most societies today, which "simply exists and blindly develops" (Adorno, 1993, p. 18). We conform at the expense of our identity, and hence, "[t]he pseudo-cultured person practices self-preservation without a self" (Adorno, 1993, p. 33).

If *Bildung* is possible in the age of *Halbbildung*, it is because *Erziehung* is programmed toward critical reflection on the latter (see Adorno, 1993, p. 38). This sort of utopian pessimism denotes that our ideal or "utopia" must not be "positively pictured" (Adorno, 2007, p. 207). Culture Industry and *Halbbildung* have become an ontological given, and we must work our way immanently. Adorno says that *Bildung* "needs what itself despises in order to survive", and furthermore, "the conditions of independent thinking on which a free society depends are determined by the unfreedom of society" (Adorno and Becker, 1983, p. 104).

The solution that Adorno arrives at is a contemporary appropriation of classical *Bildung*: "For better or for worse," Adorno (1993) says, "only isolated individuals who have not been absorbed completely in the melting pot, or professional groups who celebrate themselves as elites, still participate in culture" (p. 23). This proposed solution, I claim, seems to be a combination of Kant's theory on autonomy and Hegel's regard for high culture as well as his educative method of alienation and reconciliation.

Resurrecting Bildung: Erziehung *as education towards critical self-reflection*

That culture so far has failed is no justification for furthering its failure.
–*Theodor Adorno*, Minima Moralia

Between *Bildung* and *Halbbildung* is a proper *Erziehung*. Critical theory, which has also appropriated the German notion of *Bildung*, advocated the "commitment to exacting intellectual standards, a concern to defend high culture, and an understanding of the importance of cultural tradition" (Blake and Masschelein, 2003, p. 43). Adorno resorts to this "elitism" because those who are acquainted with high culture are perhaps going to be the last hope to recover authentic *Bildung*. But the question is, how can these "intellectual saviors" save the masses, if the masses themselves think that there is no need for saving? Herein lies the true difficulty of programming a proper *Erziehung*.

There are, to the extent of my knowledge, two available translations of Adorno's "*Erziehung zur Mündigkeit*". One translates *Mündigkeit* into "autonomy" (Adorno and Becker, 1983) and another to "maturity and responsibility" (Adorno and Becker, 1999). We can surmise that Adorno's usage of the term *Mündigkeit* may correspond to all three of the English words used: a mature individual would likely have an autonomous status, but even so, this individual does not forget that as a sociopolitical being, he or she must cultivate a sense of responsibility.

Adorno (1998b) implies that our attempt to change the objective conditions of today may already be a futile effort (see p. 192). But turning our attention to *Halbbildung* – the subjective dimension of culture industry – we could thus find a way to counter pseudo-culture, which is through a proper *Erziehung*. A proper *Erziehung*, as I gather from Adorno, "is an education towards critical self-reflection" (Adorno, 1998b, p. 193). This idea of critical self-reflection would immensely contribute to man's capability to become autonomous, which in turn would be beneficial for his self-formation. He is free insofar as he need not conform simply to survive or sustain his being.

Adorno uses Kant's definition of Enlightenment (see Kant, 1963, pp. 3–10) as a springboard for articulating the importance of "autonomy and independent thinking" in a democratic society (Adorno and Becker, 1983, p. 103). This, however, does not go unhindered. Culture Industry has rendered people passive. If an education for *Mündigkeit* is the precondition of authentic *Bildung*, then the premier task of *Erziehung* would primarily be intellectual emancipation.

Becker says, however, that although we can possibly establish an educational system that guarantees autonomy, it would be difficult for the individual to maintain it while being "in a world that increasingly seems to determine him through external mechanisms of control" (Adorno and Becker, 1983, p. 104). Furthermore, it would appear that we are merely convincing individuals to adapt to a "new culture" because theirs is not good. Even this call for autonomy can be twisted and can thus, instead, result to a suppression of it (Adorno and Becker, 1983, p. 108). This is why Adorno did not simply issue instructions for resistance, which could only be ideologized and would thus only make his agenda no different from that of Culture Industry's (see Thompson, 2006, pp. 75–76).

Adorno and Becker's conversation somehow evokes the feeling of gradually losing hope. For every posited solution, a problem ensues. But the way out of this, Adorno maintains, "is only through thought – and precisely through imperturbably and persistent thinking" (Adorno and Becker, 1983, p. 105). Beyond an encouraging aphorism, the gist of Adorno's proposed solution may actually be found here: a call for a culture of thinking. This does not mean, however, that *Mündigkeit* is a "kick against every kind of authority" (Adorno and Becker, 1999, p. 26; cf. 1983, p. 106). Being critical is different from the utter rejection of everything.

This tonal shift seems to set the tone for Adorno's appropriation of classical *Bildung*. That classical *Bildung* is detached from society means that it cannot be easily assimilated into Culture Industry. Case in point, Adorno (1993) says, "A senior handyman who, in his yearning for something higher, took on the *Critique of Pure Reason* and ended in astrology, ostensibly because only there was he able to reconcile the moral laws within us and the stars above us" (p. 30). This example attests to the fact that products of classical *Bildung* cannot easily be fragmented and, thereby, assimilated by pseudo-cultured people. In that famous passage from Kant's (2002) *Critique of Practical Reason* (see p. 203), the "stars above us" represent his metaphysics, while the "moral laws within us" correspond to his deontological ethics, specifically, the categorical imperative.

The failure of the handyman was that he was not able to contextualize the phrases vis-à-vis Kant's system. Attempting to fragment the work so that it could easily be assimilated, he thus ended up in astrology, misunderstanding the reference made to the starry heavens above us.

Because of the status of these works as part of the high culture, Adorno was hopeful that though it may seem paradoxical, succumbing to this ideology could nevertheless provide the solution to *Halbbildung* (see Stojanov, 2012, p. 129). Adorno thus envisages:

> I could envision one attending commercial films in high school (but in the grammar schools, too) and quite simply showing to the students what a fraud they are, and how full of lies, etc., or in the same way immunizing them against certain Sunday morning radio programs that play happy and carefree music as if we were still living in a 'healthy world' (a term that gives true cause for alarm); or reading a magazine with them and showing them how they are being taken for a ride by an exploitation of their own instinctual needs; or I can imagine a music teacher who does not happen to come from the youth music scene analyzing hit songs and showing why these hits are incomparably worse than a movement of a Mozart or Beethoven quartet, or a really genuine piece of modern music. Thus, one simply tries first of all to arouse the awareness that men and women are constantly being deceived, for the idea that "the world wants to be deceived," applied globally, has become the mechanism of immaturity today.
> (Adorno and Becker, 1983, p. 109)

This solution, however, tends to be utopic, if not "naïve" (Stojanov, 2012, p. 129), for it places the sole burden of education to the pedagogues, whom we presume not to be assimilated into pseudo-culture. Moreover, how do we convince people that the alternative offered to them is, in fact, better, when they are contented with the status quo?

This is where the fullness of the term "*Erziehung*" comes in. The term does not simply mean scholarly education, but it also connotes "upbringing." How we are brought up at home determines, to a great extent, our readiness to be in a larger social group, which is the school. Formal education, in turn, should be geared toward developing the individual to enter civil society. Parents and teachers must thus work hand in hand to ensure that children are prepared to receive and engage the cultural objects of *Bildung*.[4] But, apropos of the age-old distinction between theory and praxis, we must now ask, how can we convince people that this "theoretical" education is more important, if not as equally important, as "practical" education?

I do not think we have ever given a direct answer to the question "what is the value of philosophy?", for whenever such a question arises, we instinctively first try to address the meaning of "value". The difficulty comes with the people's refusal to encounter something unfamiliar, something that could shake the foundations of their thoughts. Anything of this sort is "not valuable".

With reference to authentic *Bildung*, Hegel's (1961) model, for instance, espouses an educative process of alienation from and reconciliation with ourselves through acquaintance with Greco-Roman languages and classics (see pp. 327–328). This education requires an attitude and mind-set of desiring to be lost in the foreign, only to return to oneself anew.

If this is the case, are we not simply saying that "my taste is better than yours?" Today's cultured class would generally appreciate a piece of jazz more than digitally produced music. But in retrospect, Adorno himself was very critical of jazz! Are we not simply developing a desire for this anachronistic belongingness, as if not to belong to one's age means that one is superior than others who do? Nevertheless, there is also something good in this, for we are able to picture a better, alternative reality aside from what is immediately given. And so, for the pseudo-cultured, if the problem is not that they cannot picture an alternative, it is that they refuse to.

Following this, Adorno offers a solution that seems to be a combination of immanent critique and Freud's psychoanalytic theory of identification. Adorno explains that

> children . . . generally identify with a father figure, i.e., an authority, they internalize it, appropriate it, and then in a very painful process that always leaves scars, they learn that the father or father figure does not correspond to the ego-ideal that they learned from him; and thus break away from him. Only in this way do children become mature people.
> (Adorno and Becker, 1983, pp. 106–107)

Becker affirms this immanent process by saying that our formation would necessarily involve an encounter with authority (see Adorno and Becker, 1983, p. 107).

Contradiction is a key ingredient of dialectics. Explaining this in a Hegelian tone – which I think Adorno, in this particular context, is quite faithful to – a fundamental desire for survival that developed in the age of culture industry is through conforming. The child would thus primarily need an authority figure with whom he can identify. But as the child can also have a different [pseudo-] formation, it is possible that the ideals of the authority figure and the child would soon drift away from each other. The child would become aware of the inherent deficiencies of the authority figure, which would generate a desire for emancipation. The child is thus able to control his or her formation despite conforming. This painful process of identification and detachment, which "never occur without scars" (Adorno and Becker, 1983, p. 107), is akin to the process of alienation and reconciliation – of *Aufhebung* (sublation).

Authority is thus a necessary evil – one that provides the very condition for our emancipation from it. However necessary, it must not be used to "glorify and remain satisfied with this stage" (Adorno and Becker, 1983, p. 107) This idea of contradiction, identification, detachment, and necessary evil is very evident in Adorno's critical theory of education. *Bildung* needs *Halbbildung*, and autonomy needs tutelage. The latter in the pair may in fact be a necessary condition but one which we must always learn to gradually overcome.

Adorno's critical theory of education today: emancipation from *Halbbildung* via immanent critique

Beyond the confines of the home, this psychoanalytic approach to *Halbbildung* may also work in schools, wherein a child could find an authority figure with whom he or she can identify. Becker agrees with Adorno on this and says that at some point, "the teacher must clearly see that his task consists in making himself superfluous" (Adorno and Becker, 1983, p. 107). We could derive two ideas from this. First, a good pedagogue is one who knows how to cultivate the minds of the students and, at the same time, knows when to step aside not to hinder further growth. Second, while this seems to be an immense burden on the part of educators, it is unnecessary to place all the load on them. Students who received proper upbringing in the family level would more likely be open to cultivation.

I thus argue for a collaborative effort, for oftentimes, we expect too much from the teachers to the point that they are already substituting for what the parents ought to do at home. These idealistic young educators would often get drained early, and consequently, they let themselves get caught in the capitalist machinery, merely considering teaching as paying jobs rather than a vocation upon which the bearers of authentic culture have entrusted the role of cultivating the children. The educational institution, no matter how problematic we may find it today, could play a great role in the salvation of our culture. It is on this note that we must work in the same spirit.

Toward the end of Kant's (1963) treatise on Enlightenment, he says that we do not live in an *enlightened age* but, rather, in an *age of enlightenment* (see p. 8). This is a riveting play on words, for the latter's message is certainly distinct from the former. The former suggests an accomplishment, an actualization (note the past tense of the term), while the latter suggests potency. But perhaps more ostensibly, as Adorno puts it, enlightenment (and hence, autonomy) is a "dynamic category, as a becoming and not a being" (Adorno and Becker, 1983, p. 108). Kant's favoring of the latter could attest to our thesis that *Bildung*, as a process and a goal, is a constantly moving target.

As such, tutelage must not be so negatively construed. For one, no education has ever taken place without some form of tutelage. This has been the case since the time of ancient Greeks. Hegel (1984) even said, "The beginning, precisely because it is the beginning, is imperfect. Pythagoras demanded four years' silence of his followers. The philosopher at least has the right to ask the reader to keep his own thoughts quiet until he has gone through the whole" (p. 293). Moreover, that "[e]nlightenment is man's release from his self-incurred tutelage" (Kant, 1963, p. 3) could mean that tutelage, after all, is a prerequisite of enlightenment. The autonomy we are aiming for, I presume, is not so much about simply thinking for our own selves through our own reason, for such kind of "autonomy" may only prove to be dangerous at best and catastrophic at worst. Again, while we need to overcome tutelage and authority, it is also something necessary.

Therefore, autonomy must not be taken radically. We have to understand that a powerful disease – this social pathology of *Halbbildung* and culture industry – must be treated with an equally powerful drug. As such, between the two extremes of tutelage and autonomy, we must find a solution that lies somewhere in the middle: a grounded education that should later on develop to *Mündigkeit*. Adorno may indeed be conforming to classical *Bildung*, but this did not happen blindly rather after a series of long and well-thought reflections. We *cannot not* conform, and as such, we must develop an attitude of informed criticality.

We must not resign to the idea of "*Mundus vult decipi, ergo decipiatur*". Going against culture often results in failure in one way or another; however, this notion of a "damaged life" and the "wrong state of things" (see Adorno, 2007, p. 11) must be our motivation to liberate ourselves from it. One is a slave insofar as one recognizes another as master. But it is only through the recognition of such a pathological relationship that the slave works his or her way toward freedom. The value of any tragic situation lies in our capability to transcend it.

Adorno's pessimism could lead us to one of the shortcomings of his theory. With grave mistrust for any product of culture industry, Adorno was not able to see that some products have much to offer for critical thought, if only we have the trained eye to see it. Some of these products take advantage of consumerism to present to people the inherent pathologies in pseudo-culture. The power of mass culture can pollute the minds of the masses, but granted that it has strong influence over the people, it can also be an avenue by which the deficiencies of culture industry are made apparent.

For instance, American-produced television programs such as *Boston Legal* (2004–2008) and *Mr. Robot* (2015–), if understood well, are actually a critique against U.S. imperialism and techno-capitalism, respectively. We also have critical political dramas such as *The West Wing* (1999–2006) and *House of Cards* (2013–). In addition, satire is a timeless example! Just recently, a parody film trailer in the Philippines has become viral online after it supposedly showed how typical Filipino films and television series have produced countless sequels with recycled plots (see Lasic, 2016). The tone of such critiques was very similar to what Adorno and Horkheimer (2002) puts forward in the "Culture Industry" chapter of the *Dialectic of Enlightenment* (see pp. 94–136). My point is that Adorno's idea of the homogeneity of the culture industry should be revisited because aside from educational institutions, we have these on our side. After all, "Remaining faithful to the critical spirit of the Frankfurt school seems much more of a tribute than an unquestioning acceptance of all it said or did" (Jay, 1973, p. xvii).

Adorno, I suppose, departs from the classical model of *Bildung* as the latter tends to be detached – practising a kind of ivory tower philosophizing. However, we can arrive at a solution if we meet halfway: we have to step down to raise them up. We must no longer practice the elitism of "my culture, age, or taste is better than yours". We have to step down to the level of students so that they can easily identify with us and use such a relationship to awaken them to the reality of the present circumstances. The children are most vulnerable to the effects of Culture Industry. But if we can guide them to become selective and train them to have a critical outlook, then surely, such tools would play a great role in their formation.

Truly, the task of education is indeed complicated and problematic! But we must work hard for it should we want to see ourselves beyond this situation, for as Adorno (2005) says, the "[w]rong life cannot be lived rightly" (§18). As educators and practitioners of philosophy, we only need to be reminded about the great task that is entrusted upon us. In the end, "The work is too much for us. The work is never enough for us."[5]

Acknowledgments

A truncated and earlier version of this paper was presented in the COMIUCAP International Conference on *Civil Society and Human Formation: Philosophy's Role in a Renewed Understanding of the Meaning of Education*, held at the Australian Catholic University, Melbourne, Australia, July 20–22, 2015. I would like to express my utmost gratitude to some friends and colleagues in the Graduate School and the Department of Philosophy of the University of Santo Tomas for their helpful insights, most especially to two of my mentors and constant sources of inspiration, Prof. Dr. Alfredo Co and Dr. Paolo Bolaños. Special thanks as well for some of the attendees of the congress who shared their thoughts and insights regarding the previous version of this piece. Last, a most genuine gratitude goes to Prof. Jānis Ozoliņš for considering this work for publication and for all his patience and kind considerations.

Notes

1 I have only used works that directly dealt with "education", although as would be detailed later on, there would be an interplay between "education" and "culture". Moreover, I have opted to leave out *The Authoritarian Personality* as the sections on education there would be better interpreted by an empirical researcher.
2 I am only referring to the critical theory of the Frankfurt School. However, critical theory today has become a more encompassing field of study whose thinkers come not only from the Institute of Social Research but from around the globe.
3 Originally, Hegel (1961) uses the word "ancient", but I have opted to change it to "translated" (enclosed in brackets) to remain faithful to the context in which I was using the passage (see pp. 326–327).
4 In this instance, one may raise the problem as to how such could be possible when both parents and teachers are integrated into the system of Culture Industry. Parents and teachers need not be "cultured" in the sense of classical *Bildung*, but keeping an open attitude toward it could be enough to pave the way for the proper formation of children.
5 Response of Eduardo Calasanz during the *Luncheon in Honor of the Retirees of the Loyola Schools*, March 18, 2015, Faber Hall, Ateneo de Manila University (Manila, Philippines).

References

Adorno, T. W. (1991). Culture Industry Reconsidered. Tr. A. G. Rabinbach. In J. M. Bernstein (Ed.). *The Culture Industry: Selected Essays on Mass Culture* (98–106). London: Routledge.
Adorno, T. W. (1993). Theory of Pseudo-Culture. Tr. D. Cook. *Telos, 95,* 15–38.
Adorno, T. W. (1998a). Why Still Philosophy? Tr. H. W. Pickford. In *Critical Models: Interventions and Catchwords.* (5–17). New York: Columbia University Press.
Adorno, T. W. (1998b). Education after Auschwitz. Tr. H. W. Pickford. In *Critical Models: Interventions and Catchwords.* (191–204). New York: Columbia University Press.
Adorno, T. W. (1998c). Resignation. In *Critical Models: Interventions and Catchwords.* (289–293). New York: Columbia University Press.
Adorno, T. W. (2005). *Minima Moralia: Reflections from Damaged Life.* Tr. E. F. N. Jephcott. London: Verso.
Adorno, T. W. (2007). *Negative Dialectics.* Tr. E. B. Ashton. New York: Continuum.
Adorno, T. W. and Becker, H. (1983). Education for Autonomy. Tr. D. J. Parent. *Telos, 55,* 103–110.
Adorno, T. W. and Becker, H. (1999). Education for Maturity and Responsibility. Tr. R. French, J. Thomas, and D. Weymann. *History of the Human Sciences, 12* (3), 21–34.
Adorno, T. W. and Horkheimer, M. (2002). *Dialectic of Enlightenment: Philosophical Fragments.* Tr. E. Jephcott. Ed. G. S. Noerr. Stanford, CA: Stanford University Press.
Althusser, Louis. (2014). *On the Reproduction of Capitalism: Ideology and Ideological State Apparatuses.* Tr. G. M. Goshgarian. London: Verso.
Blake, N. and Masschelein, J. (2003). Critical Theory and Critical Pedagogy. In N. Blake, P. Smeyers, R. Smith, and P. Standish (Eds.). *The Blackwell Guide to the Philosophy of Education.* (38–56). Oxford: Blackwell Publishing, Ltd.
Blake, N., Smeyers, P., Smith, R., and Standish, P. (Eds.). (2003). Introduction. In *The Blackwell Guide to the Philosophy of Education* (1–18). Oxford: Blackwell Publishing, Ltd.
Bronner, S. E. (2011). *Critical Theory: A Very Short Introduction.* New York: Oxford University Press.
David, Pascal. (2014). Bild. Tr. S. Rendall, C. Hubert, J. Mehlman, N. Stein, and M. Syrotinski. Tr. and Ed. E. Apter, J. Lezra, and M. Wood. In B. Cassin (Ed.). *Dictionary of Untranslatables: A Philosophical Lexicon.* (107–111). Princeton, NJ: Princeton University Press.
Espagne, M. (2014). Bildung. Tr. S. Rendall, C. Hubert, J. Mehlman, N. Stein, and M. Syrotinski. Tr. and Ed. E. Apter, J. Lezra, and M. Wood. In B. Cassin (Ed.). *Dictionary of Untranslatables: A Philosophical Lexicon.* (111–121). Princeton, NJ: Princeton University Press.
Gadamer, H.-G. (2004). *Truth and Method* (2nd edn.). Tr. J. Weinsheimer and D. G. Marshall. London: Continuum.
Giroux, H. A. (1983a). *Critical Theory and Educational Practice.* Melbourne: Deakin University.
Giroux, H. A. (1983b). *Theory and Resistance in Education: A Pedagogy for Opposition.* South Hadley, MA: Bergin and Garvey.
Giroux, H. A. (2010). Rethinking Education as the Practice of Freedom: Paulo Freire and the Promise of Critical Pedagogy. Retrieved from: http://www.truth-out.org/archive/item/87456:rethinking-education-as-the-practice-of-freedom-paulo-freire-and-the-promise-of-critical-pedagogy
Gramsci, A. (1971). *Selections from the Prison Notebooks.* Tr. and Ed. Q. Hoare and G. N. Smith. New York: International Publishers.

Hegel, G. W. F. (1961). On Classical Studies [Appendix]. Tr. R. Kroner. In T. M. Knox (Ed.). *On Christianity: Early Theological Writings* (321–330). New York: Harper Torchbooks.

Hegel, G. W. F. (1977). *Phenomenology of Spirit*. Tr. A. V. Miller. Oxford: Oxford University Press.

Hegel, G. W. F. (1984). *The Letters*. Tr. C. Butler and C. Seiler. Bloomington, IN: Indiana University Press.

Humboldt, W. (1988). *On Language: The Diversity of Human Language-Structure and Its Influence on the Mental Development of Mankind*. Tr. P. Heath. Cambridge, UK: Cambridge University Press.

Jay, M. (1973). *The Dialectical Imagination: A History of the Frankfurt School and the Institute of Social Research, 1923–1950*. London: Heinemann.

Kant, I. (1963). What Is Enlightenment? In L. W. Beck (Tr. and Ed.). *Kant: On History*. (3–10). New York: Palgrave MacMillan.

Kant, I. (2002). *Critique of Practical Reason*. Tr. W. S. Pluhar. Indianapolis, IN: Hackett Publishing Company, Inc.

Lasic, G. (2016). Cinemalaya's Promo Video Hilariously Attacks Recycled Plots in Pinoy Fantasy Films [News]. Retrieved from: http://pop.inquirer.net/2016/08/cinemalaya-s-promo-video-hilariously-attacks-recycled-plots-in-pinoy-fantasy-films/

Mendelssohn, M. (1996). On the Question: What Is Enlightenment? Tr. J. Schmidt. In J. Schmidt (Ed.). *What Is Enlightenment: Eighteenth-Century Answers and Twentieth Century Questions* (53–57). Berkeley, CA: University of California Press.

Nietzsche, F. (1974). *The Gay Science*. Tr. W. Kaufmann. New York: Vintage Books.

Stojanov, K. (2012). Theodor W. Adorno: Education as Social Critique. In P. Siljander, A. Kivelä, and A. Sutinen (Eds.). *Theories of Bildung and Growth: Connections and Controversies between Continental Educational Thinking and American Pragmatism* (125–134). Boston, MA: Sense Publishers.

Thompson, A. J. P. (2006). *Adorno: A Guide for the Perplexed*. London: Continuum.

Tristan, J. M. B. and Giroux, H. (2013). Henry Giroux: The Necessity of Critical Pedagogy in Dark Times [Interview]. Retrieved from: http://www.truth-out.org/news/item/14331-a-critical-interview-with-henry-giroux

Tylor, E. (1920). *Primitive Culture: Researches into the Development, Mythology, Philosophy, Religion, Language, Art, and Custom*. Vol. 1. London: John Murray.

Walton, David. (2012). *Doing Cultural Theory*. London: Sage Publications, Ltd.

12 Contestation of the ends of higher education and the disciplinary voice

John G. Quilter

Contesting the ends of higher education: a good thing

We seem to live in times when public debate about higher education policy questions is informed by economic policy stances, assumptions about the merits 'for the sector' of competition among 'providers' of higher education services and about what is owed 'consumers' (i.e., students) of the service in the way of 'consumer protection' and improving graduate 'satisfaction with the service', and the need to improve the 'productivity' of labour understood in terms of costs per unit of output, for instance, the costs of getting a student through a course of study to graduation.[1] If one listened only to such voices contributing to debates about higher education, it would be natural to think that higher education is a service much like hotels provide a service to travellers or car mechanics provide a service to those who needs their vehicles maintained and repaired. On such an 'economistic' view, the exact nature of the service provided has nothing to do with the evaluation of how well it is conducted in particular instances. In general, what matters on such a view is efficiency, meaning the most productive allocation of resources, which in turn, means that allocation of resources which produces the greatest levels of satisfaction with the service among those who consume it, thus generating the greatest value outcomes for the input of resources. That is the end of higher education as it is for any activity subject to the economic conception. For many of us in the academy, this is an all-too-familiar conception of the point of our work amongst managers.

Such voices are not the only voices contributing to discussion of higher education. I will not be able to survey or evaluate the voices in the debate at all comprehensively. However, before moving on to what I do want to address here, it is useful to observe that not all the voices in contemporary discussion are as reductive, or reductive in the same way, as the economic conception just sketched. Some, animated by a moral conception of the political significance of higher education, ask us to think of it as an engine of social mobility. Amongst other things they do, universities train young people from groups that tend to be in lower socio-economic strata of society to become members of professions which enable them to rise into higher socio-economic strata. Presumably this benefits the graduates concerned, and their families, as well as the professions they enter, irrigating them with enhanced social diversity. Universities also provide the economy with bright ideas for innovation in industrial and cultural applications. From the broader, macroeconomic perspective, universities provide the economy with trained professionals for increasingly technical areas of the modern economy – well-educated young people for the sophisticated work and innovation of the future. Similar points can be made about the contribution of universities to culture. On such conceptions, the point of higher education is not merely to produce what it produces efficiently. It is to contribute technical training, intellectual and cultural skills in critical and creative thinking, and application of knowledge that will improve the future of our social world – including but not limited to economically productive activity. This is not, or should not be, criticised as a reductive understanding of higher education. For it goes to the way we live, not just to the way we produce and consume: a modern society is dynamic, well-informed and educated, constantly working to push back the boundaries of ignorance and inability, it values its citizens' welfare and fulfilment and their opportunity to contribute positively to our common life, it needs a strong and innovative economy and system of social and cultural life to sustain itself in the ways of liberal democratic values . . . and so on.

It is unsurprising, then, that with the sophistication of a modern, liberal democratic, economically and culturally complex society, there should be numerous demands on higher education and correspondingly diverse conceptions of 'what it is for'. This diverse range of conceptions of 'what it is for' also affects other traditional institutions of such communities – like the law, school education, the social welfare system, the public service, the political system of government and so on. The ends of such institutions are a constant theme of public debate and properly so. I have no problem, then, with the diversity of contributions to debate about what *universities* are for. It is only to be expected in societies where universities have contributed to a wide range of social ends and played a part in a wide range the activities of our social lives together. The strength and support of the university as a social institution is part of how modern societies live and operate. Unsurprisingly, then, each area of social life to which it has contributed or in which it has operated will have some claim to make on the point of the university. And this is not anything that only universities are subject to. Further, it is a healthy feature of a modern society in general that there should be such debate and controversy.

Now for the 'however'. All that said, the university is in quite some trouble. In my view, in a lot of respects it has lost its way, and part of this is because it is unclear to many in the university what the university is for. I want to address this question. I will begin by sketching a couple of areas where I believe university practice and thinking is quite seriously problematic. I will then urge that at least a significant element of why this is so arises from divergent pressures on the university, which can only properly be resolved with the right understanding of what the university is 'for' and how this question should be answered in the first instance. I shall argue that the perspectives of disciplines that make up the university on this question are especially authoritative voices which should be heard more in the debates about the university and taken more seriously. To give this latter idea some content, I will sketch responses from my own discipline of philosophy. However, important though philosophy be to the identity of an institution of higher learning and understanding such as a university, each discipline needs to articulate its conception of this idea of what the university is for.

Troubles in paradise

There are quite a lot of changes to the higher education scene that one might inveigh against: managerialism,[2] an often unreflective insistence on and use of student evaluation of units and of teaching,[3] bureaucratisation of the teaching of units, the rush to online and related modes of delivery without serious attempt at evaluating their educational efficacy and value,[4] the casualisation of the teaching workforce, the increasing split between research and teaching . . . to name a few.

I will discuss two examples of trends in universities which, I argue, manifest the confusion about the ends of higher education which I shall argue need to be addressed in a particular way. I want to discuss (i) the contemporary support for so-called constructive alignment and (ii) the way we are now managing higher degrees by research.

Constructive alignment ideology

'Constructive alignment' in higher education teaching theory is a name for the theory of John Biggs and Catherine Tang in which they bring together two lines of thought about teaching practice in higher education.[5] One is from the thought that students learn by constructing their worldview and practice by actively engaging with what they are studying and addressing applications of it, solving problems with it, evaluating its success in practice and hence more deeply probing its depths and limitations. The other is that teaching practice needs self-consciously to target objectives ('learning outcomes') that are intended outcomes for the student-targets for their development as a result of their taking the unit or course. These aims then guide the teacher in designing/planning activities that the student is to do to attain or at least grow in the attainment of those learning outcomes. The aims also guide the teacher in designing assessment tasks for the students which work either to add to their growth in the learning outcomes (formative assessment) or to enable the teacher to evaluate how successfully the student has attained the intended learning outcomes. Both learning activities and assessment tasks are aligned to the learning outcomes of the unit. Good teaching, then, is constructively aligned in this way.

Put this way, constructive alignment is really the merest common sense in higher educational teaching. Given that the point of teaching is that students learn, there is no serious alternative than to do what is necessary or conducive to their learning. The learning sought in higher education should be of the highest cognitive skills attainable by students at the level of their development. These should be higher cognitive skills of the order of critical evaluation, applying and extending a theory, theorising for themselves, putting and testing or evaluating an hypothesis to explain something and the like rather than merely describing, memorising, restating and so on. Higher education aims at developing independent, critical thinkers with suitably responsible creative and insightful intellectual abilities. To form the young (or others) in such skills, they need to be given every opportunity to practise them in what they do, make mistakes and get it right, apply them in a widening field of applications, integrate their understanding in a comprehensive worldview and so on. *They* need to do this work. Merely approaching teaching as if one is filling an empty vessel with information or facts is simply a mistake. This is hardly new: Plato made the same point in the *Meno* when bringing out a point about knowledge and learning with the slave boy (Plato, 2005, 82a–85e, pp. 114–123).

Biggs's concern is primarily with professional education in the university. Exposition of theory should be oriented towards the practical application students make with it in their professional lives. It is not something done for its own sake in grand abstraction from practice. Practice and practical skill here is all. But it is not so with all disciplines in the university. In fact, without those disciplines for which this is not the case, disciplines for which the point is just to know the truth and explain things in the world for their own sake, including ourselves and our behaviour, the professions' knowledge bases, though they would not be nothing, would not be as deep as they are where they have deep theory to draw on as foundational. That 'practice', in the sense of professional education, is not everything in all university disciplines is very important. We will come back to this shortly.

At its best, constructive alignment reminds the teacher that a certain kind of unity is required in a good unit of teaching: that student development is the target, development in those abilities that enable them to participate actively in a stage appropriate way in the discipline they are studying, to exercise its distinctive ways of enquiry, reflection and creative work, to engage and benefit from the challenges of its canon, to elaborate its insights and understanding and so on. And that the topics and theories taught, skills practised by student learning activities, assessment tasks set and so on form a coherent set directed at the students' development in the discipline.

However, there is more to it than this. This line of thought cannot simply be taken at face value. For unity can be achieved in many ways. If teaching activities are to be aligned to learning outcomes and assessment tasks are to be aligned to learning outcomes, two pitfalls are possible, indeed tempting under certain conditions, consistent with achieving certain kinds of unity in a unit. The first is to simplify the conception of the alignment of learning activities to learning outcomes in such a way as to finesse their relation to assessment. That is, if it is thought that learning activities ought to be focussed on assisting students understand content and develop skills put on trial in assessment, even if the assessment is aligned to learning outcomes, the result is a highly reductive conception of what the unit ought to be about: it becomes about assessment from the point of view of the student and about anything else secondarily to assessment. Some will argue that this is right anyway. Students first focus on assessment with a view to their results and construct their work in the unit around that objective. In focussing learning activities on assessment and thus focus them on the learning outcomes, we are serving student demand and meeting their needs. I demur from such an argument but will return to it later.

A second pitfall is that the alignment doctrine puts an inordinate weight on the explicitation of learning outcomes. One is to formulate explicitly what the learning outcomes of the unit are. This is taken to be a necessary condition of students' being able to understand what the unit is aiming at so that they can pursue as self-consciously as the learning activities assist them to. Further interpretants of the learning outcomes are put in place such as rubrics for levels of achievement in assessment. But these are to be made explicit in statements and descriptions of these levels of achievement. The pitfall is to think that such explicit statements, including learning outcomes, somehow capture what is essential for the unit as an exercise in the discipline of which it is a part. This is a mistake. My reasons for resisting the pitfalls are related.

Firstly, why do I demur from the thought that meeting student need in a unit is a matter of the reductive conception of the unit in terms of the focus on assessment? The reason is that simply put, there is more to what a unit can and should do for a student than assist them to get the results in the assessment tasks that they seek. Instead, a unit of teaching is an element in the immersion of the student in the discipline that is their becoming a, stage-appropriate practitioner of the discipline. Since a discipline is more than a set of explicit statements of abilities to be developed and topics in whose treatment those skills are acquired and practised, it is more than good results in assessment tasks aligned to the learning outcomes stating those abilities and content. It is misleading to hope that a set of learning outcomes could satisfactorily articulate what the unit is for in the way of student development. They are helpful, to be sure. But they are not a sufficient condition. For a discipline not only is characterised by what can be made explicit in such statements as learning outcome statements. It is, more particularly, the set of inarticulable and informal values, practices, attitudes and habits of mind and the like that constitute the discipline's culture. That is an essential part of what the student's formation in the discipline involves. They cannot simply become self-consciously proficient in the explicit theories, debates and skills of the discipline. For without competence in the ways these things are done in the discipline and in the commitments that inform explicit practice and formulation in the discipline, 'proficiency' in what can be formulated explicitly becomes a counterfeit or malapropism of the real thing. An example of this in philosophy is certain thinkers who think of themselves as philosophers but who really practise the content, skills and so on of philosophy more as an exercise in, say, literary studies or theology but who lack the philosophical *habitus* that marks the philosopher. A unit in a discipline sequence has to go beyond the explicitly stated aspects of the discipline in the unit. As much as or more than this, it is part of the formation of the student in those informal and inexplicit aspects of the disciplinary culture. Learning activities ought to be as much directed towards this as to students' learning explicit skills relevant to successful completion of the assessment tasks or to the meeting of explicitly stated learning objectives.

Secondly, this point also explains my misgivings concerning the weight put on explicit learning outcomes and constructive alignment. For, to talk about my discipline, hoping that students can become philosophers by attaining explicitable learning outcomes alone is to miss the point just made. Some who do well at the explicitly spelled-out aims of a unit and achieve high marks simply nevertheless do not 'get' what being a philosopher is. Attainment of learning outcomes may be a necessary condition for successful development, at a stage-appropriate level, of status as a practitioner of the discipline. But it is not sufficient. For that, the acquisition of the informal, inarticulable attitudes, values and so forth is also called for. And that requires more than learning outcomes, not to mention more than aligning assessment to them.

Yet, we find ourselves increasingly hectored to get our units into constructive alignment in the reductive sense already suggested. That is, learning activities which have no direct bearing on achievement in assessment is seen to be pointless or, worse, a distraction. Some proponents of constructive alignment may reply to my criticism that I am putting up a straw man or, at best, looking at degraded examples of constructive alignment. There is nothing in constructive alignment itself that necessitates this kind of reduction of a unit to its assessment tasks. Well perhaps that is true. However, in rejoinder, I'd make a couple of observations. First, surely tellingly, one finds in Biggs's own work comments like the following:

> In fact, it was difficult to separate what was a TLA <teaching and learning activity> and what was an AT <assessment task>, as is the case in an aligned system (Biggs and Tang, 2011, p. 103). In designing TLAs it helps to consider them as the assessment tasks as well – then you have excellent alignment. For example, the teaching/ learning activity is simply applying that concept to a case study and the most appropriate assessment task is how well that concept is applied to the case study.
>
> (Biggs and Tang, 2011, p. 162)

The picture seems to be that constructive alignment in a unit is maximal where teaching and learning activities (TLAs) subserve the performance by the student of the skills in the assessment task. It would follow that TLAs which foster other skills or practise the student in disciplinary skills or knowledge not specific to or broader than those required for the assessment tasks would render the unit less than perfectly aligned and so of lower quality. Thus, though it may not be an explicit commitment of proponents of constructive alignment that a unit is reducible to its assessment tasks, the ideology of constructive alignment has a tendency towards this conception.

Secondly, the emphasis in Biggs's own work on (i) rising to the challenges of teaching a more diverse studentship, one not necessarily very well prepared for higher education studies, (ii) one whose motivations for university study are not knowledge and academic values for their own sake but professional qualification to get a well-paid job and (iii) student-centred teaching conspiring to reduce the point of a unit to its assessment and the student's performance on it. Students fitting the descriptions in (i) and (ii) tend to focus on the assessment tasks. As such, student-centred teaching can easily become a job of giving the students what they want – to learn how to do the assessment tasks. TLAs then become focussed on that, and the unit's benefit to the student is reduced to getting them through the assessment tasks. A criterion-referenced system of grading surely would only tend to magnify such effects.

Thirdly, extrinsic pressures furnish circumstances in which this reasoning can become compelling. Pressures of this sort include though are not limited to: (i) those arising from a university's need to retain students; (ii) pressures of teaching staffs' workload and the imperative to publish – requiring simplification of the work involved in teaching; (iii) the growing tendency of departments to be obliged to review final results and seek explanations from teachers if results are not at least fairly normal statistically; (iv) the increasing stress on student evaluation of teaching for promotion and so on. In the special case of teaching to conscripts who cannot understand and resent doing a particular unit, this pressure can become overwhelming. Teaching to the test is derided as poor teaching practice. Tests don't always enable students to learn deeply, and teaching to them does not give students the opportunity to attain the higher order cognitive learning that should characterise higher education. However, though we rightly deride teaching to the test, we risk becoming 'teachers to the assessment tasks' and selling students short on their development by immersion into the culture of the disciplines they are studying if we don't take a critical bead on constructive alignment ideology. We risk, and in common circumstances of contemporary universities we easily slide into, reducing their learning to learning how to get marks on assessments. This surely misses the point of higher education.

Higher degree by research studies

In my view, thinking about higher degree by research (HDR) studies is confused in Australia. The traditional model of the Ph.D. is that it can take about five years and the thesis submitted will be between 80,000 and 100,000 words long. The jump from a first in honours to this kind of research work is significant. In particular, in most undergraduate programmes, a student takes 10 units in the discipline over four years. One hopes that this exposes the student to the main sub-disciplines of the discipline but it is not always so. Thus, the distance between the knowledge of the discipline that even a highly successful honours student can be expected to have and the state of the discipline itself is very, very large. Yet, when students embark on a Ph.D., they are required to write something passing original in a sustained argument over 100,000 words. Traditionally, this meant that the student needed first to get across the sub-discipline of his or her Ph.D. topic and address those issues in it that are relevant to the topic and then, having argued a position in that constellation of debates, hone in on the specifics of the topic itself of the Ph.D. Typically, doing this requires about 100,000 words. But it also takes longer than the three years for which Ph.D.s are currently funded. Typically it requires about five years in my experience. Such, roughly, is the British influenced model. Further, once the Ph.D. is completed, the graduand can take full-time work teaching and researching. Teaching typically requires disciplinary knowledge wider than that of one's Ph.D., which is highly specialised. But in the British model, there has been no course work component of the Ph.D. programme, and so, coming by the necessary knowledge of the wider discipline for teaching takes time, which a good head of school will make for the newly employed academic, with an eye to his or her development in the profession.

The US system is quite different. It takes four to five years or more but includes a course work component to prepare the student in advanced studies in the discipline in a wider range of sub-disciplines than the preparation of the thesis requires. This has two effects. It bridges somewhat the gap between the disciplinary knowledge attained by undergraduate studies and that required for preparing the thesis. And it equips the graduand with a breadth of disciplinary knowledge that makes the transition to teaching easier once he or she is employed. Of course, the thesis is significantly shorter – a maximum of about 80,000 words. Originality is still required, but the need of the students getting across the relevant central debates of the sub-discipline of the PhD topic is obviated considerably. Hence, they can, in principle at least, drill down more efficiently and in fewer words on the specifics of their topic. But of course, such a system requires more than three years. The thesis takes no less than two years, and the course work requires at least two. Typical programmes will take five years.

It seems to me that in Australia we have selected the more difficult features of both these systems but in doing so have won none of the better features. Government now funds universities for students to take three years to complete a Ph.D. Thus, the incentives are on taking in students who are already well advanced towards the definition and partial completion of their thesis. The problem here is that, but for exceptional students, this is not a plausible picture of things. In particular, students graduating with honours, even with a first, simply do not have the breadth or depth of disciplinary exposure to know whether what they want to do will work in their discipline as a research topic for a Ph.D. There is simply too wide a gap between what is attainable having done undergraduate studies in the discipline (10 units at fairly basic level) and what is required to write a Ph.D. and stand on one's own two feet as a researcher in the discipline's research culture. And the thesis they must write is still generally between 80,000 and 100,000 words. Doing that well without graduate course work preparation requires four to five years for which the government will not pay. On the other hand, we could reduce the length of the thesis. But to do that and enable the graduand to have produced a thesis solid enough to be acceptable in the contemporary research culture of any discipline I can think of requires that students have a foundation in two years of graduate course work. Again, the government will not pay for this.

So, contemporary HDR studies in Australia face a dilemma: universities can either (i) retain the traditional model from the British influence and do not get paid by government for the extra years of student research studies beyond the three years they are currently paid or (ii) shorten the required length of the thesis, get paid for it, but present students with the challenge of preparing a thesis that can stand on its own two feet in the discipline's research culture and pass examination but do so without the advantage of the students doing two years of graduate course work to prepare for this.

One might urge that this dilemma can be avoided by the Masters by course work in a discipline taken at the student's own expense. The rejoinder to this is contained in the adjectival phrase ending that sentence: 'taken at the student's own expense'. This would cost students at least $15,000 on most reckonings. Students are unlikely to find this an attractive alternative to getting a job and working in their discipline in their spare time – not exactly a formula, excepting exceptional individuals, for high achievement in the discipline. The only alternative is to set up scholarships for either the extra years of HDR studies under option (i) or for the Masters by course work studies as a remedy for the problems of option (ii). But we are not a philanthropic nation for higher educational scholarships except to a very limited extent – an extent which does not encourage confidence that it could be a general solution for all our HDR challenges. So for all practical purposes, the dilemma stands as best as I can see. We don't really know what we want for HDR studies.

At the moment, we seem to be handling this dilemma by more or less pretending it does not exist and putting pressure on the admission and confirmation processes to filter out students who may require more than three years to complete. Given the nature of the gap between what is attainable in undergraduate education in a discipline and the advanced state of research work in our disciplines, this effectively will limit the students in HDR studies to only the most exceptional. But these are so few, by definition, that the future for HDR studies in Australia looks bleak if we continue on our present path.

The question "what is a university for?"

I have expressed a relaxed attitude about the fact that the answer to this question is contentious in a liberal, modern democratic society, and there are many voices in the debate about it. I now need to qualify this. For there is one voice which should have a certain privileged position in answering a question like "What is university for?" After all, if we were to ask "What is medicine for?" or "What is architecture for?", we would not ask accountants or advertisers. We would ask doctors and architects, respectively. Of course, it might be thought that the level of consultation by government with and lobbying by organisations like

Universities Australia (UA) constitutes asking universities. But while that is relevant, it is also a kind of category mistake. For universities and UA are not like, say, the Australian Medical Association. UA consists of university managers and bureaucrats. The AMA consists of doctors, and its elected officials speak for the interests of the profession of medicine. In contrast, university managers and administrators are a species in the university world more comparable to the CEO of the hospital or the head of an area health board. As managers and bureaucrats, they have particular agendas arising from the constraints and aims of management and administration. As such, their agendas are 'topic neutral' in a way that enables them to import ideas about management and administration from entirely unrelated fields – generalisations that are not specific to the university, generalisations which concern technique, systems and so on. But these are *means* which serve ends they don't themselves posit. They do not, therefore, have what it takes to answer the question "What is the university for?". If management and administration as such have anything to offer, it is only after our question has been answered.

In contrast, universities are for the pursuit of knowledge, truth and *according to the disciplines of the disciplines*, or lest that sound too peculiar a turn of phrase, universities' work is a pursuit whose subject matter, nature, methods and standards of success are defined by the disciplines themselves – by physics, biology, psychology, social science, mathematics, English literature, art history, history, religion studies, culture studies and so on. These disciplines are what the university consists of, and the most serious and authoritative answer to our question can come only from such disciplines. As for medicine and architecture, the questions "What is medicine for?" and "What is architecture for?" are questions internal to the disciplines themselves. So too for the university, "What is the university for?" is a question in whose answering the answers of the disciplines which constitute the university as a distinctive institution have or should have a privileged voice. But in recent years, it is arguable that that its voice or those voices have been rather marginalised. But it is a voice which can give direction where currently, arguably, we are rather disoriented.

The tendency of the ideology of constructive alignment towards a reduction of the unit of study to the students' performance on the assessment tasks can be countered or balanced with the voice of the discipline. As I have averred, a unit of study is an element in the immersion of the student, in stage-appropriate ways, into the form of life that the discipline is. This does not just involve student learning in skills and content that can be given explicit articulation but also education in the informal practices, values, attitudes and ways of enquiry and application of standards of success in disciplinary work that cannot be formulated explicitly and consist of the way things are done in the discipline. This immersion in the informal and inexplicit ways of the discipline takes the student a longer way towards internalising the discipline's values and habits of thought and standards of successful disciplinary practice than explicitly stated learning outcomes and TLAs serving them. This is not to say we should not have explicitly stated Intended Learning Outcomes (ILOs). It is only to say they are only part, and perhaps not the most important part, of the story. Recognition of this fact is called for to resist the tendency to reduce the unit of study to its assessment. But recognising this fact is at the same time taking into account the distinctive sense of the discipline of its own purpose: for example, it shows the student how to do philosophy or what good philosophy is and how to take its challenges seriously and what doing philosophy is for. And it invites to and involves the student in doing it herself. From that vantage point, from internally to doing philosophy herself, she is best positioned to understand what doing philosophy is for, and she can 'get it'. But this is not a possibility if the only thing one relies on is the prescriptions of constructive alignment alone with the emphases we saw it to have in Biggs's work. There will always be students for whom a unit of study is only and always about the assessment and getting through. *Pari passu*, such students will not become philosophers. But if we lose sight of the points about what the discipline is for that I have been trying to make, those students who would become philosophers will have to suffer under the limitations that arise from teaching only for those who never will – the tendency to teach to the assessment. The point of a unit is not merely to pass or to get a high distinction. The point is to grow in the discipline, and both TLAs and assessment tasks should serve *that* end. And that will typically take the unit well past what assessment and explicitly stated TLOs require.

Similar points help put the issues about the HDR dilemma into perspective too. For the Ph.D. is the final stage of immersion into the discipline. It is the final stage whereby the student graduates as a practitioner in the discipline who 'has her wings'. Though an 'early career researcher', she has embarked on her career as a philosopher (or physicist or mathematician). As such, it is reasonable to expect a somewhat comprehensive understanding of her discipline and an ability to contribute as a teacher in competent ways across a goodly portion of the discipline. Either the traditional model or the US model would meet this state of disciplinary development. For either model permits the student to attain a sense of her relation to the rest of the discipline as a fully participant member. And that is what is sought from HDR studies in a discipline. She has a sense of the point of doing philosophy from the years of working on her own project and her study of the discipline's broader concerns. To be in a position to write a Ph.D. thesis and have it pass implies a conception of the standards of successful conduct of philosophy in one's own voice. Thus, such a student has internalised standards of successful philosophical work as her own. This perspective affords the vantage point of a conception of the ends of the discipline. As such, it is a partial answer to the question "What is the university for?" It is, in part, for *that*.[6]

But, in ordinary conditions, the unhappy condition of the contemporary HDR student will not underwrite such a stage of disciplinary development for the student. She has to write 80,000–100,000 words of sustained argument that will pass examination in the advanced state of discipline research achievement, do so on the comparatively thin basis of what is attainable in undergraduate studies in the discipline and produce a thesis of some originality, all in three years,

Further, she has to know what she wants to write about and what will work as a thesis in *much* less time than this. That is too tall an order even for excellent students and unrealistically hopes for the exceptional student or none in all cases. Reasonable disciplinary input at this point about the ends of HDR study in the discipline could avoid this invidious choice. Of course, it would not necessarily hold a great deal of sway with government decisions about funding. However, it should. The voice of the disciplines about the point of the university is ignored at our peril in HDR studies as much as in undergraduate studies.

Conclusion

I have argued that the ends of higher education are contestable given the involvements of HEIs in the wide range of aspects of modern society that it is involved in and the mutual obligations arising from its funding. I have also argued that these ends are properly contested in a modern liberal democratic society and that many voices should be heard about this matter. I have argued further that the particular voices of the disciplines, which it is the point of the university as such to serve, have a particularly authoritative voice in such debates but that they have been marginalised. I have argued that this disciplinary voice adds important and telling insights and constraints on certain matters in teaching and learning in undergraduate education and in understanding the point of HDR studies more cogently and organising them sensibly. However, these are but illustrations of a general importance the disciplines have in the university but which, I fear, have been downplayed in the name of management and administration to our cost. We need to reclaim these voices and give them a more serious hearing than we have done recently if the university is to rise above the clamour of voices who would claim its purpose. Each discipline has responsibilities here. We all must state our case or be victims of our silence.

Notes

1 It is not as if such debates are new exactly, though they are relatively recent compared to the history of the university as an institution. For instance, see Coady (2000) in which our question is given quite a lot of direct and indirect attention in a variety of guises; in this collection, see particularly, Coady (2000a), Gaita (2000) and Langtry (2000).
2 Which could be overstated – see Krücken, Blümel and Kloke (2013).
3 For a slice of the very complex study of the merits and pitfalls of student evaluations of teaching, cf. Stehle, Spinath and Kadmon (2012).
4 Cf. Dreyfus (1998) and Waggoner (2013).
5 The central text is Biggs and Tang (2011); see also: Biggs (1996).
6 I bring together interests in the informal, inexplicit factors forming students in a discipline and HDR students in Quilter (2013)

References

Biggs, J. (1996). Enhancing Teaching through Constructive Alignment. *Higher Education, 32* (3), 347–364. Retrieved from: http://www.jstor.org/stable/3448076

Biggs, J. and Tang, C. (2011). *Teaching for Quality Learning at University: What the Student Does* (4th edn.). Maidenhead, UK: McGraw Hill.

Coady, T. (Ed.). (2000). *Why Universities Matter*. St. Leonards, New South Wales: Allen & Unwin.

Coady, T. (2000a). Universities and the Ideals of Enquiry. In T. Coady (Ed.). *Why Universities Matter*. (3–25). St. Leonards, New South Wales: Allen & Unwin.

Dreyfus, H. L. (1998). Education on the Internet: Anonymity vs Commitment. *The Internet and Higher Education, 1* (2), 113–124. Retrieved from: http://ac.els-cdn.com/S1096749499801743/1-s2.0-S1096749499801743-main.pdf?_tid=0780e578-59f6-11e6-912e-00000aab0f27&acdnat=1470282570_e5ce4104c39407014fd46e4477e09834

Gaita, R. (2000). Truth and the University. In T. Coady (Ed.). *Why Universities Matter*. (26–48). St. Leonards, New South Wales: Allen & Unwin.

Krücken, G., Blümel, A., and Kloke, K. (2013). The Managerial Turn in Higher Education? On the Interplay of Organizational and Occupational Change in German Academic. *Minerva, 51,* 417–442. doi: 10.1007/s11024-013-9240-z.

Langtry, B. (2000). Ends and Means in University Policy Decisions. In T. Coady (Ed.). *Why Universities Matter*. (85–97). St. Leonards, New South Wales: Allen & Unwin.

Plato. (2005). *Meno and Other Dialogues*. Tr. R. Waterfield. Oxford: Oxford University Press.

Quilter, J. G. (2013). The Contribution to Research Students' Development as Independent Researchers in Philosophy Made by Their Participation in Disciplinary Research Seminar Series. *Res Disputandae, 19,* 78–99.

Stehle, S., Spinath, B., and Kadmon, M. (2012). Measuring Teaching Effectiveness: Correspondence between Students' Evaluations of Teaching and Different Measures of Student Learning. *Research in Higher Education, 53* (8), 888–904. doi: 10.1007/s11162-012-9260-9.

Waggoner, M. (2013). Cultivating Critique: A (Humanoid) Response to the Online Teaching of Critical Thinking. *Liberal Education, 99* (3), 38–43. Retrieved from: http://go.galegroup.com.ezproxy2.acu.edu.au/ps/i.do?id=GALE%7CA345617436&v=2.1&u=acuni&it=r&p=AONE&sw=w&asid=40e3d8af855ca2a84035223b263ed12b

13 "The confessing animal"
Michel Foucault and the making of a responsible individual

Wendyl Luna

Introduction

There is a grave danger that a neoliberal approach to education as a commodity rather than a public good may subvert education's role in developing the rounded individual to the benefit of society as that individual takes his or her proper place.

A key role of education is to produce responsible individuals. To achieve this outcome requires the communication of the teacher as well as the student's acceptance of the relevant "truths." Foucault would say that a key outcome of the Catholic technique of confession is also to produce responsible individuals via the production of truth, enabling the Western person to 'become a confessing animal' (Foucault, 2008, p. 59).

These responsible confessing individuals are able to contribute to society through their knowledge of truth and their proper knowledge of themselves. The Catholic conception of confession falls within the educational paradigm in creating truth and responsible individuals who can contribute meaningfully to society, key outcomes of the educational process.

While Foucault saw the potentially positive effects of confession, he also engaged in robust critique of confession and its role in creating responsible individuals. In critiquing confession, Foucault uses the conception of sexuality as a focus for his examination. This focus involves an analysis of the role and effect of confession in the context of sexuality and the connection between confession and what he terms *parrēsia*, the discourse of truth. Confession can be seen as one manifestation of *parrēsia* in which the confessee by his confession declares the "truth" of the matter being confessed. Such a confession is a declaration by the confessee both to himself and to his confessor, thereby educating each of them as to the truth of the matter. This education occurs by way of internalization and reinforcement for the confessee in addition to the actuality of the declaration itself toward the confessor.

In the course of exploring Foucault's view of the nature of confession, we will try to outline Foucault's criticism of confession in general terms, seeking to answer the question of why he is critical of confession. After completing this outline, we will then determine the structure of *parrēsia*, which is a way of speaking the truth. I would argue that the key to making a responsible individual for Foucault might be found in the structure of *parrēsia*. We now raise the first question: what does Foucault's critique of confession consist of? Why is he critical of confession? For this purpose, we will be examining confession primarily in the context of sex and sexuality, as this is a key focus for Foucault. As with most things, for Foucault, sexuality is all about power relations, and we should keep this overarching theme in mind as we proceed to explore the concepts of confession and truth telling.

Parrēsia, generally, and via its manifestation in the form of confession is a form of education in that the confessee and the confessor are engaged in and exposed to a truth telling process by which each communicates and receives truth. The end result of the process, applied properly, and with knowledge of the impact of power relations, is the creation of responsible individuals. The impact of power relations in the context of confession and *parrēsia* translates readily into a consideration of the operation of power relations in the broader educational context.

The role and effect of power relations in the educational context is seen in the relentless drive toward monetization and commoditization of education. Neoliberalism converts education from a tool to create responsible individuals into an end in itself, namely, a profit-making scheme. At the extreme end, the creation of responsible individuals becomes an incidental and nonessential outcome.

Foucault teaches that no subject matter can be considered without accounting for the structures and power relations within and behind it. In the case of education, identifying the role of neoliberalism in subverting or subsuming the primary purpose of education assists us in seeking to reassert the core role of education in truth telling and creating responsible individuals.

Foucault's critique of confession

We can find Foucault's history or genealogy and criticism of confession in *La Volonté de savoir*, the first volume of *The History of Sexuality*. For convincing reasons, many commentators solely refer to this work to explain Foucault's criticism of confession, considering it to be the definitive source of understanding such criticism. However, as Dave Tell tells us, to understand the scope and extensiveness of Foucault's criticism of confession, it is not enough to rely exclusively on the first volume (Tell, 2010, p. 98). To obtain the complete picture of Foucault's criticism of confession, we would need to read all those works in which Foucault discusses confession, but this is not the main concern of this paper. Aside from *The History of Sexuality, Volume I*, Foucault also talks about confession in the following works: Foucault (1993, pp. 198–227, 2001, pp. 1–89, 2003, 2014).

The West, according to Foucault, is 'the only civilization to practice *scientia sexualis*.' Western civilization, he continues, 'is the only civilization to have developed over the centuries procedures for telling the truth of sex which are geared to a form of knowledge-power. . . . I have in mind the confession' (Foucault, 2008, p. 58). Despite its brevity, this sentence is quite dense. There are at least three things that I think Foucault wants to say with this statement: (i) "scientia sexualis," (ii) confession began with Christianity, and (iii) confession and sexuality are a construct.

With regard to the first point: the West has developed ways and means by which we speak the truth about sex. Now, this does not mean that its counterpart, the East, has not developed any procedure for telling the truth of sex. In fact, as is well known, Foucault distinguishes between the East's *ars erotica* or erotic art and the West's *scientia sexualis* or science of sexuality. In *ars erotica,* the so-called sovereign will of the master is needed for the transmission of truth. The master alone knows the hidden truth about sex and is the only one who can transmit this truth, the dynamics then being said to be coming from above. On the other hand, in *scientia sexualis*, a master or at least an interlocutor is still needed but is not considered to be the repository of truth. Instead, the truth about sex is derived from the 'obligatory act of speech' of the speaker or 'confessee' himself. Here is Foucault: confession is 'a ritual in which the expression alone, independently of its external consequences, produces intrinsic modifications in the person who articulates it: it exonerates, redeems, and purifies him; it unburdens him of his wrongs, liberates him, and promises him salvation' (Foucault, 2008, p. 62). In other words, it is the utterance or the act of confessing itself that while transmitting the truth, transforms the person. Unlike *ars erotica*, therefore, the dynamics is such that the transmission of truth does not come from above but from below. So, it is this *scientia sexualis* that the West has developed, which is made up of these procedures of telling the truth about sex. That's the first point.

The second thing we can derive from Foucault's statement is that confession, which Foucault describes as 'one of the West's most highly valued techniques for producing truth,' has a long history (Foucault, 2008, p. 59). In Foucault's account, confession slowly developed from the confessional practices in the Catholic Church, particularly the sacrament of penance, and permeated into the human sciences such as pedagogy, medicine, and psychiatry. There is a slight discrepancy in Foucault's claim: whereas in *The History of Sexuality, Volume I* Foucault traces the history of confession back to the Middle Ages, in his 1979–1980 lectures *On the Government of the Living*, he identifies its origins as being grounded in early Christianity, around the third, century with Tertullian. Despite this very minor discrepancy, it is clear that he does not trace it as far back as the Greeks, although he acknowledges that they themselves practiced confessional techniques that he distinguishes from the Christian approach. He posits that what we are, that is, our being confessing animals, could be traced to one of the two poles of Christianity's 'regime of truth.' For Foucault, those two poles are the pole of confession and the pole of faith. However, Foucault is quite definite that our status of confessing animals arises from the pole of confession rather than the pole of faith (Foucault, 2014, pp. 134–135). Perhaps this is not entirely surprising given the obviously strong connection between confession and confessing.

Shortly we will see that Foucault has some issues with the practice of confession. However, I don't think that, by tracing the history of the development of confession back to Christianity, Foucault is saying that the Church is the culprit for people becoming confessing animals. It would go too far to say that the Church for Foucault is the one to blame for what happened. In tracing the origins of Western confession, he is only saying factually that the history of confession began not with the Greek practices but with ecclesiastical practices. From there, he shows that the technique of confession did not remain as an exclusive property of Christianity but was adopted by various disciplines in secular society, such as politics, medicine, and psychiatry. Nevertheless, as it is part of the development of confession, the pole of confession in Christianity's 'regime of truth' is subject to Foucault's critique. It is important to keep in mind, therefore, that when we talk about Foucault's criticism of confession, he is not only criticizing the secular practice of confession the West has developed but the Christian practice of confession as well. That's the second point.

The question now is, what's the problem with confession? Why does Foucault have something negative to say about it? The answer to this question is the third point we can derive from Foucault's statement; that is, to quote Foucault again: '[truth-telling procedures] geared to a form of knowledge-power.' Foucault is critical of confession because for him, it is a construct. To be honest, I tried very hard to look for a quotation that directly supports this, but I failed. All I could find is this statement from Foucault that by implication, supports our claim. Foucault talks about the various mechanisms and strategies of knowledge and power that revolve around sex, for example, hysterization of women's bodies, pedagogization of children's sex, and others. He explains that these strategies themselves, among others, are the ones responsible for 'the very production of sexuality.' He continues:

> Sexuality must not be thought of as a kind of natural given which power tries to hold in check, or as an obscure domain which knowledge tries gradually to uncover. It is the name that can be given to a historical construct . . . a great surface network in which the stimulation of bodies, the intensification of pleasures, the incitement to discourse, the formation of special knowledges, the strengthening of controls and resistances, are linked to one another, in accordance with a few major strategies of knowledge and power.
>
> (Foucault, 2008, pp. 105–106)[1]

It is very clear here that sexuality, according to Foucault, is being produced and constructed in order that there may be more reason for modern power to exercise its control and increase its influence, subjecting us to new modes of power.[2] What this means is that, as Dave Tell argues, sexuality for Foucault is constructed by modern power to function in a metonymical way; that is, the term 'sexuality' is used as an abstract concept or rhetorical device that is used to lump together things that are not supposed to be lumped together (Tell, 2010, pp. 98, 107). This is reminiscent of Foucault's critique of continuous history in *The Archaeology of Knowledge*, which sees or posits continuity or unity among discontinuous things (Foucault, 1972). For Foucault, things have to be left in their discontinuity or dispersion, hence, his criticism against any theory or methodology that ascribes false unity to discontinuous and disconnected things and, in this case, 'sexuality.' A question may be raised at this point: this is Foucault's criticism against sexuality – what does this have to do with his critique of confession?

Earlier in the first volume of *The History of Sexuality*, Foucault states that 'sexuality [is] correlative of that slowly developed discursive practice which constitutes the *scientia sexualis*' (Foucault, 2008, p. 68). The discursive practice constituting *scientia sexualis* Foucault is talking about here is none other than confession itself. With this, it is easy to see the relationship between sexuality and confession. Whereas confession is the discursive practice that comprises the science of sexuality itself, sexuality is that which confession reveals. Surely there is no problem with expressing as much as one possibly can, nor is there a problem with revealing one's subjectivity or sexuality. The problem comes when we fail to recognize that confession and sexuality are constructs that we have been made to believe to be true, good, and natural. For me, Foucault's critique of confession is captured by the following statement: 'The obligation to confess is now relayed through so many different points, is so deeply ingrained in us, that we no longer perceive it as the effect of a power that constrains us' (Foucault, 2008, p. 60). In other words, the problem lies in failing to see confession or sexuality as an effect of power. This is Foucault's critique of confession. While there are issues with confession, Foucault would say that it is good thing to be a confessing animal, if and when confession leads to the production of truth and the creation of responsible individuals. But, he also argues, that can only happen if we recognize and react against the potentially constraining power relations inherent in the Western confessional practice.

We have mentioned that confession is a 'production of truth of sex.' I would like to bracket 'sex' now and focus on what Foucault describes as the 'production of truth.' This production of truth occurs equally in the general educational sphere as much as it does in confession of sexuality, a more specific form of the production of truth and education in that context.

Production of truth

In "Truth and Power," Foucault discusses the role of the 'specific' intellectual (Foucault, 1980, pp. 126–133). In contrast to the 'universal' intellectual who acts as a universal consciousness or master of truth, the 'specific' intellectual engages the present from a particular standpoint, addressing problems that are specific and contingent or nonuniversal. Foucault has a deep-seated suspicion and rejection of the universal intellectual, namely, that disconnected, power-imbued, and ultimately imaginary master-maker-controller of truth.

He prefers the specific individual who is tied to a specific context or to the particular place where he is working (e.g., the hospital, prison, laboratory, university, or family). The 'specific' intellectual is concerned with concrete, 'real-life' things and is closer to them than the theoretical 'universal' intellectual. Gone are the days of the 'writer of genius' who grasps universal truths and values that are discoverable in every society and applicable to all people. It is now the time of savants and experts who, according to Foucault, are exemplified, among others, by Darwin. Although they have specialized knowledge, they are the ones who nevertheless have significant roles in society. These individuals are important to society not only because they are knowledgeable experts but also, and more importantly, because they can determine and constitute 'a new politics of truth,' applicable to that moment in time and tied to its particular issues and problems. What then is this 'politics of truth'? What is this 'truth'? And how does it relate to these knowledgeable experts?

'Truth' for Foucault is not a group of statements given the status of 'truth' for having represented or corresponded to whatever they describe actually is. Foucault then does not subscribe to what the correspondence theory says about truth: a statement is true if what we say corresponds to the reality we are talking about. Neither is 'truth' an ensemble of universal, immutable truths lying in wait to be discovered. Rather, truth for Foucault is produced by and results from power relations. He explains,' "Truth" is linked . . . with systems of power which produce and sustain it, and to effects of power which it induces and which extend it. A "régime" of truth' (Foucault, 1980, p. 133). These power relations have in them an ensemble of 'rules' that govern the formation and production of 'truth' itself; truth then is not outside of power but can be found within it.

When we say 'rules,' we do not have in mind some structure that implies a predetermined outcome. Rather, the term 'rules' refers to the outcome arising from the application of power relations to the particular circumstances. Here is Foucault's definition of 'power relationship':

> a power relationship can only be articulated on the basis of two elements which are each indispensable if it is really to be a power relationship: that "the other" (the one over whom power is exercised) be thoroughly recognized and maintained to the very end as a person who acts; and that, faced with a relationship of power, a whole field of responses, reactions, results, and possible inventions may open up.
>
> (Foucault, 1983, p. 220)

Moreover, in *Discipline and Punish*, Foucault talks about 'specific' regimes of power; for example, 'disciplinary power,' which is different from forms of government such as 'juridical power' (Foucault, 1977). So, by 'rules,' we mean a definite outcome resulting from the interaction of the specific elements identified by Foucault, even though that outcome is fluid. In this sense, 'rules' can also be expressed as 'context-dependent possibilities.'

With this, it is not difficult to see why the 'specific' intellectual is important for this 'régime' of truth. Being connected to what Foucault calls the specific 'politics of truth' in our society, the specific intellectual with his or her own position occupies an important place in this network of power relations that is responsible for producing 'truths.' Therefore, the work of these specialists has a tremendous impact on society not because these experts are the leaders in their fields but simply because they have a certain relation to the truth, forming part in its production and sustenance.

The role of the specific intellectual Foucault describes in "Truth and Power" resonates well with the function of the present-day examiner or analyst he describes in "Critical Theory/Intellectual History." In this interview, Foucault explains that it is not the task of the analyst of the present to characterize what we are, but rather, it is his task to understand 'why and how that-which-is might no longer be that-which-is' (Foucault, 1988, p. 36). In other words, the role of the one who engages with the present is not to blindly accept as 'true' whatever has been accepted to be true; but rather, his or her role is to question such 'truth' and refute the claim that 'because this is, that will be.' There is just no truth to a fact remaining always a fact or to some truth remaining always true. It is the same with falsity: whatever is false might be proven otherwise or might become otherwise. This truth and falsity is an ephemeral reality (but still a reality) shaped by the particular power relations of the day or time.

It is the role of the intellectual to point out the transitory or 'dependent' character of truth and falsity and to describe that the 'truth' or that which is (i.e., fact) and falsity will not always remain the same and should not always remain the same. The reason for this is that 'truth' (and, perhaps, we can also include falsity'), if we take Foucault's definition of it, is always contingent on the network of power relations – a network of power relations that is malleable and constantly changes, being itself dependent on various players such as the specific intellectuals and institutions. Because in the end both deal with the status of truth; the specific intellectual and the analyst of the present have interchangeable roles. Ultimately, the two do the same thing, and that is to determine the malleability of truth, cognizant of its ever-changing status.

A good example of showing the malleability of truth or its dependence on institutions and/or specific intellectuals is the work of Canguilhem (who was Foucault's mentor) in the history of biology, which points out the historicity of biological concepts. Another example would be Foucault's own work of historicizing universal forms of rationality or historicizing reason, which before were thought to be ahistorical. He shows the concepts of rationality and reason to be malleable, based on the network of power relations existing at different points in time. We can see the important role history plays in this approach; for, as Foucault says, it shows that 'that-which-is has not always been' (Foucault, 1988, p. 37). History or contingency is the basis then for determining the status of truth or the status of anything for that matter, including those that seem to be outside the realm of history. Having examined the production of truth, we now turn to Foucault's explanation of *parrēsia*, the discourse of truth, which probably we can say is his ideal form for the production of truth.

Parrēsia: the discourse of truth

Within the general framework of the so-called government, which Foucault describes as 'techniques and procedures designed to direct the behavior of men,' the problem of examining one's conscience and of confession was studied (Foucault, 1999, p. 154). The main question is:

> How is it that within Western Christian culture the government of men requires, on the part of those who are led, in addition to acts of obedience and submission, 'acts of truth', which have this particular character that not only is the subject required to speak truthfully, but to speak truthfully about himself and his faults, his desires, the state of his soul etc.?
> (Foucault, 1999, p. 154)

Discussed in the context of 'government,' *parrēsia* is the main topic for Foucault's (1983) course at the Collège de France (Foucault, 2010). Even though it is impossible to fully characterize *parrēsia* in just a few paragraphs, we will still say something about it. First and foremost, *parrēsia* is a way of speaking. As a way of speaking, *parrēsia* is distinguished from Austin and Searle's speech acts or 'performative utterance': whereas in speech acts the effects are known (e.g., the chair's utterance that opens the meeting), in *parrēsia* they are not known (Foucault, 2010, pp. 61ff).[3] The 'parrhesiast' or the speaker of truth does not know if the listener accepts the truth of which he speaks. Likewise, whereas in speech acts the status of the subject has to be taken into account, in *parrēsia* it is not really important. The speaker of truth may be a politician before an assembly, prince's counselor, philosopher, farmer, noncitizen, or foreigner. That is, no matter what his status is or no matter what state he is in, for as long as he speaks the truth and binds himself to both his statement and the truth he is speaking about, he is a 'parrhesiast.' One's status in life is entirely independent of him being the spokesperson of truth, or the truth in the statement of truth remains the same regardless of the speaker's status. In this, we see parallels with the concept of the confessing animal. Whoever binds himself to his statement of the truth is a truly confessing animal, a responsible individual, who confesses, that is, speaks the truth.

Second, *parrēsia* is a way of speaking the truth. It is distinguished from other ways or strategies of telling the truth, such as demonstration, rhetoric, and pedagogy (Foucault, 2010, pp. 52ff). As a way of speaking the truth, *parrēsia* does not merely demonstrate or point to the truth one is talking about. Likewise, unlike rhetoric that persuades the interlocutor or addressee to believe that what one is speaking is true, and unlike pedagogy that teaches the interlocutor something, *parrēsia* is not a matter of persuasion or teaching but a way of truth telling. In this way of telling the truth, the speaker binds and commits himself to his statement of truth and to the truth of what he says. It is a courageous act of freedom that is dangerous or risky for the one who speaks the truth. More often than not, it is his life that the 'parrhesiast' puts at stake.

In this courageous act of speaking, it is not so important to know what the truth really is. What is more important is the speaker's willingness to take risks and identify himself with the truth he is saying. Therefore, whatever 'truth' that we are saying, the question we must confront is, are we ready to risk speaking about it? Are we ready to pay the price of our truth telling, the price that can be as high as our own death? Here is Foucault: 'parrhesiasts' like Plato and Dion, who risked their lives advising the tyrant Dionysius, 'tell the truth, and in telling the truth lay themselves open to the risk of having to pay the price. . . . And it is not just any price that they are ready to pay and that in telling the truth they affirm they are ready to pay: the price is death' (Foucault, 2010, p. 56). In *parrēsia* or the discourse of truth, then, what matters is the subject speaker's willingness to tell the truth, whatever that truth may be, even at the point of risking one's own life.

The following then are the key elements found in *parrēsia*: the speaker of the truth who has the freedom and courage to say it, the truth of what he says, and the risk involved in speaking the truth. If one element is missing, there will be no *parrēsia*.

We can find a close affinity between Kant's injunction, 'Sapere aude!' ('Dare to be wise' or 'Have courage to use your own reason!'), found in his essay, "Was ist Aufklärung?," and Foucault's elaboration of *parrēsia*, which for the Greeks, Foucault argues, does not only mean frankness or bluntness but also a courageous way of speaking the truth (Kant, 1996, p. 8:35, 2007, p. 29). Courage is obviously needed when one makes an *Ausgang* (exit) out of his 'self-incurred tutelage' or when one breaks free from the book or its author, spiritual director, and the doctor – the so-called authorities of our understanding, moral conscience, and will. Likewise, both speak of the same condition from which one needs to escape: self-incurred tutelage or 'the condition of minority' (Kant) and the controlled, subjugated, or oppressed state of the one to whom *parrēsia* is addressed (Foucault). If one is in either state, one needs to get out of it either through one's own effort of self-awakening or through the help of those who have achieved enlightenment. The enlightened ones include the specific intellectuals discussed here in the exploration of the production of truth.

However, there appears to be a slight difference here: whereas Kant calls for the autonomy of the individual to precisely reject any external authority so that he can freely exercise his own reason, the idea behind *parrēsia* is that one may need another person to help him properly care or govern himself and others, and that person is the 'parrhesiast' who speaks the truth. If we compare the enlightened individual with the one to whom *parrēsia* is addressed, then we find no connection between 'sapere audere' and *parrēsia*. However, if we consider the 'parrhesiast' and the enlightened or autonomous individual, then we can see the connection between the two. The political adviser, the prince's counselor, the philosopher, and the humble farmer in *parrēsia* are the same as Kant's enlightened or autonomous individual. If we are to use Kant's terminology, both have achieved a certain level maturity or freedom from any authority.

The question now is, if *parrēsia* is distinguished from pedagogy or education and if it not so much about teaching or imparting the 'truth' to someone else, is it still possible to use *parrēsia* in educating other people or in producing responsible individuals? The short answer is yes, but how? *Parrēsia* is not about truth telling for the sake of truth telling. We have to keep in mind that the goal of *parrēsia* is the 'proper' governance of self and others. With this goal, even if the effect may not be ascertained from the very beginning, it is still hoped that as the 'parrhesiast' engages in *parrēsia*, the interlocutor may change his views, if not transform himself into a better person. In *parrēsia*, there is the invitation or challenge to know the truth and to bind oneself with both (i) his true statement and (ii) the truth of what he is saying. If we accept this challenge, whatever 'truth' we speak about, no matter how context dependent or historically determined it is, we are still courageous enough to speak about it. We may not believe in or subscribe to every 'truth' we hear; we nonetheless speak as truthfully as possible. It is in speaking the truth (about ourselves or whatever) or in being 'parrhesiasts' (i.e., speakers of truth) that we, confessing animals, become responsible.

Conclusion

How do we draw all this together? At the core of education is the promotion of truth and the creation of responsible individuals who realize their potential and contribute positively to society. This too is the goal of confession, which we can describe as a type of *parrēsia*. Through confession, a person becomes the 'confessing animal' and a responsible person. We have mentioned that, although Foucault is critical of confession, it need not be seen in a bad light. For, as he writes: 'An immense labor to which the West has submitted generations in order to produce . . . men's subjection: their constitution as subjects in both senses of the word' (Foucault, 2008, p. 60). In other words, there are two sides of the word 'subjection': subject of power and the person as a subject.

The practice of confession should be properly viewed in light of this. It is indeed something negative in that it is a 'historical construct' devised by modern power to exercise its influence and expand its control over us. So, confession, a potentially beneficial exercise, succumbs to the inevitable application of power relations as people use that which is inherently good to accrue power to themselves. However, as Foucault makes it clear, we should not fail to recognize the positive side of confession; namely, that it is transformative, allowing one to become a true subject and a responsible individual engaged in the discourse of truth. Hence, even if it is often the result of power relations, confession is still beneficial in functioning as a form of *parrēsia*, achieving the positive outcomes associated with the practice of *parrēsia*.

The structure of *parrēsia* makes this clear. In this discourse of truth in which the confessee or *parrēsiast* is engaged, he does not just say what the truth is, but he binds himself to that truth no matter what it takes, even if his life is at stake. If we say the truth, no matter how ephemeral and fleeting it is, or how subjective, if we know how to bind ourselves to the truth of our statement or, to put it simply, if we mean what we say, then we are not far from becoming responsible individuals, which I think should be the main goal of the government of others and of self, that is, education.

As the confessee is a 'parrhesiast,' so too is the educator. The most effective educators are those who reflect the true characteristics of the 'parrhesiast' in declaring the truth that they teach. The parrhesiast-educator binds himself to the truth of what he is teaching as much as communicating that truth to his students. In turn, the educator becomes an effective creator of his students as responsible individuals, having acted with consistency and integrity in his discourse of truth.

If education is not simply transmission of knowledge, much less is it a commodity to be bought or sold. We follow Foucault in understanding education to be directed to the promotion of the proper government of self and others. In turn, we understand *parrēsia* as the discourse of truth, with confession being one of its forms. The true goal of the 'parrhesiast,' whether as confessee, or counselor to a tyrant or educator, is the creation of responsible individuals, both for oneself and others.

We are reminded that these worthy goals should not be made hostage to the pursuit of profit. Recognizing the inevitability of the impact of power relations in education as elsewhere, we identify unbridled neoliberalism as a potentially unhelpful influence on the fundamental goals of education. The all-pervasive effects of neoliberalism cannot be overcome given its entrenchment in the power relations of education. However, once we correctly identify the dangers of neoliberalism, we can seek to counter its more pernicious effects and encourage a return to the primary purpose of education as a form of truth telling directed toward creating responsible and productive individuals.

Notes

1 Foucault also writes: '[Sexuality,] I mean a notion that refers to a single entity and allows diverse phenomena to be grouped together, despite the apparently loose connections between them' (Foucault, 1985, p. 35). In another passage, he writes: '[Sexuality] made it possible to group together, in an artificial unity, anatomical elements, biological functions, conducts, sensations, and pleasures, and it enabled one to me use of this fictitious unity as a causal principle' (Foucault, 2008, p. 154).
2 To elaborate, here is Foucault: 'Sex as a political issue. . . . [I]t was tied to the disciplines of the body. . . . [I]t was applied to the regulation of populations. . . . It fitted in both categories at once, giving rise to infinitesimal surveillances, indeterminate medical or psychological examinations, to an entire micro-power concerned with the body. But it gave rise as well to comprehensive measures, statistical assessments, and interventions aimed at the entire social body or at groups taken as a whole' (Foucault, 2008, pp. 145–146).
3 This is not the first time that Foucault distinguishes something from Austin and Searle's speech acts. In *The Archaeology of Knowledge*, he distinguishes 'statements' from speech acts, saying that statements and speech acts are not identical (Foucault, 1972, pp. 83–84).

References

Foucault, M. (1972). *The Archaeology of Knowledge*. Tr. A. Smith. New York: Pantheon Books.

Foucault, M. (1977). *Discipline and Punish: The Birth of the Prison*. Tr. A. Smith. New York: Random House.

Foucault, M. (1980). Truth and Power. In C. Gordon (Ed.). *Power/Knowledge: Selected Interviews and Other Writings 1972–1977*. Tr. C. Gordon, L. Marshall, et al.. New York: Pantheon Books.

Foucault, M. (1983). Afterword: Subject and Power. In H. Dreyfus and P. Rabinow (Eds.). *Michel Foucault: Beyond Hermeneutics and Structuralism* (208–226). Chicago: Chicago University Press.

Foucault, M. (1985). *The Use of Pleasure: The History of Sexuality*. Vol. 2. Tr. R. Hurley. New York: Pantheon Books.

Foucault, M. (1988). Critical Theory/Intellectual History. Tr. J. Harding. In L. Kritzman (Ed.). *Politics, Philosophy, Culture: Interviews and Other Writings 1977–1984* (17–46). New York and London: Routledge.

Foucault, M. (1993). About the Beginning of the Hermeneutics of the Self: Two Lectures at Dartmouth. *Political Theory, 21* (2), 198–227.

Foucault, M. (1999). Course Summary: Government of the Living. Tr. R. Townsend. In C. Jeremy (Ed.). *Religion and Culture by Michel Foucault* (154–157). Manchester, UK: Manchester University Press.

Foucault, M. (2001). Truth and Juridical Forms. Tr. R. Hurley and others. In J. Faubion (Ed.). *Power: The Essential Works of Michel Foucault 1954–1984*. Vol. 3. (1–89). New York: The New Press.

Foucault, M. (2003). *The Abnormal: Lectures at the Collège de France 1974–1975*. Tr. G. Burchell. Ed. A. Davidson. London and New York: Verso.

Foucault, M. (2008). *The History of Sexuality*. Vol. 1. Tr. R. Hurley. Victoria: Penguin Books.

Foucault, M. (2010). *The Government of Self and Others: Lectures at the Collège de France 1982–1983*. Tr. G. Burchell. Ed. F. Gros. London and New York: Palgrave MacMillan.

Foucault, M. (2014). *On the Government of the Living: Lectures at the Collège de France 1979–1980*. Tr. G. Burchell. Ed. A. Davidson. New York: Palgrave MacMillan.

Kant, I. (1996). What Is Enlightenment? In M. Gregor (Tr. and Ed.). *Practical Philosophy: The Cambridge Edition of the Works of Immanuel Kant* (11–22). Cambridge, UK: Cambridge University Press.

Kant, I. (2007). Was ist Aufklärung? Tr. L. Hochroth and C. Porter. In S. Lotringer (Ed.). *The Politics of Truth* (29–37). Los Angeles: Semiotext(e).

Tell, D. (2010). Rhetoric and Power: An Inquiry into Foucault's Critique of Confession. *Philosophy & Rhetoric, 43* (2), 95–117.

Index

accountability 33, 43; lack of 35; moral 58; social 43
Adorno, Theodor 178–93
aim of a university education 113
Aquinas, Thomas 105, 119n3, 172
Aristotle 12, 14–18, 28n6, 29n8, n11, 151, 158, 160
Ariyaratne Ahangamage Tudor 92–6
assessment tasks 198–202, 205–6
Augustine 61–2
autonomy 23, 49, 133, 180, 186–8, 191–2

being-centred education 131
Benedict XVI 39–40, 124, 129
Berry, Thomas 96
Bildung 144, 180–92
British model 203
Buddhism 97, 100
Buddhist education 99; formation 99; studies 98

Canadian universities 36
Cartesian foundationalism 152
Cartesianism 109
casualisation 198
casuistry 157
Catholic intellectual tradition xi, 4, 14, 161–2
Catholic philosophical tradition 104, 107
Catholic philosophies of education 37, 38, 45
Catholic philosophy of education 42–3
Catholic school 39
Catholic university 104–7, 117, 161, 163–7, 169–71, 173–5
Centre for Sustainable Development 100
Champaran Schools 91
character 160–1, 215–16
choice 127–8, 132, 167, 172
Christian education 130–2, 134

Christian Gospels 66, 79
Christian values 130–1
civil society 4–5, 8, 13, 18, 20–6, 100, 139, 141, 151, 156, 160, 189
commodification of knowledge 78, 118
common good x–xi, 4–5, 9, 12, 14–15, 18, 20–2, 24–5, 35, 37, 39, 41, 43–5, 107, 135
confession 209–13, 216, 218–19
conformist society 186
Confucian Golden Rule 53–4
Confucian secular education 68
consensus among moral agents 156
constructive alignment 198–9, 201–2, 205–6
consumerism 84, 93, 96, 98–9, 184–5, 192
core of education 218
core values 168
crafts 50, 88, 90–1, 95
crisis of modern education 179
crisis of society 145
criterion referenced system of grading 202
critical function of institutions 143
critical pedagogy 178–81
critical theory 180, 187, 190, 215; of education 180
culture 146, 169, 178–80, 182–93, 197, 200–2
culture and traditions 18, 34
culture industry 178, 180, 183–4, 186–8, 190, 192–3
culture of consumerism 184

Da Xue (Great Learning) 56, 60–1
dehumanization 68–9, 72, 130, 186
democracy 5, 11–13, 26–8; civil society and 20–5; concept of 14–20
democratic institutions 19–20
democratic states 11
democratic values 13, 19, 22, 26–8, 197
despair 66–71, 76, 78, 80, 125

dialectics 190
difference 72, 142
dignity 39, 43, 45, 60, 86, 123, 125–6, 129–31, 134, 163, 170, 174
disciplinary culture 201
discipline of philosophy 198
discourse ethics 21
discourse of truth 209, 216–19
duty *Yi* 57

education: as a commercial transaction 17; and the democratic society 25–8; as service 86
educator 70, 72–3, 74, 78–9, 167, 173, 219
emotivism 153
encounter with God 131
end of Higher Education 196
ends of HDR study 207
enlightenment 59, 96–7, 154, 183, 191, 217
Enlightenment Literacy 93, 96
epistemological consensus 151, 158
epistemological crisis 152–3, 156, 159
epistemological virtues 75
Erziehung 181, 187–9
essence 127, 129
ethical formation 165–7, 168, 171, 173, 175
ethics 69, 96, 99, 152, 159–60, 166–7; Christian 125
ethics and spirituality 96
Ex Corde Ecclesiae 163, 166

Fa (law) 58–9
false values 125–6, 128
Father-Son relations 55
Formation *see* human formation
formation of persons 4, 43, 45
forms of wisdom 116, 118
Foucault, Michel 209–10; critique of confession 210–13; truth for 214–15
framework of seven pillars 173
Francis 41, 128, 133
Frankfurt school 179–80, 192
freedom 12, 14–15, 17, 19–20, 39, 122, 128, 130, 132; academic 49, 78; inner 99, 130; spiritual 41–2
Freire, Paulo 66; on despair and hope 66–72; on oppression 73–4; pedagogy of great convergences 76–80; philosophy of liberation 76

Gandhi, Mohandas 77, 85–7; religion 87; Satyagraha Ashram 89–91; Tolstoy farm 88–9; Wadhra scheme of basic education 91–2

Gentile, Mary C. 163; GVV Curriculum 167–8; values 168, 174
Giroux, Henri 26–7, 179
global values 122, 130
God 106–7, 124, 128, 130–1, 133–4, 138, 164, 166, 182
good 6, 15, 19, 38, 41, 44–5, 60, 105, 107, 115–18, 124, 161, 164, 172–3; the good life 11–12, 158–9; *see also* common good
good for humanity, the 164
good life, the 11–12, 158–9, 161
GVV curriculum *see* Gentile, Mary

Halbbildung 178, 181, 183–9; emancipation from 191–2
heart of the Church 163–4
Heidegger, Martin 1, 147–8, 157
hierarchies of values 127
Higher Degree by Research (HDR) studies 202
holistic education 84, 91, 98–101
holistic formation 85; Ariyaratne's 92–6; Sulak Sivaraska 96–9
hope 62, 144, 147, 188; critical 27; pedagogy of 66–76
Human dignity 123, 174
human flourishing 43, 106, 158, 160
human formation 117–18
humanism 52, 145, 157
humanization 68–70, 72
human-person 39, 116, 123, 126, 163–6, 169–72, 174–5
human values 99, 169

incommensurability 151–3, 156–7
indigenous culture 99
individualism 26, 31, 35, 93, 95–6
institutionalized negative secularism 139

Jesus Christ 134, 164
Ji Xia Academy 50
jobs 32, 43, 92, 94, 97, 191
John Paul II 40, 122, 129, 130, 133, 134, 163, 164, 165–6, 168, 174
Jun Zi 60–1

Kant, Immanuel 142, 153, 160, 171, 179, 188, 191, 217
Kong Zi see Confucian secular education

learning outcomes 198–201, 205; intended 205
Li (propriety) 52, 58–9
liberal university 111

liberation 69, 72–6, 79–80, 99, 130, 140, 153
lifelong learning 42
linguistic hospitality 144
love 40, 53, 66, 75, 79, 87, 89, 94, 107, 129–30, 134, 148, 165 ; of God 62, 131; of self 62; of wisdom 59
Lun Yu (The Analects) 52, 56

MacIntyre, Alasdair 22, 104–5, 151; critique of philosophy and theology 105–6; educated public 111; epistemological crises 159–61; incommensurability 151–9; revitalising the university 111–17; theory of rational vindication 108–11
man of culture 146
manual work 86, 88–9
Maritain, Jacques 39–42, 44, 124, 133
mass culture 192
metaphysical realism 108, 170, 172
Midnight University 101
mission statements 37
Modernity 100, 126, 138, 156–7
modern society 93, 95, 197, 207
MOOCs 2–3, 25
moral agent 59, 154, 157, 159–61
moral education 151
moral enquiry 105, 108, 151, 153, 156, 159
moral philosophy 8, 151, 154, 155–6, 163
moral progress 154
Mündigkeit 187–8, 192

nature of education 1, 17
neoliberalism 74, 80, 210, 219
Nussbaum, Martha 33, 169

oppression 6, 22, 66, 68–9, 72–6, 79–80, 86, 178, 183
oppressive social order 68
origins of universities 49
outcomes 9, 20, 31, 33, 34; behavioural 1; key 209; measureable 1; student 33; value 196; *see also* learning outcomes
Ozolins, Jānis T. 115–18, 173

parrēsia 209–10, 216; discourse of truth 216–17, 218–20
pedagogical convergence 77
pedagogy of great convergences 76–8, 81
personalism 126, 170–2
person-centred education 40
PhD 203
phenomenological analysis of ethical action 172

philosophy 5, 8, 27, 32, 52, 62–3, 104–5, 108, 115–17, 154–5, 156–8, 165–6, 170–1, 179, 189, 193, 198, 200, 206; in the Catholic university 105–7; of education 36–9, 43, 45–6; German 182; of liberation 76; between theology and 146–8; *see also* moral philosophy
Plato 11, 14–15, 61, 199, 217; ideal state 12
political technics 138–40
politicization of education 34, 44
politics of truth 214–15
post-Encyclopaedic university 111
power relations 210, 213–15, 218–19
power relationship 214
practical rationality 154–5
practical wisdom 17, 160–1
practices 9, 68, 74, 76, 78–80, 87, 187, 200; confessional 211; of enquiry 111; Greek 212; informal 205; meditational 93, 101; religious 126; thick 159–61; work 24
production of truth 209, 213–16, 217
professional education 199
pseudo-culture 184–5, 188–9, 192
public space 21–2, 24–5, 142, 156
purpose of Christian education 132
purpose of education 5, 26, 36–9, 42–3, 46, 131, 210, 219

rational agent 158, 160
rational enquiry 105, 108, 111–12, 114, 117, 154, 160
regime of truth 211–12, 214–15
relationship of theology to philosophy 105
religion 14, 26, 62, 79, 87–9, 94–5, 98, 137–9, 146–7, 174; and culture 20, 38, 51, 141
religious education 87, 90, 146
Ren 5, 52–4, 59; *Da Ren* 58; *Ren Min* 58; *Xiao Ren* 58
responsibility to the wider community 45
Ricoeur, Paul 76, 141, 147; critique in and of institutions 142; education and cultures 143–4; education and humanity 145–6; and secularism 137–40
rival moral traditions 153, 159
role of institutions 138

Samarkand 50–1, 63
sanctity of life 126
sanctity of the world 237
Sarvodaya Shramadana Movement 95
Satyagraha Ashram 89
Scheler, Max 129, 130, 171
scientia sexualis 210–11, 213

Index

scientism 96
search for truth 8, 27, 140–1, 165
secularism 7, 104, 143, 145–7; of abstention 140; of confrontation 140–1
secularization 138
Senior Brother-Junior Brother 55–6
Senior friend-Junior friend 55–6
Sevagram Ashram 91
sexuality 9, 209–13
Silk Road 50
Sivaraksa, Sulak 6, 84; spirit in education movement 100–1; *see also* holistic formation
social diversity 197
social justice 23, 26, 84
social media 24–5
speaking the truth *see parrēsia*
specific intellectual 213–15
Spirit in Education Movement *see* Sivaraksa, Sulak
spirituality 79–80, 92, 96, 99–100, 101
spiritual life 42, 88
subject, the 124, 142, 216–17

task of education 113, 143, 193
teacher 25, 49, 63, 73, 81, 87, 89–90, 129, 134; pre-school 95; and pupil 130, 133
teaching activities 199
teaching and learning activity (TLAs) 201–2, 205–6
teaching ethics 163, 165, 167
technics 137–8, 145; and cultures 143–5; political 138–40
telos: of human life 159, 161; of medicine 160; of perfected science 109; of truth 109
theory of liberation 72, 75–6, 80
theory of rational vindication 105, 107, 108–10, 114, 117
Three Obediences and Four Women Virtues 56
TLAs *see* teaching and learning activity
Tolstoy Farm *see* Gandhi, Mohandas
tradition 8, 14–15, 100–1, 105–8, 110, 112, 151–2, 154–5, 157, 160–2, 164–5; Buddhist 101; Catholic educational 41; cultural 185, 187; of rational enquiry 114–15, 117
translation 141, 143–6, 148, 181

truth 28, 40–1, 87, 89, 104, 110, 129, 132–3, 140–2, 154, 159, 164, 199, 205, 209; claims 7, 21, 117; and the good 105, 111, 115–18; meaning of 174; politics of 9, 214–15; production of 213–14; search for 165–6; about sex 211, 213; telling 210, 212, 216–18; *see also parrēsia*
types of literacy 93

universal intellectual 213–14
universe of the word 140–1
university 40, 44, 49–51, 63, 104, 140–2, 197–9, 204–7; as agapeic 165; community 174; corporate 27, 118; education 8–9, 35, 92, 94, 98, 101, 104, 106–7, 113, 115–18, 151; research 165; secular 107, 117, 137; students 116, 166; *see also* Catholic university
US system 203
utopianism 112

values 4–5, 7, 39–41, 84, 122, 145–6, 147, 163–6, 167–8, 171–4, 197, 201–2, 205, 214; common 18; ethical 97, 168; global 122, 130; human 99, 169; moral 93; public 27; spiritual 93; traditional 93, 138; universal 131, 134; world of 123–4, 127–8, 133; *see also* democratic values

way of truth-telling 232
Weil, Simone 69, 76
will, the 134, 171–2, 173–4; of God 134; of the leader 19; of the people 16; of those in power 20
wisdom 6, 7, 27, 42, 45, 78, 88, 94, 96, 98, 100, 105, 115–18, 124, 131, 134, 168; authentic 99; *panna* 99; practical 17, 160–1; *see also* Zhi
Wojtyla, Karol 124–5, 129, 131–2, 134, 164, 168–73; *see also* John Paul II
Word, the 147–8
Wu Lun 54–5

Yi (duty) 52, 54–5, 57–8

Zheng Ming 54, 58
Zhi (wisdom) 52, 59